Developing Innate Abilities

Experiencing Assessment Center Exercises

Second Edition

Linsey C. Willis

Florida Atlantic University

Kendall Hunt
publishing company

Cover image © Shutterstock.com

Kendall Hunt
publishing company

www.kendallhunt.com
Send all inquiries to:
4050 Westmark Drive
Dubuque, IA 52004-1840

Table of Contents

About the Author

Dr. Linsey C. Willis, with more than 39 years of human resources (HR) and management experience, is currently president of L. J. CRAIG & Associates, Inc., a management and organizational consulting firm. Her firm's clients represent a diverse mix of organizations from the public, private, and not-for-profit sectors in the United States, the Caribbean, Canada, Thailand, and Dubai. Linsey serves as an expert witness for attorneys in the employment law and personal industry disciplines. Dr. Willis is also a full-time instructor for Florida Atlantic University's College of Business. She is on the faculty of its Management Department and teaches management and HR undergraduate and graduate courses. She also teaches for the university's Executive Education Department, leading courses granting HR certification and advanced HR certification. Linsey is the author of Mastering the Assessment Center Process: The Fast Track to Promotion (2017), Charles C. Thomas Publisher, LTD.

Dr. Willis holds a doctorate in Public Administration from Nova Southeastern University, a master's degree in Forensic Studies from Indiana University, a master's degree in Public Administration from Florida Atlantic University, and a BA in Political Science from the University of Kentucky. Linsey has also earned certification in HR from the Human Resources Certification Institute, which has certified her as a senior human resources professional (SPHR).

Acknowledgements

Writing this book was a labor of love and was written for students, employees, and anyone who wants to develop their innate abilities. The commitment and perseverance it took to complete this would not have been possible without the genuine support of my husband J. Frank Willis. He is always there to share stories about my teaching and consulting projects. I also want to thank Robert S. Sloat, PhD, an associate, colleague, and friend of over 37 years who reviewed and edited the first draft. He was also a reviewer and editor of another book I wrote that was published in 2017 entitled, *Master the Assessment Center Process: The Fast Track to Promotion*. This book was written for law enforcement officers who want to be promoted. I also want to thank two of my teaching assistants Tyler Reis and Rachel Cumming who were content reviewers for this book when it was first launched and used only as an eBook. Their youthful perspectives were very important to obtain. Their feedback and comments, particularly, with the scenarios and exercises and the multiple-choice questions were invaluable. I also want to thank Pamela Feit, a graduate student who contributed one scenario which I modified for use in the 2nd edition. Finally, I want to thank my boss, Roland Kidwell, PhD, chair of the Management Department of the College of Business at Florida Atlantic University. Not only was he interested when I told him I was writing the book, but he was instrumental in facilitating the establishment of a student fund from which the royalties from the book sales could be used to benefit students. He was even considerate enough to advise me that the fund would be established in my name.

Linsey C. Willis

Preface

Most of you purchased this book to use for the course, others purchased for self-development, prepare for a job interview, or a promotion where you work. Regardless of the reasons, you made the right investment. I wrote this book because there is a skills shortage of employees looking for jobs or are currently in a position and lack the skills that are necessary to be successful (e.g., customer service skills, adaptability, dealing with people, and teamwork skills). Regardless of how you are going to use this book, you will learn a great deal about

- Yourself by first completing a self-evaluation questionnaire.
- The importance of developing your innate abilities.
- A brief history of the assessment center process.
- Several universal abilities that are important to be successful at work, in social situations and in life.
- Some seminal research findings about the different abilities.
- Emotional intelligence.
- How abilities can be measured to an extent by reading scenarios, subordinate counseling exercise, and an in-basket exercise by answering multiple-choice questions.
- Why note-taking when reading scenarios and exercises will help you to later demonstrate your innate abilities.
- Examples of when and how the abilities (weak or strong) were used.
- About yourself by rereviewing your self-evaluation exercise when you have read the book and completed the exercise, and reflecting on the extent to which you feel you improved your abilities.

CHAPTER 1
Introduction

OVERVIEW

Welcome to a new way to develop your innate abilities using the assessment center process methodology. Everyone has innate abilities, which are part of their genetic makeup. Because you probably know yourself well, you know what your strengths and weaknesses are. For example, you may be weak at public speaking but may be a much stronger writer. You may be able to make sound and logical decisions because you deliberately take the time to analyze the different options or pros and cons and do not rush to judgment. But, you are not very good at dealing with people because you are introverted. You may perceive that you have excellent interpersonal skills but your subordinates find you to be cold, aloof, and uninterested in them. Another example is about planning and organizing. You may be strong at writing an action plan but weak at implementing it. There are a multitude of other examples but you will be provided with many others throughout the book.

In my second job, out of graduate school, I learned a great deal about the assessment center process and all aspects of the methodology. Throughout my career I have continuously utilized the knowledge and hands-on experience I acquired from 1982 to the present. I am an international expert on the methodology and used this methodology to write this book for you. The experience I acquired from developing and scoring assessment center exercises helped me to develop my abilities as well as learn that one of my weaknesses was problem analysis. Regarding problem analysis, at times I over analyze a situation, get lost in the detail and then make mistakes.

I wrote ***Mastering the Assessment Center Process: The Fast Track to Promotion***, which was published by Charles C. Thomas Publishers, Ltd, in September 2017. This book was written for law enforcement officers who are preparing to participate in an assessment center process. Then I decided to write a similar book for college/university students, so they could develop their innate abilities. I decided to strike while the iron was hot.

A brief history of what an assessment center is will help you understand the methodology I used to to develop the exercises in this book. The following excerpt is from my 2017 book.

A BRIEF HISTORY OF ASSESSMENT CENTER METHODOLOGY

The first major documented use of AC procedures in American industry was a monumental study called the Management Progress Study which was conducted at AT&T beginning in 1956 (Bray, 1964; Bray, Campbell, & Grant, 1974; Bray & Grant, 1966). The study involved 422 recently hired males whose progress had been followed to determine their range of professional growth and the characteristics which led to their success in management. The results of the initial 8-year "predictive validity study" were quite positive. Eighty-five percent of the individuals who successfully reached the middle management level had been correctly identified by the assessment process (Bray & Grant, 1966; Thornton & Byham, 1982).

For over 60 years, the AC method was used in the private sector. In companies such as AT&T and JC Penny, the method was used to study adult development and has expanded to a great many countries (Lievens & Thornton, 2005). After its use became common in the United States it gained acceptance in the United Kingdom and then was adopted by Germany, Japan, South Africa, and then other country participants, who attended one of the International Congress conferences on the AC method, including Sweden, South Korea, India, Indonesia, Kuwait, Brazil, Venezuela, Russia, China, Singapore, and Malaysia (Thornton & Krause, 2009). Based on research by Thornton and Rupp (2006), the method has gained acceptance in other fields during the last 50 years, including developmental planning and advanced training. And soon after the AT&T Management Progress Study (Howard & Bray, 1988) was completed, other large corporations found that the AC method was able to identify those who had managerial talent (Thornton & Byham, 1982; Thornton & Krause, 2009).

With that background, let's go back to the years before the AC was widely adopted by private industry. The use of AC assessment and selection methods had been evolving and accelerating since its first use in this country by the Office of Strategic Services, which later became the Central Intelligence Agency. That agency assessed 5,391 persons in the United States between December 1943 and August 1945 (Mackinnon, 1977; Office of Strategic Services (OSS) Assessment Staff, 1948).

During the first year of the OSS in 1942, a large number of recruits whose performance was later deemed questionable were hired, since selection was not based upon any professional or uniform screening process. In later years, an AC methodology was utilized to predict an applicant's likelihood of success as a spy. The actual techniques and exercises used included varied and the process and methods used by the OSS involved identifying behaviors related to successful performance.

The same methods are currently being used. Moreover, a multitude of scholarly journal articles and books have been written on the methodology. Among them, Thornton and Rupp (2006) wrote Assessment Centers in Human Resource (HR) Management: Strategies for Prediction, Diagnosis, and Development *and Thornton and Gibbons (1982) published "Validity of Assessment Centers for Personnel Selection" in the* HR Management Review.

In 1970, an article by William C. Byham, appeared in the Harvard Business Review. The article based upon his experiences, as well as others, in the implementation of the AC process for J.C. Penney, captured and communicated to the general business community the enthusiasm for the evolving AC concept and the validity evidence obtained up to that point. Bray, Campbell, and Grant (1974) have also succinctly explained why it is that ACs make sense. These authors formulated the requirements of management into two basic categories. One category relates to the technical aspects of a job and to the procedural and informational foundation of effective performance. The second category encompasses various features of a managerial skill nature, including communications, motivation, influence, and leadership. Each position in a managerial hierarchy represents some blend of the two categories, that is, technical skill and managerial skill. Specific technical competencies are not measured because the Assessors are required to concentrate upon the more universal aspects of effective management performance working with and through other people (Willis, 2017).

WHAT ARE INNATE ABILITIES?

Innate abilities are also referred to as "soft skills." Soft skills have many different definitions. For example, soft skills include both intra and interpersonal abilities necessary for self-development and success in the workplace (Kechagias, 2011). Soft skills are also sought by company recruiters, which include dealing with people and being able to coordinate with others (Simpson, 2006). Soft skills are also defined as characteristics that effect a person's social interactions, job performance, and career advancement (Parsons, 2006).

Additionally, Saunderson (2017) noted in an article he wrote for training.com that soft skills are less tangible and harder to quantify than technical proficiencies. He also provided several ways a person can develop their soft skills (i.e., apprenticeship, group activities, mentoring, game-based learning), none of which included the assessment center method. He referred to the examples he summarized as situational learning which is also an excellent way to develop skills.

I did some research to find out whether there are a lot of journal articles about soft skills. There are multitudes. In fact, based on the articles I read, it is a fact that many college graduates lack soft skills. As an expert in testing and assessment, I know that soft skills are critically important. According to a study done by Adecco Staffing, United States, "forty-four percent of executives said a lack of soft skills was the biggest proficiency gap they saw in the U.S. workforce" (Feffer, 2016, p. 57). Furthermore, 67% of HR managers reported that even if a candidate lacked the technical skills, they would hire someone who possessed strong soft skills (Feffer, 2016). The latter figures were based on a report from three different organizations: the International Association of Administrative Professionals, Office Team, and HR.com.

Soft skills have also been examined in terms of whether they are important for a person's employability (i.e., a person's capability to obtain the education and skills to obtain a job). Sharma (2018) conducted a literature review of research conducted from 2000 to 2013 on employability skills. A summary of his review includes:

- Seventy-five percent of long-term job success rests on people skills, while only 25% is dependent on domain knowledge (Klaus, 2010).
- Hard skills contribute only 15% to one's success, whereas 85% of success is due to soft skills (Watts & Watts, 2008 as cited in John, 2009).
- Wilhelm's (2004) research found that employers always look out for graduates who are socially mature and adaptable for entry level positions.
- A competent workforce comprised of workers who use their soft skills to handle global business situations is needed (Caudron, 1999; Himmelsbach, 1999; Sharma, 2018, p. 27; Solomon, 1999.

The absence of soft skills is not just a problem in the United States. It has also been reported in the United Kingdom. According to Clarke (2016), the United Kingdom is dealing with a deficit in soft skills. She cited a report published by Development Economics, Ltd, for McDonalds, United Kingdom, which pointed out that by 2020 it is forecasted that well over a million workers' careers will be held back because they do not possess soft skills (Clarke, 2016). The soft skills identified in the report include the same ones lacking in the United States: communication and teamwork. Furthermore, according to the British Chamber of Commerce, 88% of employers surveyed felt that 57% of young people do not have communication, resilience, or team working skills (Clarke, 2016).

Matsouka and Mihail (2016) obtained the opinions of HR managers and university graduate's about the skills required in the labor market and following were necessary:

- Initiative
- Teamwork
- Being ethical
- Communication
- Being professional
- Demonstrating emotional intelligence
- Being able to set goals

In an article by Lauren Weber (2018) in *The Wall Street Journal* about career options for a changing economy, several career path options were provided based on whether a person possessed a high school diploma, a vocational credential, or a bachelor's degree. Paul Daugherty, chief technology and innovation officer at Accenture PLC, commented that executives will just hire new employees when their skills become obsolete. Weber noted that employers must invest in the skills of their current workers. She noted that besides technical skills, jobs require "creativity, interpersonal skills, adaptability and the capacity to continue learning" (Weber, 2018, B6).

Kyllonen said:

> One exciting development is the use of soft-skills assessment in college-placement testing. Traditionally, placement testing has been strictly cognitive—students take a mathematics test to determine their readiness for college-level mathematics coursework. Those who do not make the cutoff are assigned to take a non-credit-bearing developmental or remedial course prior to being eligible for the credit-bearing course. But perhaps non-cognitive skills, such as motivation and determination, can compensate to some extent for deficient mathematics skills. A determined student is likely to do what it takes to pass an entry-level course, whether that involves doing extra homework, studying nights and weekends, or working with a tutor.
>
> (Kyllonen, 2013, p. 20).

Kyllonen (2013) makes another very important point,

> There is considerable interest in the idea of a standardized soft-skills assessment that avoids the problems of ratings. Standardized tests of soft skills, such the MayerSalovey-Caruso Emotional Intelligence Test (MSCEIT), ask examinees to identify the emotions (e.g., happiness, fear, sadness) expressed in a picture of a face; the emotion one might feel if given additional work; or to recognize how much an action (e.g., making a list) might affect one's mood. Such assessments are beginning to be used in industry. It is likely that efforts to develop such measures will continue. (p. 22)

It is difficult to measure a person's innate abilities through a multiple-choice exam that taps into their knowledge of a certain academic discipline. But knowledge is different from abilities. I am sure you have read many different job descriptions and each one lists the knowledge, skills, and abilities that are necessary for the job holder to be successful at completing the various job tasks. If an interview process (i.e., a structured vs. an unstructured interview process) is content valid and includes scenario-type questions, a person's innate abilities can be measured to an extent. Without going into a long discussion of what abilities are (see the end of this chapter for an exhaustive list of abilities), let me just state that by reading and experiencing the contents of this book you will learn a great deal more about what your abilities are and how strong or weak you are in demonstrating them. The questions you are probably asking include: How can reading a textbook help me develop my innate abilities? What if I do not possess some abilities? How will learning about my strong and weak abilities get me a job or a better job? Is this just another textbook with assignments that are just busy work? The answers to these and other questions will be covered in each chapter.

For a start, the following are a few important reasons why you should develop yourself:

- For promotional opportunities
- For job enrichment
- To stay ahead of your competition
- To add value to the company you work for
- Self development can be intrinsically motivational
- For a sense of accomplishment

Why You Should Develop Your Innate Abilities

Whether you know it or not, you need to start working on developing your innate abilities because it is never too late. If you are already in a management position or just in a staff position, you might know that one of the most important roles a manager plays is developing their subordinates. Moreover, one of the things all effective managers do is develop themselves throughout their career regardless of whether their superior has ever been concerned with their (the manager's) development. I am sure you have heard of the saying, *"You are only as strong as your weakest link."* Well, a weak link is a subordinate who works for an organization that doesn't spend money to develop its employees. In fact, companies that spend money on employee development programs have a better track record with attracting, retaining, and motivating employees. I know this based on my years of experience teaching management and HR courses and being a management and organizational consultant.

I have read many newspaper articles that suggest a college degree is not worth the money it costs to obtain one. For example, according to an article written by Selingo (2015), "Just 38 percent of students who have graduated college in the past decade strongly agree that their higher education was worth the cost, according to results of 30,000 alumni polled by Gallup-Purdue Index." I have read other articles that include interviews from employers who have told the journalists that many of their recent hires do not have problem-solving skills, ability to deal with people, and other skills. For example, according to the NACE Center for Career Development and Talent Acquisition's 2016 Job Outlook survey, employers want leaders who can work on a team; demonstrate evidence of their leadership skills (as per their resume), written communication, problem-solving, and oral communication skills; and have a strong worth ethic.

According to research by Hart Research Associates of three of the five most important soft skills are looking for in college graduates are teamwork (83%, ethical judgment and decision making and critical/analytical thinking/reasoning (81%). Hart Research Associates, 2015, p. 4).

Why is this? Some people blame the business school curriculum, others reference the millennial and other young generations. It depends on the degree a person has obtained and whether they have ever had opportunities in school to practice or develop their innate abilities. It all depends on many intervening variables to include: the school they attended, their genetic makeup, their life experiences, who they socialize with, what part of the world they are from, how much or little work experience they have, and so on. According to Parsons (2006), soft skills are character traits that facilitate a person's interactions, job performance, and career potential (Parsons, 2006). We all develop our skills through our daily experiences.

Cappelli's Review of the Skill Gap, Skill Shortages, and Skill Mismatches

Cappelli (2015) wrote an extensive literature review about the skill gap, skill shortages, skill mismatches, and the evidence for or against. His review included many countries besides the United States. The points he made relevant to this book include the following:

- Recruiters may be the most appropriate people to ask about employer-based evidence on skills problems and since the 1980s the conclusions have been similar and focused on shortfalls with respect to conscientiousness (1995, 2015).
- A 2009 survey conducted by the Business Roundtable found that workplace attitude was one of the top seven problems.
- Oral communication skills came in eighth place (Cappelli, 2015).
- "The Institute of Director's (2010) reports argued that a biggest gap between the skills employers need and what people who have left school is in, leadership, sales, communication and customer service skills" (as cited by Cappelli, 2015, p. 262).

Training on Competencies, Emotional Intelligence, and Self-Management

Training and developing employees is a big industry, and although this book is not designed for companies' use to develop employee's abilities per say, it can help you develop your abilities, so you can get a job or be promoted at the company or organization you currently work for.

Based on the numerous police clients I and my associates have coached throughout the United States, I know that training is highly prevalent and is not only about managing conflict, but also racial profiling, active shooter, stress, and other topics. American corporations spend approximately $50 million training employees on competencies that include social and emotional intelligence. Chernis and Goleman (2001) conducted a survey of management literature pertinent to company training interventions about emotional intelligence (e.g., self-awareness, creativity, self-motivation) and determined that adults can develop their emotional intelligence competencies. The scenarios and exercises in this book have been designed to help you develop your innate abilities (aka competencies or skills), which include some scenarios about emotional intelligence (EI).

Managing yourself and modifying one's behavior is important and has been studied quite a bit since the 1970s (Burnaska, 1976; Byham, Adams & Kiggins, 1976; Moses & Ritchie, 1976; Smith, 1976 as cited by Zeidner, Roberts, & Matthews, 2009). One study found that the trained supervisor's behavior improved 6–months after the behavior modeling program (ahead of the control group) in productivity, decreased turnover, and absenteeism (Zeidner et al., 2009).

Regarding self-management training programs, based on a study done in 1986 by Kanfer (as cited by Zeidner et al., 2009), nonsupervisory employees can learn to demonstrate emotional intelligence. The proposition was that because individuals have control over the change process, they can change. Given this research and my experience with assessment center methodology, my assertion is that you can develop your abilities (including your emotional intelligence) and change your behavior if you are in control.

What does the aforementioned have to do with this discussion on why you need to develop your innate abilities? Everything, because my proposition is that once you have read and finished the experiential exercises and tests, you will not only feel that you have learned a great deal about your innate abilities, but how you can improve your weakest abilities and enhance or tweak your strongest ones. I have no doubt about this based on extensive experience using the assessment center process in many aspects of my career. A description of the contents of the book and how it will be used follows. Besides this chapter, there are 11 chapters each of which contain scenarios, a Subordinate Counseling exercise, an In-Basket (IB) exercise, and a multiple choice quiz accompanying each chapter.

The 12 Chapters

Chapter 2: Planning and Organizing
Chapter 3: Problem Analysis/Problem-Solving
Chapter 4: Judgment
Chapter 5: Decision-Making
Chapter 6: Dealing With People/Interpersonal and Emotional Intelligence
Chapter 7: Adaptability
Chapter 8: Workplace Scenarios—How Would You Handle?
Chapter 9: Subordinate Counseling Exercise
Chapter 10: Generic Management In-Basket Exercise
Chapter 11: Problem Solving Cases
Chapter 12: Reader's Feedback
Chapter 13: A Model to Reflect on and Use

Design, Organization, and the Experiential Process

This is not a typical college/university textbook. It is designed to accompany any introduction to management and organizational behavior, introduction to management, employee development, organizational development, psychological testing, and other related courses. However, the book does not cover all the standard principles and practices of the various course titles and does not have to be used strictly by college students. The book has many author citations because I summarized some of the research on each of the abilities.

The book is also designed to be used for experiential learning and can also be used by anyone who is preparing for a job interview for an entry level or management position. It can also be used by employees who will be competing in a multicomponent promotional testing process that includes simulation exercises. To recap, this book will help you develop your innate abilities by experiencing assessment center type exercises (e.g., subordinate counseling, in-basket [IB]) typically included in many processes. So as not to confuse you, a center is not a place but a process even though the exercises candidates experience take place in controlled environments. I believe that the material in this book has universal appeal because I believe most people want to improve themselves.

Finally, you will not find a book on the market like this nor will you have the opportunity to experience the types of exercises contained in the book unless you ever have an opportunity to participate in an assessment center process.

The exercises and contents simulate different business or management situations that take place in the real world. Most of the scenarios were developed based on actual situations but the names of the organizations have been changed or are made up. Moreover, when you come across a famous person's name assume that other infamous people may have the same name.

The innate abilities (e.g., planning and organizing) in each chapter are well defined and come from all the assessment center testing processes my firm has completed since 1998. None of the material in this book was borrowed from other authors. You will experience several different ways to not only learn about your abilities but how to improve them and includes:

- Completing a self-evaluation questionnaire.
- Reading many different definitions including subcomponents of universal abilities.
- Reading scenarios or exercises that tap into one or more abilities.
- Taking quizzes that are designed to measure to the extent possible with multiple choice questions, your innate abilities.
- Reading different problems solving cases and answering quiz questions.
- Reading items in an IB exercise.
- Completing a quiz about the IB exercise.
- Reading an IB assessor guide.
- Reading about a problem employee in the subordinate counseling exercise.
- Completing a quiz about this problem employee.
- Reading the subordinate counseling assessor guide.

If you did not buy this book to prepare for a promotion or for self-development purposes but to meet a college course requirement, you will be exposed to many other things that are offered within the learning management system that comes with the purchase of your book or in the CANVAS learning management system (only if you are registered as a student). These things include discussion questions, videos, and other ways to learn about innate abilities and how to develop yours.

Multiple-Choice Questions

Question 1

Soft skills are referred to as,

A

Innate abilities

B

A person's genetic make-up

C

Strengths and weaknesses

D

Likes and dislikes

Question 2

What is directly stated in the text as a reason for a worker's career being held back?

A

No technical abilities

B

Poor people skills

C

Lacks soft skills

D

Language Barrier

E

All of the above

Question 3

According to the author, what will you learn a great deal about by reading this book?

A

Innate abilities

B

Soft skills

C

How to move up the corporate hierarchy

D

Your strengths and weaknesses

E

All of the above.

Question 4

What did the British Chamber of Commerce find out about soft skills?

A

Young people do not have communication, resilience, or team working skills.

B

Millennials do not care about developing their skills.

C

According to 75% of employers surveyed, young people lack soft skills.

D

They are developed by students at all British secondary schools.

E

The most important soft skills are conscientiousness, extroversion, and communication.

Question 5

According to the NACE Center for Career Development and Talent Acquisition's 2016 Job Outlook Survey, what do employers want?

A

Motivated, energetic employees who have good problem solving and people skills.

B

Young, energetic, and motivated employees.

C

Leaders who can work on a team, and demonstrate evidence of written communication, problem solving, oral communication skills, and have a strong work ethic.

D

Leaders who know their strengths and weaknesses and constantly develop themselves.

E

Educated, technically astute workers who also possess soft skills.

Question 6

How will this book help you develop your innate abilities?

A

By experiencing assessment center type exercises.

B

By answering discussion questions.

C

Reading the exercises and writing reports.

D

A and B.

E

Taking some standardized online intelligence tests.

Question 7

What does the author write about multiple choice exams?

A

Most exams test a person's knowledge of a subject.

B

It is difficult to measure a person's innate abilities in this type of exam.

C

A and B

D

Abilities cannot be measured by taking any multiple-choice exam.

E

All of the above.

Question 8

This book is:

A

Not a typical college/university textbook.

B

Not available on the open market.

C

Used by thousands of universities around the world.

D

A new way to develop your innate abilities by using the assessment center process methodology.

E

A and D.

CHAPTER 2
Planning and Organizing

OVERVIEW

Welcome to **Chapter 2**, which is about planning and organizing. Let's start with a definition I have used in past promotional testing processes.

- **Planning and Organizing:** Plans and organizes daily work routine. Establishes priorities for the completion of work and uses time management strategies. Avoids duplication of effort. Estimates expected time of completion of work elements and establishes a personal schedule accordingly. Attends required meetings, planning sessions, and discussions on time. Implements work activity in accordance with priorities and estimated schedules. Plans, coordinates, and uses information effectively to enhance activities and production. Knows and understands expectations regarding such activities and work to ensure such expectations are met and in a timely manner. Develops and formulates ways, means, and timing to achieve established goals and objectives. Effectively and efficiently utilizes resources to achieve such goals and objectives.

Now that you have read the entire definition, you should have noticed many of the words are action verbs. The sentences are subdimensions; that is, comprise the planning and organizing ability.

ANALYSIS/DISCUSSION ABOUT PLANNING AND ORGANIZING SUBDIMENSIONS

- *Plans and organizes daily work routine.*

The following is one way to learn more about planning and organizing. Think about how you would answer the questions. If your boss asks you how you plan and organize your daily work, what would you tell him or her? If your boss asks you to write a plan for launching a new product or service, what would be your first step?

- Do you first identify the tasks you complete daily and then work on a project or report that you do not work on every day?
- Do you know how long it takes to complete all the word of your job tasks?
- Does your daily work routine involve meetings with peers and/or subordinates?
- Do you have to organize your resources every day, once a week, twice a month, and so on?

If you do not know the answers to the abovementioned questions, you should think about each question and write down what actions you currently take or plan on taking to be more effective when planning and organizing your daily routine.

- ***Establishes priorities for the completion of work and uses time management strategies***.

Every day at work, school, or in our daily lives, we have priorities and we must determine how we are going to accomplish the priorities and the order in which each priority will be handled. How do you establish priorities?

The following questions are optional but will give you greater understanding of your own planning and organizing skills.

In the box provided, check off the following tasks you complete to establish priorities:

Question 1

Write or type in the computer the things that need to be completed daily.

Yes.

☐

No.

☐

Question 2

Determine how long each task will take.

Yes.

☐

No.

☐

Question 3

Rewrite the list and put in rank order; that is, the most important task will be completed first, and so on.

Yes.

☐

No.

☐

Question 4

Determine whether the tasks that take the most time will be done first or last based on my personality preference.

Yes.

☐

No.

☐

Question 5

Ensure that I am not interrupted when completing the most difficult tasks because interruptions cause me to lose focus.

Yes.

☐

No.

☐

Question 6

Turn my cell phone to vibrate to prevent interruptions.

Yes.

☐

No.

☐

Question 7

Close my office door and let my boss, staff, or coworkers know that I do not want to be interrupted and for how long.

Yes.

☐

No.

☐

- *Avoids duplication of effort*.

When you start to work at a new company or organization, you will learn how to complete each job task and will eventually find out whether you are or someone else is completing the same task (e.g., completing a form, making phone calls, getting back with a customer). The duplication can be anything, so be imaginative and think about when this has happened to you. Think about and try to answer these questions:

- Have you ever worked at a company or other organization where different staff are completing the same tasks?

- Have you ever had to redo some of your work because you find out that someone else already completed the work?
- Have you ever had to redo your work more than once because you made too many mistakes?

There are several ways to ensure the duplication of effort does not occur. However, some of the ways listed later assume that you are in control of the situation. If you do not have total control over your work (e.g., autonomy), then duplication of effort may occur.

Let me suggest a few strategies to prevent or reduce the amount of duplication of effort you sometimes have to deal with at work.

1. Read and learn about all policies and procedures that apply to your department.
2. Find out whether any procedures are also part of another policy.
3. Evaluate whether the overlap is necessary and if so why.
4. Discuss the duplication with your boss, subordinates, or coworkers.
5. Suggest that the procedure(s) be rewritten by the person responsible for writing and updating policies and procedures.
6. If the procedure will not be changed any time soon, speak to the person in charge (if you do not have control over the situation) and suggest that the duplication stop, if possible.
7. Explain your rationale for terminating the duplication of effort so you do not offend anyone.
8. Try not to rush to complete tasks, particularly those that you dislike completing as this may cause you to make mistakes.

Summary Points

Overall, when planning and organizing, the individual must engage in many different actions to plan and organize. As you might already know, planning and organizing is not as easy as you think. It does not happen by just snapping your fingers, looking at a piece of paper or the computer screen, or scheduling an impromptu meeting with staff, and so on. It takes time, which today so many people do not have enough of which may be the result of poor planning and organizing abilities. Based on my work experience, there are many situations and statements people have made about being short on time:

- *I do not have the time to plan and organize; I get interrupted too often to write anything down.*
- *There is no need to write a plan, I have the information in my head.*
- *We have never planned here and do not need to because things just happen.*
- *I have too many things to accomplish and not enough time.*
- *I do better when the work just happens, if I follow a written plan, I get lost.*
- *Priorities change all the time around here so there is no need to write a plan.*
- *Planning and organizing is my supervisor's job.*
- *Writing a plan that includes organizing resources, takes too much time.*
- *I just do the work and the planning and organization unfolds as I do the work.*

You may be wondering, "What do the latter statements have to do with developing my planning and organizing skills?" First, if you have ever experienced any of the aforementioned, then you need to change your thinking about these two interrelated abilities. Second, the material in this chapter will help you realize that all the ***issues/problems/opinions*** can be resolved or changed.

FIVE SCENARIOS AND IN-BASKET ITEMS

The remainder of this chapter includes six different scenarios involving planning and organizing. The following will take place:

- A scenario is presented.
- You should read and think about the situation described in the scenario.
- Write some notes about how you handle or would handle the situation.
- Think about how you will plan and organize the work to solve the problem or issues.
- Read the rest of the scenarios and go through the same process.
- Take the quiz.

Carefully read and think about what the problems are. When you take the quiz, you will be provided with five planning and organizing scenarios. There are a total of 13 questions.

When reading each scenario, pretend you are at work for the company. Focus only on what is presented. Do not over analyze what is presented. In other words, do not assume things or issues that are not obvious. Also, do not worry about the size of the company, not having an organizational chart, or not knowing the names of the people described in the scenario. In summary, the only information available is what is written. Use this information to demonstrate your planning and organizing abilities.

- **Going out of town**
- **Subordinate's difficulty with job tasks**
- **Reduction in force (RIF)**
- **Newly promoted employee**
- **Planning for a promotion**
- **In-basket items**

Scenario 1: Going Out of Town

It is Monday morning and you are working diligently to complete several tasks before leaving town for 3–days for a workshop. Training and development are wonderful employee benefits offered by your company and you never miss an opportunity. Your plane leaves tomorrow morning at noon. Your boss walks into your office and tells you he needs the marketing report you have been working to complete. You are told that it must be finished today and not Friday, the day you return from the workshop. You have four other priority tasks to complete before you leave.

How do you plan and organize your work to complete everything before you leave town?

Multiple-Choice Questions: Going Out of Town

Question 1

Which below is/are the **BEST** action(s) to take regarding the other four priority tasks?

A

Review each of the tasks for importance and due dates.

B

Determine how long it will take to complete each one.

C

Delegate whatever tasks that can be delegated.

D

Handle all of them in rank order.

E

A, B, and C.

Question 2

Given that your boss has asked you for the marketing report today instead of Friday, what do you do?

A

Tell him I cannot complete it because I am going out of town.

B

Ask him what time he needs it by the end of the day.

C

Tell him I will complete the report immediately so he will have it before I leave town.

D

Tell him that I do not have time to complete it due to four other priority items I must complete.

E

Tell him that he will have it but it may be incomplete because of time constraints.

Question 3

What is/are the **BEST** plans and way(s) to organize and complete your work before you leave town?

A

Hold all calls, cancel all meetings, complete the easiest tasks first.

B

Stay at work and if necessary, take the remaining tasks home, complete, and submit.

C

Finish priority tasks and delegate the rest if possible.

D

Make sure the marketing report is completed first.

E

B, C, and D.

Scenario 2: Subordinate's Difficulty with Job Tasks

You are into the sixth month of your job as an Account Executive for a software company that writes and sells phone applications. You have three subordinates. Their former boss took a job with another company. They are very familiar with the work flow. However, two of them are having difficulties getting their tasks done on time and have missed or been late to team meetings. The situation is getting worse and you have observed this yourself and received employee complaints.

Multiple-Choice Questions: Subordinate's Difficulty With Job Tasks

Question 4

Regarding the two subordinates who have had difficulty getting their tasks done on time, what are you plan(s) of action?

A

Schedule them for a time management workshop ASAP.

B

Schedule a meeting with both of them and ask them which tasks they are having difficulty with and why.

C

Meet with them together and review the job tasks to determine how important and how long each task takes to complete.

D

Determine if any of the tasks can be handled by other staff.

E

All of the above.

Question 5

Given that two of your subordinates have missed or been late to team meetings, what is your plan for resolving this problem?

A

Track the number of times they have missed or been late to team meetings and complete disciplinary forms.

B

Schedule and hold a meeting with them and ask them why they have missed/been late to meetings; document this; advise them that they may be disciplined if this continues; monitor their comings and goings; schedule follow-up meetings with them.

C

In a prescheduled meeting, advise them that they can no longer miss or be late to meetings and outline the repercussions.

D

Tabulate how many times each person has been late or missed a meeting, provide them with the information and tell them to arrive on time.

E

Ask them when and how they will stop missing meetings and arrive on time to meetings and tell them to write up their plans and submit to me.

Question 6

Which below **BEST** describes how the employee's familiarity with the work flow relates to planning and organizing?

A

It can be used as a starting point to help them better plan and organize their work so they complete tasks in a timelier manner.

B

Knowing the work flow should enable them to indicate how long it takes to complete each task and what steps can be streamlined or eliminated.

C

It doesn't because the flow or work tasks is not planning and organizing of the tasks.

D

Employees can plan and organize how and when they will complete each task.

E

All of the above.

Scenario 3: Reduction in Force

You are a Customer Service Representative for an engineering company that manufactures parts for cars and trucks. You have held the position for 2–years and are very familiar with how things are done. The company recently went through a RIF and you are one of the few employees who kept their job. Before the RIF there were 8 customer service representatives. Now there are only four representatives and as a result your workload has increased. You are entitled to overtime pay but must ask for it in advance and management does not approve much overtime. Your job tasks include all of the following:

- Confer with customers by telephone or in person to provide information about products or services, take or enter orders, cancel accounts, or obtain details of complaints.
- Check to ensure that appropriate changes were made to resolve customers' problems.
- Keep records of customer interactions or transactions, record details of inquiries, complaints, or comments, as well as actions taken.
- Resolve customers' service or billing complaints by performing activities such as exchanging merchandise, refunding money, or adjusting bills.
- Complete contract forms and prepare change of address records, or issue service discontinuance orders, using computers.
- Refer unresolved customer grievances to designated departments for further investigation.

- Determine charges for services requested, collect deposits or payments, or arrange for billing.
- Contact customers to respond to inquiries or to notify them of claim investigation results or any planned adjustments.
- Solicit sales of new or additional services or products.
- Order tests that could determine the causes of product malfunctions.
- Obtain and examine all relevant information to assess validity of complaints and to determine possible causes, such as extreme weather conditions that could increase utility bills.
- Review claims adjustments with dealers, examine parts claimed to be defective, and approving or disapproving dealers' claims.
- Review insurance policy terms to determine whether a loss is covered by insurance.
- Compare disputed merchandise with original requisitions and information from invoices and prepare invoices for returned goods.
- Recommend improvements in products, packaging, shipping, service, or billing methods and procedures to prevent future problems.

Source: O*Net OnLine, 43-4051.00—Customer Service Representatives.

Multiple-Choice Question: Reduction in Force

Question 7

How will you plan and organize your work to complete all of your tasks in a timely manner?

A

Ask my boss which of my job tasks can be given to clerical employees to handle.

B

Determine which tasks are done daily, several times a week, bimonthly or other times; determine how long each one takes to complete and how important one is.

C

Write a to-do list every day which includes all tasks that must be completed.

D

Work through lunch and ask for overtime to ensure all works are completed daily.

E

Both B and C.

Scenario 4: Newly Promoted Employee

Assume that you are James/Janis Franco and work for Craig Industries, makers of no wrinkle, high, end business attire. The attire is custom made and fitted online via video conference meetings. The company became a multinational corporation last year and successfully raised a 120 million dollars in its initial public offering (IPO).

This week you were offered the Marketing Manager position at the conclusion of a competitive internal selection process. One of your new direct reports, a female, was interviewed for the position, but fared poorly. You start the position next week.

You will have 6 direct reports who are responsible for 49 employees (five positions are currently vacant) in four different countries. Your boss, Hugh Jackman, Director of Marketing, wants to meet with you the afternoon of your first work day to hear about your plans for the first 60–days on the job. He has a reputation for being a great strategist and visionary thinker, but he is known to be someone who is keenly interested in the important details. Expect him to ask you many specific questions.

Question 8

Which below are the **BEST** plans of action?

A

Review all policies and procedures, ethics code and work flow processes, strategic plan, budget, and identify any current problems that need to be addressed.

B

Review each supervisor's personnel file, walk around the office and speak to all employees (in small work groups and/or individually).

C

Schedule one-on-one meetings with each supervisor and then have a meeting with all employees and then set priorities.

D

Review sampling of reports (i.e., monthly, quarterly), senior staff meetings, other relevant documents.

E

All of the above.

Question 9

Which plan(s) would you prepare for and complete regarding the employee who was not selected for the position?

A

Read her personnel file, carefully observe her on the job, and meet with her, when appropriate.

B

Schedule a meeting with her and review her goals and objectives.

C

Plan to discuss why she did not get the job.

D

Be prepared with documentation in case she files a grievance against me.

E

None of the above.

Question 10

Given that Mr. Jackman has a reputation for being a great strategist and paying attention to the important details, which below are the **BEST** plans for your meeting?

A

Make sure I review the entire strategic plan for my department, update him on our accomplishments but include only the most important details.

B

Print two copies of strategic plan, prepare summary list of most important accomplishments, and prepare list of questions (and my answers) he may ask me, and review the material before meeting.

C

Allow him to run the meeting and prepare a list of questions he may ask me.

D

Contact him before the meeting and ask him what details are most important to him.

E

Conduct meeting with him by going through each goal and objective on the entire plan and fill in a few details.

Scenario 5: Planning for a Promotion

Assume that you are Document Management Specialist for LdshipEdge Corporation, a multinational management consulting firm with clients in 75 countries. You have held the position for 3–years and have just applied for a management analyst position because you have over 7–years of analytical experience. It was posted on the company's intranet and listed for current employees only. You know that two of your coworkers are applying and other employees who work in different departments may apply. A synopsis of the job description is below.

Job Description
Management Analyst

Position Overview: Conduct organizational studies and evaluations, design systems and procedures, conduct work simplification and measurement studies, and prepare operations and procedures manuals to assist management in operating more efficiently and effectively. Includes program analysts and management consultants.

Essential Duties and Responsibilities

- Document findings of study and prepare recommendations for implementation of new systems, procedures, or organizational changes.
  - Interview personnel and conduct on-site observation to ascertain unit functions, work performed, and methods, equipment, and personnel used.
  - Analyze data gathered and develop solutions or alternative methods of proceeding.

- Plan study of work problems and procedures, such as organizational change, communications, information flow, integrated production methods, inventory control, or cost analysis.
- Confer with personnel concerned to ensure successful functioning of newly implemented systems or procedures.
- Provide guidance and expert advice to management or other groups on technical, systems- or process-related topics.
- Gather and organize information on problems or procedures.
- Prepare manuals and train workers in use of new forms, reports, procedures or equipment, according to organizational policy.
- Review forms and reports and confer with management and users about format, distribution, and purpose, identifying problems and improvements.
- Develop and implement records management program for filing, protection, and retrieval of records, and assure compliance with program.
- Design, evaluate, recommend, and approve changes of forms and reports.
- Analyze information and evaluate results to choose the best solution and solve problems by using decision-making and problem-solving skills.
  - Identify the underlying principles, reasons, or facts of information by breaking down information or data into separate parts.
  - Observe, receive, and otherwise obtain information from all relevant sources.
  - Provide information to supervisors, coworkers, and subordinates by telephone, in written form, e-mail, or in person.
  - Develop constructive and cooperative working relationships with others, and maintaining them over time.
  - Translate or explain what information means and how it can be used.
  - Develop specific goals and plans to prioritize, organize, and accomplish your work.
  - Compile, code, categorize, calculate, tabulate, audit, or verify information or data.
  - Establish long-range objectives and specify the strategies and actions to achieve them.
  - Identify information by categorizing, estimating, recognizing differences or similarities, and detecting changes in circumstances or events.
  - Keep up-to-date technically and applying new knowledge to your job.
  - Develop, design, or create new applications, ideas, relationships, systems, or products, including artistic contributions.
  - Handle complaints, settle disputes, and resolve grievances and conflicts, or otherwise negotiate with others.
  - Use computers and computer systems (including hardware and software) to program, write software, set up functions, enter data, or process information.

Abilities

Active Listening—Giving full attention to what other people are saying, taking time to understand the points being made, asking questions as appropriate, and not interrupting at inappropriate times.

Critical Thinking—Using logic and reasoning to identify the strengths and weaknesses of alternative solutions, conclusions or approaches to problems.

Reading Comprehension—Understanding written sentences and paragraphs in work-related documents.

Judgment and Decision Making—Considering the relative costs and benefits of potential actions to choose the most appropriate one.

Oral Communication (Speaking, comprehension, and expression)—Talking to others to convey information effectively. The ability to listen to and understand information and ideas presented through spoken words and sentences. The ability to communicate information and ideas in speaking so others will understand.

Inductive Reasoning and Deductive Reasoning—The ability to combine pieces of information to form general rules or conclusions (includes finding a relationship among seemingly unrelated events). The ability to apply general rules to specific problems to produce answers that make sense.

Deductive Reasoning—Problem Sensitivity—The ability to tell when something is wrong or is likely to go wrong. It does not involve solving the problem, only recognizing there is a problem.

Written Communication—The ability to communicate information and ideas in writing so others will understand.

Job Specifications (minimum entrance requirements): Master's degree and extensive skill knowledge and experience working on management projects. A 4-year college degree in business, management, or a related field, and over 7–years of experience may substitute for not possessing a master's degree. Certification in project management or a related discipline will also be considered. Some experience coordinating, training, or supervising or managing the activities of others to accomplish goals is also preference.

Adapted from (https://www.onetonline.org/link/summary/13-1111.00 Summary Report for: 13-1111.00—Management Analysts)

You believe you are qualified for the position and will make the cut for the interview process. However, you are concerned about your competition and how past internal promotions were handled. Moreover, even though you have not completed your master's degree you have many years of related experience.

You recall and think about what was rumored to have happened with past internal promotional processes:

- Two employees were preselected for the position for which they applied for.
- One employee did not possess a college degree but had 15–years of experience and was referred by one of the Directors.
- The interview process included situational (scenarios) questions which none of the candidates were advised would occur prior to the interview process.
- One employee was selected because of gender and race despite not being qualified.

All candidates must complete an online application, submit an up-to-date resume, and official college transcripts for any degrees obtained since being hired by the company.

The application submission deadline is 2–weeks from today. Your calendar is booked solid and you also have an out of town business meeting you must attend.

Question 11

Which below is the **BEST** way for you to plan and organize in order to submit the required documents by the due date?

A

Clear my calendar of all meetings that can be rescheduled, in order to have sufficient free time to complete the application process.

B

Review the online application portal to ensure that I fully understand how to complete the online application; contact the HR department if I have any questions.

C

Review and update my resume; contact a resume writing service if I need help; review final document before submitting.

D

Obtain a transcript of the courses I have completed toward my master's degree and submit it with other documents; find out if the HR department will accept the credits I already completed.

E

All of the above.

Question 12

You have just been notified that you made the cut for the interview process. What plans will you make to prepare for the interview?

A

Reread the job description, find out who else has applied, set up a study group for the interview process.

B

Study the job description tasks and abilities, and find books on Amazon about situational interviews, buy some of the best books, read each one.

C

Set aside study time before the interview, and get a good nights' rest the night before.

D

Read situational interview questions and the response standards that are relevant to the position.

E

B, C, and D.

Question 13

What plans would you make if any, about how the past internal promotional processes were handled?

A

None.

B

I would obtain as much information about situational interviews by conducting research on the web and read and study the materials.

C

Try to schedule a meeting with the HR department to find out more about the interview process.

D

Contact employees in the company to find out if the rumors are true so I can prepare for not being selected.

E

A, B, and C.

The next scenario is an example of written in-basket essay. You **DO NOT** have to write an essay. Write down which items you would complete first, second, and so on, and why. Chapter 10 contains a practice in-basket with a multiple-choice quiz.

Scenario 6: In-Basket Items

It is 9:00 a.m. on Monday morning and you are in your office and have several tasks to handle today. They are

1. You have a performance evaluation meeting with one of your employees at 10:00 a.m.
2. A call has been transferred to you. It is your wife and she has an emergency.
3. A client is waiting in the lobby for you regarding a previously scheduled meeting set to start at 9:15 a.m.
4. There are 15 new e-mail messages in your inbox. The first 3 you already glanced at are very important follow-up messages from potential clients.
5. Your boss is walking in your office door and quickly tells you he has set up a staff meeting at 11:00 because of a crisis with one of the suppliers.
6. One of your peers from the Marketing Department is waiting outside your office. He has a few questions he wants to discuss with you in person.
7. You have a doctors' appointment at noon.

How will you handle 1 to 7?

CHAPTER 3

Problem Analysis/Problem-Solving

OVERVIEW

Welcome to **Chapter 3**, where you will learn a great deal about problem analysis and problem-solving (aka perception and analysis). Their definitions will vary based on the job analysis for the target organization. Moreover, these constructs can be measured many ways and by trained assessors and will determine whether a person is evaluated as being strong, average, or weak.

When I explain one of the aforementioned abilities to my coaching clients I often break down the definition of perception and analysis (aka problem analysis, problem-solving) and indicate that the various exercises they will be participating in measure one of these abilities. For your learning experience, I have presented the subcomponents of perception and analysis as questions, which you can think about and attempt to answer as follows:

1. Can I quickly identify a problem and analyze it?
2. Am I able to notice details or phenomena?
3. Am I able to distinquish between pertinent v. impertinent information?
4. Can I foresee the consequences of various alternatives?
5. To what extent can I obtain relevant information from available information and screen out fewer essential details?
6. Do I misinterpret information?
7. Am I able to demonstrate perceptions of an interaction between various aspects of a problem and between various actions taken or available to be taken?
8. To what extent am I able to use data and related information to evaluate a problem?
9. To what extent am I able to logically interpret information to solve problems?

I suspect you felt that those were difficult questions and the list could be presented with a self-report rating scale of 1 to 5 with 5 being strongly agree and 1 strongly disagree. However, you may evaluate yourself higher or lower than what your true ability reflects when participating in an assessment center process. In this chapter, you will have an opportunity to learn something about your abilities as noted in the first paragraph.

DEFINITION OF PROBLEM ANALYSIS

My definition of problem analysis, which is composed of many action verbs, focuses on a person's ability to

- Gather and analyze the most critical information needed to understand problems.
- Probe and go beyond past symptoms to determine underlying causes of problems and issues.
- Integrate information from various sources.
- Define reasonable alternatives to resolve problems.
- Base decisions to solve problems on sound logic and rationale.
- Choose the best alternative despite uncertainty.
- Evaluate pros and cons, trade-offs, legal issues, timing, customer or stakeholder issues, and available resources.

As you should have noticed, the two definitions of perception and analysis are similar and overlap. Nevertheless, your ability to solve problems is very important in your personal life and particularly at work. If you are weak at problem-solving, there are ways to improve (e.g., Mindtools), but being weak in problem analysis and problem-solving can result in

- Missed opportunities.
- Overlooking important information necessary for a report, project, purchase, meeting, feedback, and so on.
- Mistakes being made
- Wasted budget dollars.
- Delays in completing tasks.
- Delays for staff.
- Delays for your superior(s).
- Delays in work assigned by your superior(s).
- A customer complaint.
- A major political problem.
- A major risk to the company.
- A problem for a subordinate, which is not his or her fault.
- Missed review of data, which results in making the wrong decision(s).
- A reprimand or other disciplinary action taken against you.
- Loss of your job.

If this has ever happened to you then based on your weak problem analysis/problem-solving abilities, flawed, poor, or incorrect decisions were more than likely made.

SOME RESEARCH

While conducting research for this chapter, I came across a very good quote from Wedell-Wedellsborg (2017)

> What they struggle with, it turns out, is not solving problems but figuring out what the problems are. In surveys of 106 C-suite executives who represented 91 private and public-sector companies in 17 countries, I found that a full 85% strongly agreed or agreed that their organizations were bad at problem diagnosis, and 87% strongly agreed or agreed that this flaw carried significant costs. Fewer than one in 10 said they were unaffected by the issue. The pattern is clear: Spurred by a penchant for action, managers tend to switch quickly into solution mode without checking whether they really understand the problem. (p. 78)

Another way to think about and understand problem-solving is from a technical report I obtained from the National Center for Educational Statistics, Institute for Education Sciences (Dossey, McCrone, O'Sullivan, & Gonzales, 2006), which at the time was part of the U.S. Department of Education. The researchers categorized problem-solving in three ways: *decision-making*, *system analysis and design*, and *troubleshooting*.

They defined the three categories as follows:

> Decision making problems describe situations where an individual has to understand a situation, identify the relevant alternatives and constraints, and select among them to reach the best decision. System analysis and design problems characterize situations that require a student to consider and dissect a complex situation or set of requirements and the myriad relationships existing among them. Troubleshooting problems require a student to understand the main features of a malfunctioning system or device, eliminate possibilities that might explain the difficulty, and devise an explanation for the perceived difficulty.
>
> (Dossey et al., 2006, p. 10).

On the other hand, Wedell-Wedellsborg (2017) suggested three different criteria that should be used when making a decision (which is based on a person's analysis of an issue or problem). They are *must*, *should*, and *might*. He also notes that the risk factor, which is very difficult, should be included when making a decision. You should also learn why decision-making and problem-solving (aka problem analysis and perception and analysis) go together. You can also learn more about how good your problem-solving skills are by completing a variety of exercises found on the Mindtools website.

https://www.mindtools.com/pages/article/newTMC_72.htm

In fact, "a set of common factors defining problem solving appears through the literature on the subject" (see Bransford, Brown, & Cocking, 1999; Mayer & Salovey, 1997; and English 2002 for reviews of the literature; Dossey et al., 2006, p. 10). According to this research report, the factors involved in problem-solving are individually based. Questions asked include:

- Does the learner have any strategies they can use to apply their knowledge of problem-solving?
- To what extent are monitoring and control used by the individual?
- What role does an individual's beliefs and attitudes play and how willing is he/she to engage in problem-solving?
- What are the individual's cognitive preparations when he/she is engaged in problem-solving? (Dossey et al., 2006, p. 10)

My experience, over the past 39-years with assessment center methodology, has taught me that people who have initially participated in a variety of job simulation exercises demonstrate a variety of problem-solving abilities ranging from weak to strong as well as other abilities (e.g., judgment and decision-making). Examples include their verbal statements and written communication. Also, I do know that some people can learn to shore up on their weak abilities but only up to a point. Wedell-Wedellsborg (2017) stated,

> *Wrong decisions are an inevitable aspect of life, both in our personal and professional lives. We redeem them by learning the lessons they teach us, paying the fees that life charges as cheerfully as we can. But bad decisions are predictable pitfalls; they are unenforced errors. (p. 35)*

He provided, what he believes are proven processes, methods, and techniques. His key problem-solving strategies are included as a tool for you to practice. He presents his methods for understanding and solving a problem in a question format (pp. 59–60). For this book I modified his presentation as follows:

1. Document when you became aware of the problem.
2. Define the problem using your own words.
3. Determine whether there are any general solutions.
4. Be clear about your goals.
5. Include all important factors and salient facts.
6. Describe problem as simply as possible.
7. Check your main assumptions.
8. Consolidate the assumptions into a shorter list.
9. Cull your list further.
10. Synthesize remaining items.
11. Make sure to include the criteria used to judge the various alternatives.
12. Work backward, if appropriate.
13. Contact anyone else you know who has faced a similar problem (Wedell-Wedellsborg, 2017).

Finally, I reviewed chapters in *The Psychology of Problem Solving*, by Davidson and Sternberg (2003). They summarized Sternberg's triarchic theory of human intelligence that includes eight components as follows:

1. "Recognizing the existence of a problem,
2. Defining the nature of the problem,
3. Allocating mental and physical resources to solving the problem,
4. Deciding how to represent information about the problem,
5. Generating the set of steps needed to solve the problem,
6. Combining the steps into a workable strategy for problem solution,
7. Monitoring the problem-solving process while it is ongoing, and
8. Evaluating the solution to the problem after problem solving is completed" (p. 5).

As you should note, the previous definitions are similar and overlap. Also, when Sternberg formulated his theory, he may have borrowed from the literature on management about planning and monitoring. It is my opinion that Davidson and Sternberg's statement, "problem recognition, definition, and representation are meta-level executive processes" (p. 5) is valid.

The various exercises used in an assessment center process are designed to measure management abilities and problem-solving is one that is critically important. If managers can solve problems based on their careful analysis of the different elements, then the quality of their decisions is significantly better. As Einstein and Infeld (1938, p. 92) argued, "the formulation of a problem is often more essential than its solution." Choo, Nag, and Xia's (2015) study findings also suggest the importance of problem formulation in problem-solving by top management.

FIVE SCENARIOS

The remainder of this chapter includes five different scenarios involving problem analysis/ problem-solving. The following will take place:

- A scenario is presented.
- You should read and think about the situation described in the scenario.
- Write some notes about how you handle or would handle the situation.
- Think about how you will plan and organize the work to solve the problem or issues.
- Read the rest of the scenarios and go through the same process.
- Take the quiz.

Carefully read and think about what the problems are. When you take the quiz, you will be provided with five possible options.

When reading each scenario, pretend you are at work for the company. Focus only on what is presented. Do not overanalyze what is presented. In other words, do not assume things or issues that are not obvious. Also, do not worry about the size of the company, not having an organizational chart, or not knowing the names of the people described in the scenario. In summary, the only information available is what is written. Use this information to demonstrate your problem analysis and problem solving abilities.

- **Employee with outside business.**
- **Crude and sexual jokes made during shift.**
- **Promotional hiring process problem.**
- **Climate survey results.**
- **Human resources problems.**

PROBLEM ANALYSIS/PROBLEM-SOLVING (AKA PERCEPTION AND ANALYSIS) SCENARIOS

Scenario 1: Employee With Outside Business

Assume that you are a Manager at ABC Corporation. You have 6 direct reports, 2 paraprofessionals and 4 labor/trades employees. One of your labor/trades employees (an African American female) comes to you with a problem that you will have to handle, if true. There are allegations that another employee has been running his own business during work hours. This employee overheard a few of the workers talking about this individual making extra money during working hours and that he had a good thing going. You have heard that one of his customers, who frequents a local restaurant/bar in town, was talking about helping this employee make more money. These employees frequent the same restaurant/bar. You are aware that they posted pictures of themselves on Facebook.

Multiple-Choice Questions: Employee With Outside Business

Question 1

What would you say/ask/tell this employee?

A

Ask her if she would be willing to provide me with the names of her coworkers and to keep our conversation confidential.

B

Tell her that I will report the issue to the HR department.

C

Tell her that I will access the employee's Facebook page.

D

If the allegations are true tell her that he will be fired.

E

All of the above.

Question 2

Which are the most important problems addressed in this situation?

A

An employee is focusing on gossip and rumors instead of work.

B

Allegations of an employee working on his outside business during work hours.

C

Posting pictures on Facebook.

D

Possible unethical behaviors at work.

E

An employee is focusing on what another employee's actions are instead of her own work.

Question 3

Regarding posting pictures on Facebook what problems are there with this?

A

Posting the pictures during work hours and using company equipment to do so.

B

Nothing, because employees have a right to use Facebook and post pictures of themselves wherever and whenever they want.

C

The pictures might/do violate the law; for example, child pornography.

D

Nothing, because under the National Labor Relations Act, this is concerted activity.

E

Letting everyone know who your off-duty customers are.

Scenario 2: Crude and Sexual Joke and Comments Made During Shift

You work on the evening shift in the package distribution center of a large multinational corporation. The distribution center operates 24 hours a day, 7 days per week and 365 days annually. You work alongside 30 other coworkers. There are also robots which move the pallets up and down the columns and rows. Technicians handle all the problems with the robots. During the night shift there is only 1 manager on duty v. 3 during the two other shifts. The reasons are: no phone calls, less work, and a cost cutting measure.

The company is very diverse especially for those working in the packaging and distribution center. On your shift there are 19 men and 11 women. The ethnic and race breakdown includes an almost equal number of Caucasians, African Americans, Hispanics, and a few Asians.

One evening, you (a White male) and a female (Hispanic) coworker hear two males (one African American and one Hispanic) making crude and sexual jokes in front of, and directed at the three women who work in their area. It is known by everyone that one of the females is transgender. The jokes were about this as well as comments made about female body parts and sex. You are very offended and tell the men that what they are doing is wrong and offensive. They tell you to shut up and continue their banter.

Multiple-Choice Questions—Crude and Sexual Joke and Comments Made During Shift

Question 4

What problems might there be with having only one manager on duty during the night shift in this company?

A

Potential accidents; too small of a span of control (only one eye for 30 persons); only one person responsible for solving major problems.

B

If the manager calls in sick, there will be no one from management on duty.

C

Employee sabotage and theft.

D

Reduced productivity.

E

All of the above.

Question 5

Why is telling crude and sexual jokes at work a problem?

A

It may be unwelcome, hostile, or harassing behavior.

B

It is illegal under the federal law.

C

It may violate company policy.

D

It could result in a major liability to the company.

E

All of the above.

Question 6

Assume that you are the manager, on duty and the two employees report what they observed. What would you tell them about the problems?

A

That what they observed is a violation of company policy.

B

They did the right thing by immediately reporting this to me.

C

There will be no retaliation against them for having told me about this and our conversation will remain confidential.

D

They will be asked to sign an affidavit.

E

All of the above.

Question 7

What is/are the problem(s), if any, with an employee telling another employee to shut up particularly in front of other coworkers?

A

It is not only rude, but it is appropriate behavior.

B

Nothing, people have a right to speak their mind at work.

C

It could signal bigger problems with the culture of the workplace.

D

Poor dealing with people skills that need to be addressed with this employee.

E

A, C, and D.

Scenario 3: Promotional Hiring Process Problem

Assume you are a Production, Planning, and Expediting clerk and work for DCE Corporation. You have worked in this position for 3-years and it was the only position you could obtain after graduating from college with a business degree.

You have mastered the following tasks:

1. Distributing production schedules and work orders to departments;
2. Reviewing documenting, such as production schedules, work orders, or staffing tables, to determine personnel or materials requirements or material priorities;
3. Requisitioning and maintaining inventories of materials or supplies necessary to meet production demands;
4. Arranging for delivery, assembly, or distribution of supplies or parts to expedite flow of materials and meet production schedules.

You also feel that you have developed strong abilities when it comes to conferring with department supervisors or other personnel to assess progress and discuss needed changes.

(**Note:** Job tasks are from O*Net, Summary Report for: **43-5061.00—Production, Planning, and Expediting Clerks**).

Company policy for the majority of supervisory, management, and director-level positions is to promote from within. Therefore, a few weeks ago you applied for a first-line supervisory position in your department.

Your interview for this position is next week and you are very excited about the opportunity. At the end of the day you are notified by the manager of the department (who recently transferred into the position from another state), that the position will be readvertised because no one including you met the minimum qualifications. You also heard a rumor from a few other coworkers that he was planning to hire one of his relatives for the position. To say the least, you are very upset.

Multiple-Choice Questions: Promotional Hiring Process Problem

Question 8

Why is there a problem with an employee being scheduled for an interview and then being told by their manager that they are unqualified for the job?

A

There may not be a problem because the HR department may have made a mistake.

B

The manager is probably not following HR policies and procedures.

C

The employee may be able to file a formal complaint with the HR department or a grievance with the union (if applicable).

D

B and C only.

E

It is not fair.

Question 9

What, if anything, is problematic with hiring a relative to work directly under you, the manager?

A

It may violate the company's nepotism policy.

B

Favoritism and the relative may be given preferential treatment which is unethical.

C

A, B, and D.

D

The action could cause morale problems.

E

Nothing, if the company allows this.

Question 10

Which below are management problems with telling an employee they will not be interviewed for a job after they have already been scheduled?

A

Poor judgment, decision-making, and dealing with people skills.

B

Poor collaboration with HR department staff.

C

Poor planning.

D

There are no problems because managers can change their minds.

E

It is a violation of state and federal law.

Scenario 4: Climate Survey Results

Jerry Giant is an Operations Manager for Mars Associates, a 5-year old international company which sells online refabricated automobile and other mechanical parts. He has 25 employees in his department. The company is nonunionized.

Based on the results of the most recent climate survey, which was administered and scored by an outside company, with the assistance of the HR department, some open-ended feedback about two of his employees is very problematic. Like most other managers he has spoken to, the process is worthwhile because improvements have been made based on the feedback (e.g., reduced turnover, increased productivity and job satisfaction in many departments).

The problematic open-ended comments, many of which were repeated but stated differently (i.e., semantics) about his department are:

- Lack of teamwork;
- There are a few bullies who cause problems for everyone and nothing is being done about this;
- Bullies cause problems for everyone; low morale, fear of coming to work.
- Some people do not work well with others;
- No collaboration and it is needed and;
- Where is a manager when you need them? (Of which there were more than five similar comments in the feedback).

Jerry's V.P., Vincent Jokester has scheduled a meeting with him, in 2-weeks, to discuss how Jerry plans so solve the problems.

Question 11

Which below are the **BEST** ideas for Jerry to discuss with Jokester about how to deal with the bully problems?

A

Ask the HR department to conduct a workshop about how to deal with bullies and harassment and require all employees to attend.

B

Consider conducting one-on-one confidential meetings with all employees to find out if they have been bullied and by whom.

C

Find out why nothing was done about the bullies in the past and review each employee's personnel file.

D

Conduct a walk about the plant, meet with employees casually in an attempt to find out who are the bullies and then make plans to discipline each one.

E

A and B are the best options, although B is a much better option in order to maintain confidentiality.

Question 12

Which below is/are the **BEST** preliminary way(s) to solve the lack of teamwork and collaboration problems?

A

Find out through an internal investigation who is not working as a team, compile the results and make plans to meet with each problem employee.

B

Conduct a meeting with all employees and discuss the findings about teamwork and collaboration and ask for their feedback about how to deal with the problem.

C

Hire an outside consulting firm to train all employees about Total Quality Management.

D

Have the HR department conduct a mandatory workshop on teamwork, during which time examples will be provided where teamwork has decreased stress, increased productivity and job satisfaction.

E

All of the above.

Question 13

What should Jerry do about the comments concerning "where is a manager when you need them?"

A

Do a self-analysis and think about why some employees feel he is not there when they need him; facilitate an open-door policy; schedule weekly meetings with all staff on plant floor; meet with each employee individually, if they desire; ask each employee what he can do for them, and other behaviors needed to facilitate communication and feedback.

B

Nothing, as the comments are too general.

C

Meet with Jokester and find out his opinion about me not being there when employees need me.

D

Conduct small group meetings with employees and ask them what they mean by the comments; document the information; then meet with each employee privately to obtain more information; assure each employee of no reprisal for their honesty.

E

A, C, and D are all appropriate.

Scenario 5: Human Resource Problems

As a newly promoted manager working the third shift, you have come to realize there are several problems that need to be addressed, specifically:

- Some of staff are not adhering to the policies and procedures; for example, they are not following safety procedures, some come to work with unkempt clothing, others call in sick on Mondays or Fridays.
- Productivity is down because nonwork-related e-mails are being sent out by staff members.
- According to the informal grapevine, the past few managers have been lax in their supervision.
- When newly promoted persons try to establish their credibility, they are ignored.
- Some staff have formed informal groups which has resulted in a great deal of gossip occurring during work hours.

You are not sure who the main players are because you have just been promoted. Also you have yet gotten to know everyone well enough to interact with each employee on a personal level. You want to make sure you deal with this in an effective manner so you will make it past your probationary period. You also want to impress your boss.

Question 14

Regarding some policies and procedures not being followed, what will you do solve the problems?

A

Dealing with unkempt clothing can be handled immediately by meeting with all staff to discuss the consequences of this type of behavior.

B

Review the SOPS to identity the exact sick leave/attendance violations and meet with all staff to review the SOPs and the consequences of continuing to call in sick on Mondays or Fridays.

C

Document the sick leave/attendance records for all employees prior to meeting with each individual.

D

Meet with each person who has violated the sick leave/attendance policies; deal with accordingly (verbal informal warning, written warning, etc.).

E

All of the above with C and B being your initial priority.

Question 15

What would you do about decreased productivity?

A

Obtain and calculate how many work hours are being lost from time spent sending nonwork-related e-mails.

B

Further investigate the lax supervisory culture and formulate ways to change that posture and include meeting with my boss to discuss before implementing any plan.

C

Manage by walking around and being visible; for example, cut in on side meetings.

D

Schedule and hold regular meetings, as time permits, to review the staff's work, and to establish my command and my supervisory guidelines.

E

All of the above with D being your initial priority.

Question 16

What should you do about the grapevine (aka gossip)?

A

Find out who the members of the gossip prone informal groups and other groups are and get to know them.

B

Hold a meeting with all staff and discuss the problems created by gossip which can lower morale, is a time waster, can hurt the employees who are being gossiped about, and is counterproductive in respect to meeting company goals and objectives. Also discuss the need for ethical behavior.

C

Note any incidences I have observed, document and start the disciplinary process based on each case; continue to monitor the workplace; and also solicit my boss' feedback and assistance where applicable.

D

Facilitate an on-going dialogue with each person which may prevent them from gossiping because they will have a better relationship with me.

E

All of the above but B is the best way to start the process.

CHAPTER 4

Judgment

OVERVIEW

This chapter is about judgment. The word is a bit more complicated than just a simple noun. Judgment, also spelled judgement, pertains to a person's ability to perceive critical elements of a situation, analyze the elements, and arrive at sensible conclusions. Judgment is also involved in considering what decisions a person will make. More detailed definitions of judgment follow. In this chapter, only judgment, not decision-making, will be dealt with even though the two (judgment and decision-making are nouns) are intertwined.

Why is your ability to use render a judgment important? You can probably think of many reasons why being able to do so has been so important in your life thus far. Your use or misuse of your ability to render judgment is particularly critical in the workplace. If your judgment is

- flawed.
- clouded.
- based on gut reactions.
- based only on quick impulses.
- always spontaneous with little thought.
- based on limited information or too much information.
- based on sunk costs.
- due to peer pressure.
- based on who you want to please.
- not morally sound.
- not ethically sound.
- based on personal bias.
- based on stereotypes about people.
- politically motivated.

YOU COULD LOSE YOUR JOB!

The latter are only a few examples of how using bad or poor judgment is critical and important for your career and success in life. Even though judgment is one of the soft skills, the use or misuse of your innate judgment is not so soft and is in fact powerful and dangerous based on the context in which the judgment takes place.

Regarding your use of judgment, I am certain you can think of and document a long list of times you have used good or poor judgment. I want you to think about people you have interacted with during your life who

- Have had difficulty rendering judgment even when they have a great deal of information.
- Have no difficulty rendering their judgments with no information and often come up with the wrong conclusions.
- Are very spontaneous and do not even think before they act.
- Often get into trouble because they use poor judgment.
- Use poor judgment on a regular basis because, for example, they are very compulsive and do not take the time to think things over.
- Need to ask someone else what they should do because they do not feel comfortable with or have great difficulty making decision(s) (which is using their judgment to decide) without asking someone else.
- Use poor judgment because they did not perceive the critical elements and then "rush to judgment."
- Spend their money on things they cannot afford but purchase the items (e.g., a new car) anyway.
- Base their judgment on gut reactions.
- Render judgment without factual information/evidence when it is needed to make the right decision.

The examples may or may not translate to judgment on the job, so, let's turn to different workplace examples. One of the reasons you need to learn more about judgment and improve this ability is so that if you use poor judgment at work (based on what the situation and what judgment you used to make your decision), it could cost you your job!

Let's continue with a few more examples.

Using poor judgment at work can

1. Prevent you from being promoted
2. Result in lack of recognition by your peers
3. Result in you receiving a lower pay increase or no pay increase
4. Be a liability to the company
5. Result in a lawsuit against the company
6. Ruin your and others' reputations
7. Cause a serious on-the-job accident
8. Destroy relationships
9. Result in lost customers
10. Result lost credibility

JUDGMENT SITUATIONS AT WORK

This section provides various examples of good and poor judgment when dealing with work issues. While working on this section, I did a quick Google search about judgment and often decision-making appeared instead of judgment or both words appeared together. I believe that both words appeared together because the individuals who wrote about judgment and decision-making in news articles, a blog post, or other online documents know that a person's judgment impacts their decision-making.

In researching why people make bad decisions I found an interesting blog post by Mavity (2013). He opines that the reason there are workplace problems is due to poor judgment. Based on my knowledge and experience, I totally agree with him. Even though it was not clear to me what he was referring to (based on his job title), his findings are very interesting and important. His statement,

> *I no longer use the term "common sense" other than to criticize the term as having lost its meaning. The majority of the 500 or so workplace death cases I have investigated have involved poor judgment by an otherwise decent and skilled worker. Many incidents . . . demonstrated remarkably bad decision making. There is an absence out in the work world, of this so-called "common sense."*

Mavity also explored the McMillian dictionary to identify different definitions of bad judgment. For example, he found that a person who is foolish lacks good sense and judgment. Someone who acts impulsively does things without thinking in advance what the outcome will be. He also found that people with bad judgment who do things without thinking can be described as impetuous people who do things in a hurry and do not carefully plan are considered hasty. These are examples of bad judgment (Mavity, 2013).

Following are components of a definition of judgment, which I have used in the past for promotional testing processes to evaluate a candidate's judgment. The full definition includes sub-definitions as follows.

Exercise analytical judgment in areas of responsibility by

- Identifying core issues or situations as they occur and specify decision objectives.
- Effectively diagnosing problems, exercising common sense, seeing critical connections and ramifications, and identifying and analyzing alternatives to issues or solutions.
- Implementing decisions in accordance with prescribed and effective policies and procedures with a minimum of errors.
- Seeking expert or experienced advice, where appropriate, and researching issues, situations, and alternatives before exercising judgment.

Moral and Ethical Judgment

Making decisions that are moral and ethical is also important. The allegations of unethical decisions made by leaders of countries, companies, and governmental agencies over the past almost 40-years or so have inspired books and research about ethical leadership and related topics. If the leaders of any public or private sector organization or country are unethical and immoral, the behavior(s) can cascade throughout the organization. No research sites are necessary for this because it is common knowledge; that is, read any journal or listen to any television or online news site and you will learn about unethical and immoral leadership problems occurring around the world daily.

A micro example is when a subordinate observes their manager behaving unethically and even immorally, he or she may mirror the behavior. According to research, moral judgment and moral action are interrelated (Blasi, 1980) and hundreds of studies have predicted positive and negative behaviors. Helping others, whistle-blowing, resistance to pressure from management personnel or those in authority, and stealing and cheating are examples of positive or negative behaviors (as cited by Loviscky, Treviño, & Jacobs, 2007; see Greenberg, 2002; Rest & Narvaez, 1994; Trevino, 1986).

In the previous paragraph, I noted "almost 40 years" because when I started my career in 1980 I immediately experienced totally inappropriate, unethical, and immoral behavior. Because I had obtained a degree in Forensic studies at Indiana University, I was very familiar with deviant behavior, different types of criminal behavior, sociopathy, victimology, immorality, and other related topics. However, in 1980, I was yet to experience unethical, immoral, or criminal behavior in the workplace. But it did not take long to acquire the experience. The next few points summarize only some of my experiences with poor judgment and unethical and/or immoral behavior, which greatly influenced me.

- **Required to take a polygraph:** After starting a new job and working a few weeks, my manager decided to make me take a polygraph. I asked him why I had to do this and he gave me no reason other than he wanted me to. After I completed and passed the test, and no longer worked for him (I was assigned to different managers in the company) I found out later by my new manager that doing that was disallowed.
- **Practice of slipping and falling:** A coworker slipped and fell at work and went out on worker's compensation. I did not observe the incident and was only told she had an accident. When she came back to work she openly told me that she had done this in past jobs. She also bragged that one time she deliberately slipped and fell in a department store, sued them, and obtained a nice settlement. She thought it was funny. I was relieved and happy when she left the organization.
- **Soliciting me for dates with administrative assistant's friend:** While working as a senior staff associate at the police academy's assessment center operation, I met and had to interact with the administrative assistant for the assistant police chief. I was participating in a project the assistant chief was working on. Each time I arrived at the assistant chief's office, the administrative assistant greeted me and never failed to ask me whether I wanted to be fixed up with his friends. Each time I declined. Years later he became the police chief (without competing for the Sergeant, Lieutenant, or Captain positions), and then the city manager. Later, I read in the *Miami Herald* that he was stealing from the charity he set up for poor children, lost his job, and later went to prison. I was shocked and dismayed because I knew him when he was a rising star and moved up the hierarchy and eventually became the city manager.
- **Accepting a bribe:** A man I served with on a professional association board worked for county government and then became an elected official for a local city. He later went to prison for receiving from a local business owner, among other things, a Tag Hauer watch. I read about him in *The Palm Beach Post*.
- **Absent without official leave (AWOL) and slip and fall employee:** A former employee of mine, who was our recruiter, was away from work without leave (AWOL), came in late frequently by sneaking through another employee's office (which happened to be in a part of the office, which had two doors), and after about 6-months on the job, I was finally allowed to put him on probation. My boss was reluctant to discipline him but finally relented. A few days before the employee's termination meeting, he slipped and fell in the main lobby and went out on worker's compensation. I found out from the risk manager (who should have never told

me this) that he had a history of slips and falls in previous jobs. That same week, the recruiter was indicted for being involved in a resume kickback fraud operation when he was a recruiter for the aerospace industry. I felt vindicated because I tried to fire him soon after we hired him but received little support from my boss. He had a reputation for being afraid to fire people.

- **After acquired evidence about employee ignored:** One of my staff found out that an employee who had already started work in a job in the IT Department had falsified her application. This is referred to as after-acquired evidence in a hiring process, which can be used to terminate an employee. Subsequently, this employee should have been fired because not only had she lied on her application but did not possess the type of college degree written in her application, which was a minimum qualification for the job. My boss chose not to fire her. I am quite certain a few of the reasons were (a) her boss put pressure on my boss to not fire her, (b) her husband was a local city manager, and (c) my boss was a "good ole boy" who did not rock the boat.

NINE SCENARIOS

Over the new few pages, nine scenarios are presented that I would like you to carefully read and think about how you would handle each one.

- **Irate customer**
- **Rumor about an affair and peer pressure**
- **Subordinate on-the-job accident**
- **Sexual harassment of female**
- **Alleged employee theft**
- **Problem employee with negative personality**
- **Sick leave usage**
- **Unsafe workplace**
- **Coworker training and ethics violations**

When you take the quiz, you will be provided with five of the best possible ways to handle each question about the scenario.

When reading each scenario, pretend you are at work for the company. Focus only on what is presented. Do not over-analyze what is presented. In other words, do not assume things or issues that are not obvious. Also, do not worry about the size of the company, not having an organizational chart, or not knowing the names of the people described in the scenario. In summary, the only information available is what is written. Use this to render your judgment.

Scenario 1: Irate Customer

You started work as a Customer Service Representative with a new company 3-months ago and are now considered past the probationary (also referred to as introductory) period. You received 3-weeks of on-the-job training which included reading many of the company's policies and procedures. You also shadowed another coworker who taught you a great deal.

You receive a call from a customer who wants to return a product they received and wants their money credited to their bank immediately. He is irate, rambles on about some of the company policies and procedures and tells you that you are incompetent. You did your best to explain the policies and procedures but again, he raises his voice and asks to speak to your boss.

Multiple-Choice Questions: Irate Customer

Question 1

What would you do after he continues to raise his voice?

A

Put him on hold and transfer him to my boss.

B

Apologize for the inconvenience, listen to him, and after he calms down, attempt to resolve his problem.

C

Tell him to stop raising his voice.

D

Hang up on him because I should not have to put up with an abusive customer.

E

Put him on hold for a few minutes, get back on the phone and reinitiate the conversation.

Question 2

What type of training, if any, do you, as a new employee need?

A

How to handle irate customers.

B

None as he or she (you) just completed 3-weeks of training.

C

There is not enough information provided in the scenario to determine.

D

Training on policies and procedures.

E

All of the above.

Question 3

What should an employee do, if anything, when a customer calls them incompetent?

A

Tell the customer that they are not incompetent.

B

Advise the customer that they are sorry that the customer feels this way.

C

Nothing because there is nothing the employee can do to change the customer's opinion about them.

D

Nothing because as the customer is always right.

E

Just listen to the customer and try to help them.

Scenario 2: Rumor About an Affair and Peer Pressure

You have been recently promoted to a Supervisor, Technical Service Group at Company X. You do not know any of your subordinates very well. However, you do know that five of them are hardworking employees and have longevity with the company. One of your male peers from another department comes to your office, asks if he can speak with you for 5 minutes, and he states, "There is a rumor going around that one of your female employees is having an affair with your boss. Both are married"; before you can respond. He also tells you that the two of them leave work early and go to a hotel. He suggests that you need to do something about this ASAP or your supervisory position may be in jeopardy.

Multiple-Choice Questions: Rumor About an Affair and Peer Pressure

Question 4

What do you say to this employee about the rumors he shared with you?

A

Nothing initially.

B

"You should ignore rumors as they are none of your or my business."

C

I would thank him for the information.

D

"It is totally inappropriate that you even told me about this rumor."

E

"Thank you for the information but this rumor should not be repeated or spread."

Question 5

What will you do, if anything, about his suggestion, "You need to do something about this ASAP, or your supervisory position may be in jeopardy?"

A

Nothing.

B

Tell him he is out of line.

C

Walk away.

D

Tell him that my position will not be in jeopardy.

E

Both A and D is a viable option.

Question 6

What should be done about the possible fact, that one of your subordinates is having an affair with your boss?

A

Call the female subordinate in to my office and ask her if she is having an affair with my boss.

B

Confer with the HR Director about this and tell him/her about the rumor.

C

Nothing because I do not have enough information and it may, in fact, only be a rumor.

D

Tell my boss what I have been told.

E

All of the above.

Scenario 3: Subordinate On-the-Job Accident

You are a Manager in the manufacturing plant of a company that makes paper and plastic supplies. You have held the position for 1-year but are still learning about the culture of the company and how things are done around the plant. You are aware that more workplace accidents occur because employees are not using safe workplace protocols. You have voiced your concern to the Director of Safety on one or more occasions. Fortunately, none of your direct reports have had any accidents.

You are walking through the plant and you see from a slight distance an employee falling from a scaffolding. A few other employees are gathering around. As you get closer, you see that the person, a male, is one of your newly hired employees who is still in training. You arrive on the scene of the accident.

Shortly thereafter, he is taken to the hospital and has serious injuries. Immediately after the incident is over, your boss sends you a text message and asks you to meet with him the next day at 9:00 a.m. sharp.

Multiple-Choice Questions: Subordinate On-the-Job Accident

Question 7

What is your immediate course of action?

A

Respond to my boss' text message.

B

Find out how he fell and then check to see if he is okay.

C

Go to my supervisor's office and speak to him.

D

Try to help the employee until EMS arrives; talk to him; let him know I am concerned about him.

E

Help him, check for debris, keep other people away from him.

Question 8

In the meeting with your boss, what, if anything, do you tell him?

A

Nothing, unless I am asked (keeping my mouth shut is the best option).

B

I will tell him that the employee is still in training.

C

I will tell him that the Safety Department staff are not keeping the workplace safe and something should be done about this.

D

Wait until after he asks me question(s), so I can provide him with the most accurate information.

E

I would tell him that the employee should probably be fired.

Question 9

Regarding the information provided in this scenario about the employees not using safe workplace protocols, which is the **BEST** course of action?

A

Discuss this with my boss and suggest all employees be sent for refresher safety training.

B

Call the Safety Director and address my concerns.

C

Nothing now as Safety is not my department.

D

Ensure that my employees immediately use safe workplace protocols.

E

Review the records of all employees to find out which ones are deficient and prepare counseling documents for each.

Scenario 4: Sexual Harassment of a Female

You are the Food and Beverage Manager of XYZ Hotel, a Four Star hotel. You have 30 employees working in your department and 4 supervisors. You have received a great deal of training which is one of benefits of working for this company. You feel you have a lot of knowledge regarding how to handle situations. A component of the company culture is employee empowerment.

One day a female employee, who is a bartender, comes to your office and tells you she wants to file a complaint with you and then the HR Department. She says, "I am being sexually harassed by Johnny Jones (a male bartender), I have asked him to stop on more than one occasion, but he will not leave me alone. Please help me." The bartender is your daughter's boyfriend.

Multiple-Choice Questions: Sexual Harassment of Female

Question 10

What do you immediately tell your female employee?

A

"You need to report this to the HR department."

B

"I will talk to him personally, because he is my daughter's boyfriend, I apologize for what he did to you. I will make sure this never happens again."

C

"Thank you for bringing this to my attention, we can both go to the HR Department and report this and they will direct us on what to do next."

D

"I will get back with you as soon as I speak with him (the male bartender)."

E

"Why didn't you report this to me the first time this happened?"

Scenario 5: Alleged Employee Theft

You work in the Accounting department of a well-known department store which is a part of a national chain. You are an Administrative Assistant to the Accounting Manager. It is your first job after graduating from college with a degree in Business Administration. You love your job, your boss, and working for the store. One day, one of the accounting clerks comes to your office and asks to speak to you confidentially. He proceeds to tell you that your boss has been stealing money from the company. He states, "I was preparing a report for the dress shirt supervisor and found a short fall of orders versus sales and traced it back to the Accounting Manager returning some to the supplier but could not find out where the refund check was processed. It went directly to my boss."

Note: His boss is also your boss.

He then says, "I think I should report this to the HR Department or the Ethics Hotline immediately and I need your help."

Multiple-Choice Questions: Alleged Employee Theft

Question 11

Which option below is the **BEST** judgment call?

A

Tell him I will get back to him.

B

Ask him to double check his figures and get back with me.

C

Advise him to double check his figures, call the Ethics Hotline and then the HR Department.

D

Tell him to advise the Accounting Manager what he found out.

E

Tell him that I do not know and that I do not want to get involved.

ETHICS AND MORALS

The next set of scenarios integrates ethical and moral judgment issues. Please approach each scenario as you have the previous ones. The scenarios have been adapted from Loviscky et al. (2007), Managerial Moral Judgment Test. Some options for handling each one have also been adapted from Loviscky et al. (2007) and are noted as such.

Scenario 6: Sick Leave Usage

You are a supervisor and are advised by one of your subordinates that a coworker of theirs, Andrew, was not actually sick today but had taken a day off to recharge his batteries. The employee, Andrew, had just called in and told you he was not feeling well.

Scenario adapted from Loviscky et al. (2007).

Multiple-Choice Questions: Sick Leave Usage

Question 12

What **KEY** issues should you consider before taking any action regarding Andrew?

A

Are Andrew and his coworker friends?

B

Is Andrew lying and how can I find out?

C

Is Andrew violating the company's sick leave policy; and if so, should he be disciplined?

D

What is the difference between taking time off to "recharge your batteries," and telling your supervisor you are not feeling well?

E

Should a meeting be held with Andrew's coworker to find out why he advised me of their conversation.

Scenario 7: Problem Employee With a Negative Personality

You have a subordinate who is rotating through the company's training program. He has a negative, unpleasant personality and has developed a reputation for going behind people's backs. Nevertheless, his job performance has been very good. He has been assigned to work in your unit for 3-months after which time he will be moved to another unit. It is a standard operating procedure to document the daily performance of new hires and turn in a checklist and written feedback to the manager of the unit and the HR Department.

This week the subordinate made a serious mistake which caused major problems for your unit. Because he is scheduled to be rotated to another unit the following week you feel that it might not be worth your time and effort to document this. You do not want to deal with the subordinate's personality problems.

Adapted from Loviscky et al. (2007).

Multiple-Choice Question: Problem Employee With a Negative Personality

Question 13

What actions should you take regarding the mistake this employee made?

A

Meet with this employee, coach him on what he did wrong and try to help him before he moves on to his next assignment.

B

Avoid any interaction with him.

C

Advise the employee's soon to be supervisor about his mistake and other issues.

D

Complete the required performance documentation and submit it.

E

A and D are both viable options.

Scenario 8: Unsafe Workplace

John Jakes works for a multinational chemical corporation located in a Midwestern state in the United States. He is a member of the union, is 54-years old, and has made future plans to retire around age 60. He is one of the most senior persons on the crew. He loves his job because he fills in for the guys who are vacation, are out sick, or in training. He is almost always working somewhere different in the plant and has acquired a lot of different skills over the years.

On numerous occasions, as he was working at different locations at the plant, he observed many safety violations on the job. Those included:

- Employees were sleeping on the job;
- A few of the men were snoozing in the control room;
- Two men were observed smoking in the trucks; and
- Cigarette butts had been thrown on the floor in restricted locations.

When he approached any of the men they laughed at him and told him to shut-up.

Multiple-Choice Questions: Unsafe Workplace

Question 14

What should Jakes do about the violations?

A

Document what he observed and report them to his supervisor.

B

Continue to document what he observes.

C

Nothing until it gets out of control.

D

Report them to the state and federal government Occupational Health and Safety agencies.

E

A and B.

Question 15

Within 2-weeks after Jakes reports the violations to his supervisor, the following things happened to him:

- Coworkers shun him in the breakroom;
- His supervisor tells him to back off (he is also a smoker);
- Three of his coworkers surrounded him and asked him when he was retiring;
- He is called a spy and rat by one of the active union members;
- One guy spit at him as he walked by; and
- He finds a dead rat in his locker.

He reports the latter to his supervisor, and nothing was done. During the next several weeks the same behavior was repeated. What should Jakes do now?

A

Nothing because apparently his boss is not going to take any action; Jakes is a member of the union; is approaching retirement and does not want to be fired.

B

Report what happened to his supervisor's boss and the HR department.

C

Ask his supervisor to schedule a meeting with all of the workers to discuss the problems.

D

Prepare his early retirement paperwork and submit to the HR department.

E

File charges with the EEOC.

Scenario 9: Coworker Training and Ethics Violations

Adapted from: Ellis, J. E. (Ed.). (2019, December 23). Where the 737 went off course. *Bloomberg Business-week*, Aviation, pp. 14–18.

Background

Airstream XS is a 40-old multinational company known for designing high quality private and commercial jets. The company is also known for:

- What is referred to as a prideful culture;
- Pressure from top management to produce;
- A rich pay-for-performance system;
- High quality training which dates back to its Jet University which was founded in the 1960s;
- A test and design pilots and engineers club;
- A high level of collaboration and communication among staff;
- Informal and parochial relationships among the pilots (e.g., they love to discuss design); and,
- Job security and rich benefits.

However, over the past few years several changes have taken place at Airstream XS to include the following:

1. The use of more contractors with limited experience;
2. Quality of the design has slipped;
3. Pay increases have been cut significantly;
4. The union voted to double the number of unionized pilots in reaction to more contractors being hired;
5. There have been layoffs of long-term pilots and engineers and the hiring of contractors to fill the void;
6. The flight training simulator was moved from a city on the west coast of the United States to a city on the east coast and an attempt has been made to turn the training center into a profit machine;
7. Based on focus interviews with a great deal of small groups of employees, morale is bad.

Situation

Assume you are Cicero Willis, senior design engineer. You have worked on a self-managed team for 6-years. One of your coworkers, Sammy Cynicale, a 15-year employee who has conducted a great deal of the simulator training, has been acting very strange lately. Not only has he vented his anger over the aforementioned changes but he has even joked about sabotaging some of the new designs. He did not like that many of the experts in the human factors staff (i.e., those who worked with the machines) were resigning in large numbers and that 2,500 jobs were shipped to other cities. He stated, "A few of our writers have complained that the simulator software changes do not work, but management does not listen to them. If they don't care, why should I care? Communicating with people in a different time zone is not easy."

You know that some of his points are valid. For example, the company has cut back on the number of required training hours and used the money for a new customer satisfaction system.

Sammy refuses to call the HR confidential hotline which was basically established to hear harassment complaints as well as health and safety issues and management violations of the union contract.

Sammy has also commented on the number of in-house trainer vacancies, the poor communication between the engineers, pilots, and top management and the constant pressure to produce with reduced rewards.

Your boss, Travis Tricky, is on an extended leave of absence (LOA) and no one has been put in acting position. Communicating with the Design Engineering Director, Sheldon Shifty is difficult because he is either out of the office or in a meeting every time you attempt to facilitate a meeting with him. Also, most senior staff members believe that all he cares about is his salary and moving up the hierarchy.

You and Sammy are close friends and have known one another since college. You attend the same church; your wives are close friends and, on most weekends your children hang out together.

This week, you notice more changes in Sammy's behavior; he comes in late, has skipped some of the training sessions, fails to cover some new sections of the material, and spends his lunch hours talking to other union friends in small groups. Whenever you have walked by, the group disperses.

Multiple-Choice Questions: Coworkers Training and Ethics Violations

Question 16

Given your observations of Sammy's behavior what you should you do?

A

Document all of my observations and then call the HR confidential hotline.

B

Nothing because Sammy is just angry and I could get him in trouble; all employees vent and his way is more aggressive.

C

Write an anonymous note to the Director about what I have observed.

D

Report my observations to the HR Director.

E

All of the above.

Question 17

The same week one of your and Sammy's team members, Ted Tool, another employee who has conducted some of the simulator training, sees you in the plant lunch room, waves to you and comes and sits down. He states, "I need to tell you something but do not repeat it." What he tells you confirms your observations about the issues and Sammy's behavior. He indicates that he may consult with one of the HR representatives or his union representative.

What should you do?

A

Thank him and tell him that the two of you are on the same page but also tell him that if we report him the entire training program could be adversely affected.

B

Thank him for entrusting you with the information; tell him that you have already reported your observations; and ask him if both of you should speak to the Director to ensure he is in the communication loop.

C

After Ted leaves the table call the EAP counselor.

D

Contact the union President; report my findings to him or her; advise Ted of this, include any violations, where applicable so I am not perceived as a complainer.

E

All but A are acceptable judgment calls, but D is the best if any one choice was available.

Question 18

Shortly after you leave the lunch room you see Sammy in the hallway and hear him raising his voice to two employees who happen to be recently hired outside contractors. As you move closer you hear him state, "You will both be sorry if there are any accidents. The company should have never replaced long term employees with you. Just stay out of my way." The next thing that happens as he finishes his sentence is he clenches his hands into fists and is about to strike one of them.

What should you do?

A

Grab Sammy and attempt to tackle him to the ground and then call security, but only if necessary.

B

Try to stop him by pulling him away, moving in between Sammy and the men, verbally try to calm the situation, and then call security, but only if necessary.

C

Walk away.

D

Yell HELP, call the police and then grab Sammy and pull him to the side.

E

Call the Director and tell him that this behavior is not appropriate and request a sit down meeting with Sammy.

CHAPTER 5

Decision-Making

OVERVIEW

There is a great deal of research concerning different aspects of decision-making. Fitzgerald (2002) conducted a search and identified 6,681 books dealing with decision-making pertinent to business and investing, and 734 articles on business decision-making of which 170 appeared since 1999. Furthermore, he also found a 1999 study of 356 varying decisions made by people in varying size public and private sector organizations in the United States and Canada. The study findings found that 50% of senior management decisions fail (Fitzgerald, 2002), which does not surprise me in the least. Based on my knowledge of management and leadership, managers fail for many reasons including:

- their hubris
- they are not credible
- they pass the buck
- they do not know how to treat their subordinates
- they are "I" focused v. "We" focused
- they do not share the vision
- they are not able to engage and motivate their subordinates

I conducted some research to validate my knowledge of the topic and found that decision-making has been studied in terms of being a predictor of a person's accomplishment of work tasks. As per Del Missier, Mäntylä, and Bruine de Bruin (2010), Parker and Fischhoff (2005), and Parker and Weller (2015) based on predictive validity studies, lower decision-making competency is related to taking greater risks as well as behavior that is not adaptable.

MILLER AND BYRNES DECISION-MAKING MODEL AND OTHER RESEARCH

Miller and Byrnes (2001) discussed decision-making as a model, wherein a person who is able to self-regulate his or her decision-making is also a person who is able to self-regulate him or herself and can then set "adaptive targets" and also uses appropriate measures to achieve tasks (Byrnes, 2013; Byrnes, Miller, & Reynolds, 1999 as cited by Ceschi et al., 2017, p. 2). They also considered that being a competent decision maker indicates that a person is focused on making quality decisions. According to Aristotle (1953 as cited by Thiele & Young, 2016),

> *Practical judgment is not the acquisition and application of abstract principles or theories. It develops from life experience. But not all experiences produce quality results.*

And,

> *To develop practical judgment is to develop the capacity for a narrative framing of reality.*

> *(Thiele & Young, 2016, p. 39).*

Other research on decision-making focuses on the role of the decision maker in terms of being able to ensure quality control and being a gatekeeper for idea generation (Day, 2007; Krishnan & Ulrich, 2001 as cited by Mueller, Melwani, Loewenstein, & Deal, 2018). Different research has examined a decision maker's role regarding resource allocation, which is very important for control over budgetary and time allocation (Mollick, 2012), as well as generating profits (Ford, Sharfman, & Dean, 2008). Moreover, according to Stevens and Burley's research (1997), decision makers must evaluate, on average, more than 3,000 ideas to obtain just one commercial success (Mueller et al., 2018, p. 3).

I initiated a Google search and typed in "worst decisions made" and found many.

A few are:

- **"All 12 of the publishing firms that rejected J.K. Rowling's *Harry Potter and the Sorcerer's Stone*? Since their first printing in 1997, the Harry Potter books have broken publishing records; they are now considered the fastest-selling books ever."**

- **A movie named *E.T.: The Extra-Terrestrial* doesn't exactly scream "box office gold." Maybe that's what Mars candy executives were thinking back in 1980 when they passed on Universal Studios' offer to feature M&Ms in their new alien flick. Sure, Steven Spielberg was directing—he already received Oscar nominations for both *Jaws* and *Close Encounters of the Third Kind*—but his latest film *1941* had been a flop. Worse, Universal wouldn't show Mars a script. Thanks, but no thanks."**

Source: https://money.howstuffworks.com/10-worst-business-decisions8.htm

The latter bad decisions resulted in great commercial successes for the companies who decided to go forward with the offers made to them. The companies no doubt were left with some scars for having made poor judgment calls. As Thiele and Young (2016) noted, "Every scar, it is said, tells a story. For the most part, good judgment is developed from suffering the consequences of bad judgment" (p. 39) and can result in good or poor decisions being made.

I feel strongly and believe that the scenarios presented in this chapter will help sharpen your decision-making skills. You have continuously learned about decision-making during your life and work experiences. For example, more than likely you made poor or bad decisions because the judgment call(s) you made was/were flawed. I have made many poor and good decisions in my life. Each decision improved my ability to make better decisions because I made a better practical judgment call.

Excellent, bad, and other decisions:

- **Excellent decision**—I was offered two positions the same week and accepted the one that paid less money but afforded me the opportunity to be a change agent instead of a practitioner. That decision was based on a very good judgment call because I was thinking about how each position could best benefit my long-term career.
- **Bad decision**—Against my better judgment I took my ex-boyfriend up on his persistent and pleading offer to drive me from Indiana University in Bloomington, Indiana, back to Lexington, Kentucky, where I needed to return to gather some belongings before I moved to Miami, Florida. The story is too gloomy to repeat here. At the time, I felt very lucky to have made it back to Lexington, Kentucky.
- **Good decision based on good judgment**—When I was a human resources (HR) director, when a decision was made by another member of the senior management team, I wrote a memo that outlined my reasons for disagreeing with his decision. He pushed for our boss to allow his decision to be put into place without conferring with any other senior staff. The day I presented my memo to senior staff, in a meeting with all present, was the day my work environment grew ugly, hostile, and difficult to endure. But I knew I made the right decision because I was following my conscience; adhering to the principles and practices of my profession; was sure that the arbitrary decision he made (which my staff would have to implement) would eventually violate the Americans with Disabilities Act; and was doing the most ethical thing.
- **Bad decisions**—I have maintained some friendships with people whom I should have ended years before they caused me hurt, pain, and personal discomfort.
- **Poor decision that became a good decision**—I bid on a contract that after my firm was selected to do the work, I did not walk out of the room when a few of the clients (it was a multidepartment contract) made it clear to me that they preferred the other consulting firm (the firm was their long-term vendor and was always the low bidder) but the HR Department had made the final decision (poor decision). After working on the contract for a few months because of the unprofessional as well as threatening behavior (we will sue you) of one of the senior executives, I terminated my contract with their department (good decision). Despite my investment in time (and money) I felt so good that day and learned a lesson that improved my skills at negotiating business contracts.

I hope you appreciated my life decision-making stories all which made great impressions on me and helped strengthen my decision-making ability. I have learned from the many times painful school of hard knocks through a variety of life experiences where I used my practical judgment to make many decisions, some good and some not as equally good.

Thiele and Young

Upon reading Thiele and Young's (2016) article, "Practical Judgment, Narrative Experience and Wicked Problems," I learned what Machiavelli wrote about judgment. Based on Machiavelli's learned experience he maintained that "a certain kind of experience lends itself particularly well to the development of practical judgment" (Thiele & Young, 2016, p. 6). I was enthralled to learn that Machiavelli was the originator of this quote, which was cited by Thiele and Young (2016). I agree wholeheartedly that we all suffer from having made bad decisions, which were based on impractical or bad judgment calls. I also totally embrace what Thiele and Young (2016) recapped from their reading of Machiavelli's, *The Prince*, that my historical experiences have provided me with a good education for becoming a practical judge. As I was growing up, one of my mother's favorite expressions was, "It is not what you know but whom you know," which is what Machiavelli thought (Thiele & Young, 2016).

My mother and father always emphasized the importance of a college and graduate school education, but noted that until I obtained the education, the "who you know" would not be as relevant. My parents told me that my credentials would get me in the door but down the road, "who I knew" would matter more. Their good judgment and decision-making were that both my sister and I would finish college and graduate school. What does this have to do with decision-making? Once you acquire the credentials and gain work experience, you will meet many people who will guide you during your career. Some of them you may need to call upon years later for assistance, a favor, or a contact. Many years into your career, it is who you know but you would not have known these people if not for your credentials, which helped you obtain your job where you met them.

The workplace scenarios in this chapter provide you with opportunities to practice your decision-making ability. Thiele and Young (2016) noted that John Dewey (2002), author of *Human Nature and Conduct*, contends that "judgment operates by way of a 'dramatic rehearsal' whereby one plays out competing storylines of action, habits, desires and impulses in imagination . . . Practical judgment is, by and large, an act of intellectual and moral imagination operating in a narrative mode. The decision-maker engages in dramatic rehearsals—or perhaps better said, dramatic prehearsals—discerning how events are likely to unfold given the characters involved and circumstances at hand." (p. 43)

NINE SCENARIOS

The remainder of this chapter includes nine different scenarios involving decision making. The following will take place:

- A scenario is presented.
- You should read and think about the situation described in the scenario.
- Write some notes about how you handle or would handle the situation.
- Think about how you will plan and organize the work to solve the problem or issues.
- Read the rest of the scenarios and go through the same process.
- Take the quiz.

The basis of each of the following scenarios is true but they are camouflaged stories that I created so as not to reveal their origins. Each scenario includes events that took place and should be read as if they are taking place in real time. Each scenario also includes characters.

The best way to handle each one is not included, but when you take the quiz you will provided with five possible ways to handle each situation. When reading each scenario pretend you are at work for the company. Focus only on what is presented. Do not over analyze what is presented. In other words, do not assume things or issues that are not obvious. Also, do not worry about the size of the company, not having an organizational chart or not knowing the names of the people described in the scenario. In summary, the only information available is what is written. Use this to demonstrate your practical judgment and decision making skills.

- **Sunk costs**
- **Criminal background check issue**
- **Team problems**
- **Employee drinking problem**
- **Peer issue**
- **Unethical boss**
- **Disciplinary and promotional actions**
- **Off-duty employee behavior**
- **Workforce needs for cloud computing**

DECISION-MAKING WORKPLACE SCENARIOS

Scenario 1: Sunk Costs

Assume that you are Jason/Jennie Statham, manager, Facilities and Operations for the ABC Corporation. ABC manages properties for other corporations throughout the United States. ABC has a strategic plan with goals and objectives that cascade down to the operational and strategic levels. The most important goal (which you fought hard to gain approval for) on your departmental plan is to purchase, implement, and test a property management software package. For several months you worked with a cross-functional task team to select the software and the project is underway. The cost for the system to include the beta testing is $250,000.

You have invested a great deal of time and energy with this project already (i.e., late evening hours and some weekends). Moreover, you spent many hours preparing and then presenting a plan to the senior management team. The support for the project barely made it through a final vote. As of today, the project is in its sixth month. You negotiated a contract with three payments (i.e., 50% down and two more increments of 25% each). The expected time for completion is 12-months.

It has been brought to your attention that on more than one occasion the software has many "bugs," which you thought had been corrected. You just finished a call with one of your clients and now one of your project managers, Jack Black, is standing outside your office door and asks to see you. You motion him in, and he sits down. Based on the look on his face, he is upset. He proceeds to tell you that his team has discovered more bugs and problems. The company is in the process of migrating to the new system and complaints from the end users are mounting. He states, "Boss, based on the evidence documenting all of the problems we have had, I strongly recommend that we cancel the contract with the company."

Multiple-Choice Questions: Sunk Costs

Question 1

Given the project is the top goal in the strategic plan for your department and 50% of the contract cost has been spent, **WHICH** decision would you make and why?

A

Continue with the project due to the money expended.

B

Call or e-mail my boss to discuss the situation with him; he should decide; do not cancel the contract until after I have reviewed the documentation with my project manager.

C

Withhold judgment given the limited information available.

D

Call the President of the software company and read him/her the riot act and threaten to cancel the contract if corrections are not made immediately.

E

B and D.

Question 2

How would you deal with the cross-functional task team and end users who have been adversely affected?

A

I would not need to deal with them because they are no longer a working team.

B

Schedule a meeting with them and any other end users and explain the situation.

C

I would not deal with them given the limited information.

D

Have my Project Manager draft an announcement summarizing the problems, and how we will handle them and then disseminate it over the Internet.

E

Both B and D.

Scenario 2: Criminal Background Check Issue

Bradley Cooper is a Project Manager with the RZP company and has been with the company for 5-years. RZP has 1,500 employees throughout the United States, Canada, and Mexico. The company makes specialized parts for the automobile industry. Over the past year the company was sued for negligent hiring, supervision, and retention because of the hiring of an employee whose criminal background information was not obtained until after he started work. He was subsequently fired. His actions cost the company well over $1 million dollars in legal fees and fines.

Now the company has instituted a new policy and procedures for periodic criminal background checks on all employees. The checks are done randomly by the HR Department.

A Customer Service Representative, one of your 8 direct reports who has worked for the company for 3-years, is one of your best employees and is being considered for a promotion. Subsequently a criminal background check was conducted. You met with a staff person from the HR Department and they reported he was arrested for selling cocaine and assaulting a police officer and his case is pending. You are then told that the Vice President (your boss' boss) over your division, has directed the HR department to ignore the results. You are then told (and did not know this previously), that the employee is the VP's nephew, he will retain his job and the background check will not be considered.

Multiple-Choice Questions: Criminal Background Check Issue

Question 3

What is your judgment call and why?

A

Ignore the results because I have no control over what a Vice President decides.

B

Ask the HR staff person to advise my boss; it should be his judgment call.

C

Tell the HR staff person that this is unacceptable to me even though the charges are pending against the employee, and I will speak to my boss about this ASAP.

D

Do nothing given the information available is insufficient.

E

Any of the options reflect good judgment.

Question 4

Let's assume that you are forced to retain this employee and a few weeks later, you receive a call from a local newspaper reporter who asks you if you are aware of the fact that your employee was just arrested (again) for selling cocaine, and then proceeds to ask you why he is still allowed to work for the company.

What is your judgment call and decision?

A

Immediately refer him to the HR Department and then inform my boss about the call.

B

Hang up on him as it could be a prank call.

C

Advise him that I did not know this and proceed to tell him that it was not my call to retain the employee.

D

Tell the reporter I will call him back ASAP.

E

Tell him I did not know, that I have a meeting to go to and will call him later.

Scenario 3: Team Problems

Jack, Jim, Mike, Susan, and Delia work for DEF Corporation and are a self-managed team. Overall, they work very well together. They are all Systems Engineers and are of the same status. They are empowered to decide what annual pay for performance increase each member gets because the company has team-based pay. They have worked together for 3-years and were provided with extensive team training during their first 3-months on the job.

The roles they assumed have worked very well over the years. Jack is the team leader, Jim handles the team communications, Mike runs the meetings, Susan is team scribe, and Delia is the planner and organizer person. Subgroups have formed on the team which is common and for this team Jack and Mike are the subgroup and have become very good friends outside of work. However, their friendship has not caused any problems for the team (e.g., group think).

The past meeting and this weeks' meeting were problematic because Jack arrived late for both meetings, raised his voice at Susan and Delia and ended both meetings early even though their updates and tasks had yet to be reviewed. When Jack walked out, the rest of the members were very upset to say the least.

Multiple-Choice Questions: Team Problems

Question 5

If you were a member of the team what would be your first suggestion (i.e., decision)?

A

Suggest to the rest of the team that they call a meeting with Jack to find out if he is okay and to advise him of their concerns about his behavior.

B

Advise the team that the department manager should be told about Jack's behavior.

C

Suggest to the team that we should wait another week to see if Jack's behavior has changed.

D

Ask Mike if he could have a private meeting with Jack to find out what is going on.

E

Both A and D.

Question 6

Assume that Jack tells the team that he is having serious marital and family problems. You observe that his effectiveness as a leader of the team continues to decline. If you were a member of this team what would be your practical judgment and decision?

A

Suggest to the team members that we rotate roles which will free Jack from being the leader for the time being.

B

Suggest to the team members that Jack be asked to leave the team.

C

Ask Jack what he wants to do about being the team leader.

D

Both A and C are viable, but A is preferable.

E

All of the above.

Scenario 4: Employee Drinking Problem

Assume you are an employee and work for the IZZY Corporation. Your job title is Customer Care Coordinator. You have worked for the company for only 6-months and are still getting to know everyone. You feel you have established good working relationships with the coworkers you have gotten to know well since you were hired. You love your job and respect and admire your supervisor.

Two characteristics of the company culture which you do not like are secrecy and confidentiality. You do not know, nor have you been told by anyone why this is the case. However, you were told by another area coordinator that there have been workplace problems in the past (e.g., accidents in the plant, drinking on the job, and tardiness). One coworker told you, *"Your best option is to keep your mouth shut at all times so you will not lose your job."* You considered that this employee may be disgruntled or may have just wanted to share past problems with you.

Several days later you are in the lunch room and the employee is sitting next to you. No one else is around. He reeks of alcohol. You say nothing. Then you both leave the lunchroom simultaneously and as he walks down the corridor just a few feet ahead of you, he is not walking straight and almost stumbles.

Multiple-Choice Questions: Employee Drinking Problem

Question 7

Considering you are not his supervisor, what would be your decision?

A

Take a picture of this with my cell phone, send it to the HR Department and then advise my boss.

B

Call the safety department.

C

Go to him to ensure he does not stumble and ask him if he is okay.

D

Assist him and relate what happened to my boss ASAP as he may have a drinking problem.

E

Ignore it and walk away as it is not my problem or business, and I must keep my mouth shut.

Question 8

The following week one of your employees, Steve Astute, comes to your office and advises you that he observed the same employee outside during a break drinking something covered by a brown paper back. He also smelled alcohol on the employee's breath. He then states, "I did not know what to do but I am concerned about him."

What decision(s) below do you make?

A

Call the employee's supervisor and advise him/her what Astute told you he had observed.

B

Ask Astute to document what he observed and submit the document to you which will be sent to the employee's supervisor.

C

Advise Astute about what happened a week ago with this employee.

D

Contact the HR department.

E

Both A and B.

Scenario 5: Peer Issue

Assume that you are the Finance Manager for the Jolly Corporation, an international company that creates, builds, and sells miniature mechanical toys for children. You have worked there for 2-years and have gotten to know many of your peers in terms of their management styles, personalities, and work ethic. Jolly has a decentralized, open, collaborative culture. The top leaders are well respected and are known to do what they say they will do (Kouzes & Posner, 1993); in other words, they walk-the-talk.

However, on numerous occasions you have had to deal with some managers whom you believe do not represent the culture. One day you receive a call from one of these managers, Henry Hubris, Manager of Manufacturing. His tone of voice is condescending, rather loud and what you perceive as caustic. He states, *"Well this has happened once again, another rejection of supplies ordered and another delay. What is your department, the Gestapo? You are a bunch of Nazis."* You explain to him that the order was rejected because it was way over budget and that this is the second time in 1-month this has happened. There is a pause on the phone and then he continues with his rant and tells you he will be going over your head to get the order approved. Then he hangs up.

Multiple-Choice Questions: Peer Issue

Question 9

What practical judgment call and decision would you make?

A

Obtain the rejected purchase order, review it, and then advise my boss of what transpired.

B

Call Hubris back and advise him that I will be reporting his behavior to my boss.

C

Call Hubris back and tell him I will be filing an ethics complaint against him.

D

Call Hubris' boss and tell him what happened and that I will not put up with this.

E

Contact the company hotline and file a complaint against him.

Question 10

Assume that one or more of your staff overheard Hubris' statements because your phone was on conference call. After the call one of them, Greg Guts, says, "I am sorry that happened, he spoke to me like that last week."

What would you do about Guts' comments?

A

Nothing.

B

Thank him for his concern.

C

Ask him to come in, take a seat and describe in detail what Hubris said to him and document it.

D

Schedule a meeting with my boss and review the situation as Hubris' behavior could result in more serious problems for the company.

E

Both C and D.

Question 11

If Hubris was one of your subordinates and you were advised of his behavior and statements, **WHICH** option below would be your judgment calls and decisions?

A

First, verify if in fact he made the comments to another peer; speak to the recipient of his comments and obtain as much information as possible.

B

Review the company policy and procedures manual and/or ethics code to determine if he violated any policies or codes and inform your supervisor.

C

Schedule a meeting with him to review the situation; make sure he understands the consequences of his behavior.

D

If he has never been disciplined before, (i.e., check his personnel file) consider preparing a written warning, and if he has to adhere to the progressive disciplinary continuum.

E

A and B only.

Scenario 6: Unethical Boss

Andrew Analyticas, is a recently hired Contracts Supervisor for a fast-growing national Employee Wellness company Health Teks, Inc. He has been in the position for 9-months, worked for one of the company's competitors, Health Data Points and was hired by Health Teks. One of reasons Andrew was offered the job was his undergraduate degree in accounting but also his master's degree in Forensic Accounting.

Health Teks has 200 employees, contracts in 20 states in the United States and 2,000 clients. During the third year the company was in the business the CFO was fired because he was arrested for violating his previous noncompete agreement; he had stolen some critical files on a USB drive and allegedly provided the data to the company he later went to work for (i.e., Health Teks). Because of the scandal shortly thereafter the HR department wrote an Ethics Code manual, contracted with a company with expertise in Ethics training and required all newly hired employees to attend an 8-hour workshop as well as all current employees.

Andrew loves his job and enjoys working with the well trained and energetic staff. He is slowly getting to know people in the company. Given his degrees in accounting, he is extremely detail oriented and scrutinizes reports a minimum of three times, and reports any inaccuracies to the Senior Contracts Manager, Catherine Curvaceous.

He likes Ms. Curvaceous but notices that she usually leaves the office early on Fridays, spends a great deal of time in senior management meetings and attends other staff meetings infrequently. She is pleasant and courteous to staff but not overly communicative. Even though she says she has an open-door policy her door is usually almost closed all the way.

Andrew heard through the informal grapevine that Curvaceous is politically connected and some people think she always supports top management staff even if she disagrees with their decisions. She has also received annual performance increases above the maximum allowed per the compensation policy.

One day Andrew is checking the consulting contract file for invoices to approve and forward for payment and notices a new account for a company (Your Health Buddy) he has never seen before with an invoice for an excessively large amount; $25,000. He does not know how the paperwork appeared in the file because a standard operating procedure (SOP) requires his approval and initials on all new contracts. He also notices that the company did not submit any documentation for the travel and per diem expenditures. When he has finished reviewing the other paperwork he sends Catherine an e-mail about this. She responds back in less than 10 minutes, tells him to pay it; advises him that the documentation will be submitted later, and that she has approval from the CFO. Andrew feels very uncomfortable about this and makes a note to the file. He is curious as to why the CFO, Michael Monied, approved this instead of the V.P. of Contracts Management, Joe Drudge, but makes the assumption that the V.P. knows about the situation. Overall, he thinks the situation is unusual and not a standard operating policy and procedure (aka SOPs).

Question 12

Regarding Curvaceous' direction to pay the invoice, what should be Andrew's next course of action?

A

Send an e-mail to Curvaceous and request to meet with her to find out when the documentation will be submitted and why the company was exempted from the SOPS.

B

Nothing, since it is not his business to question his boss.

C

Contact a trusted peer in the Finance department, advise them of the situation and ask them if sending the invoice for payment will put me in jeopardy.

D

A is the best option but there is nothing unethical about contacting someone in the Finance department for their advice (option C).

E

Report the situation to the HR department hotline before the situation gets out of hand.

Question 13

About 2-weeks later Andrew is checking his files to find out if the documentation has been submitted. Nothing has been submitted. He also contacts a peer in the Finance department, Lenny Lazy, and asks him if a new account (i.e., Your Health Buddy) has been set up. Lenny looks it up and says it has not been set up and has no paperwork on it.

What should Andrew do?

A

Make a note to the file.

B

Nothing.

C

Forget about the entire incident.

D

Ask Curvaceous about it.

E

None of the above.

Question 14

One evening during the same week Andrew asks Lenny about the account. Later that week, Andrew is at a restaurant in the city during happy hour. He is with a few coworkers. He happens to be looking across the room and sees Curvaceous and Monied checking in with the maître de, and notices that they are holding hands and Monied kisses Curvaceous on the neck. He knows that neither one is married but his immediate thought is, does their relationship have anything to do with the invoice submitted with no paperwork?

At this point in time what should Andrew do?

A

Go to their table and say hello. This way they will both know that he is aware of that they are together.

B

Nothing other than storing this in his long-term memory; the information may be useful at a later date.

C

Ask Curvaceous for a meeting the next day and advise her of his overall concerns.

D

Nothing and keep his mouth shut about seeing them.

E

All of the above are viable options.

Question 15

A week later Andrew receives another invoice to pay and instead of asking Curvaceous about it he checks with Lenny and is told again there is no account in the system for this company. Shortly thereafter Curvaceous sends him an e-mail and directs him to sign off on the second invoice. He does so but makes another note to the file. Then he decides to conduct some research about the company. He finds the name in the state listing of corporations. He does further research and finds out that there are two owners of the company; Monied and Curvaceous.

Which below is/are the **BEST** decisions for Andrew to make?

A

Document this; ask to meet with the Ethics Officer and before providing the information make sure the conversation will remain confidential and that he will not be retaliated against for reporting this; and as a safeguard set up a meeting with the HR Director.

B

Turn the documents over to the police department.

C

A is the best course of action, but E is also a viable option.

D

Nothing because there is nothing illegal about two people owning a business together even if they work for the same company.

E

Write a letter to the corporate attorney outlining all of the events, include copies of the documentation, do not use his name and send it through the U.S. mail.

Question 16

A week after Andrew's research when he found out that Monied and Curvaceous are co-owners of Your Health Buddy, he is notified by the receptionist that two police officers are there and want copies of his e-mails, all correspondence about the company, and want to ask him a few questions. She also advises him that Monied and Curvaceous have just been arrested for embezzlement. What should he do?

A

Go to the front reception area and advise them that it will take him a few minutes to compile the material, tell them that they can wait, or he can call them when the documents are ready.

B

Tell the secretary to refer them to his boss.

C

Tell the secretary to tell them he is in the middle of a meeting, and he will call them tomorrow.

D

Tell them he will be glad to answer their questions but needs to advise his supervisor first; also ask them if they met with anyone else other than Andrew.

E

Both A and D.

Scenario 7: Disciplinary and Promotional Actions

In all military branches, the relationship between enlisted and officer personnel can be difficult. This is more pronounced among the higher ranks. The three ranks, Sergeant (Sgt.), Lieutenant (Lt.), and Captain (Cpt.) are part of this scenario. Each person is involved in different parts of the scenario.

John Doe, Sgt., works for a branch of the military. Within 24 hours of an infraction, he received a "letter of reprimand" from his supervisor, Nate Noaction, Cpt.

The discipline was well justified with a thoroughly documented "paper trail." At this time Sgt. Doe was in the process of being promoted. Doe's supervisor's Cpt. Noaction was fully apprised of Doe's problem and the contents of his personnel file. He totally supported Sgt. Doe's promotion.

Shortly thereafter Cpt. Noaction called Doe into his office and told him he was suspending his promotion for no less than 6-months. The order was given verbally but not in writing which violated SOPs. Doe's promotion was occurring within a month and after the verbal order a few weeks passed and no documentation was submitted based on Cpt. Notation's verbal order.

Dudley Dilligence, a newly promoted Lt., has just been temporarily assigned to supervise the Sergeants. He is made aware of Sgt Doe's situation and the missing documentation. Given that Lt. Dilligence has to go out of town for training for a temporary assignment he asks another administrative person to follow-up. Before he leaves town Sgt. Doe approaches him and inquires about the discipline and the promotion and asks if Lt. Dilligence could help him. Lt. Dilligence is unable to give Sgt. Doe an update because the phone rang, and he had to rush off to handle an emergency which took the rest of the afternoon.

Question 17

While on his temporary assignment what actions should Lt. Dilligence take to ensure that the paperwork regarding Sgt. Doe is expedited so he will know what will happen to him?

A

Nothing because Dilligence delegated the follow-up to another staff person.

B

Follow-up with the staff person via e-mail or cell phone.

C

Nothing as he is on leave and is not responsible.

D

Both B and E.

E

Check in with Doe to find out if has heard anything.

Question 18

Lt. Dilligence continues to touch base at least once a week to find out how things are progressing and is on each occasion by the staff person he delegated the follow-up process to that things are moving along. However, when Lt. Dilligence returns a few weeks later he is told that Sgt. Doe's promotion date came and went, and Cpt. Noaction has not completed the paperwork. Lt. Dilligence is then advised by Cpt. Noaction that he is planning to pursue the disciplinary action against Sgt. Doe which will be harsher than the original discipline. He also tells Lt. Dilligence that Sgt. Doe is not wearing the correct uniform for his rank and that Doe received the pay increase because of his promotion and should not have.

Which below is/are the **BEST** courses of action for Lt. Dilligence considering he has been dealing with the situation for quite some time and Cpt. Noaction did not follow SOPs?

A

Contact someone from the HR department, fill them in on the details and discuss what can be done.

B

Nothing.

C

Thank Noaction and walk away.

D

File a complaint against Noaction.

E

A, C, and D are all appropriate.

Question 19

A few days later Lt. Dilligence is advised by an HR representative that because Sgt. Doe has already assumed his new rank (despite not wearing the appropriate uniform), an order to suspend his promotion is no longer possible and that more severe disciplinary action will now be taken against Sgt. Doe; that is, he will be demoted to a lower rank.

What should Lt. Dilligence tell the HR representative?

A

The order to not put Doe into the next rank was verbal only and the official forms were not completed by Cpt. Noaction.

B

Cpt. Noaction is the responsible party, not him (Dilligence) and he will be reporting this to Cpt. Noaction, his boss, the Major, and all other involved parties.

C

All of the choices are acceptable.

D

Tell him or her not to do this.

E

A is the best response, but B is also appropriate.

Question 20

A few days later Cpt. Noaction pressures Lt. Dilligence to pressure Sgt. Doe into signing falsified documents (i.e., backdated forms). Lt. Dilligence is also pressured by a senior administrative officer who works for Cpt. Noaction.

Which below is/are the **BEST** way(s) for Lt. Dilligence to deal with the pressure?

A

Talk to some of his peers to provide him with support so he can hold the line and not submit to Cpt. Noactions' pressure.

B

Speak with Cpt. Noaction's superior (a Major) about the situation and ask for a group meeting with all involved persons (other than Sgt. Doe).

C

Ask the Major to ask Cpt. Noaction to stop pressuring him to push Sgt. Doe to sign the falsified documents; also advise him that he will not engage in unethical activities that violate SOPs.

D

Tell Cpt. Noaction and the Major that he always supports his superior's decisions when they are legal, moral, and ethical; he owes it to Sgt. Doe to not be pressured into signing falsified documents; and that he should not be fearful of reprisal for doing the right thing.

E

All of the above.

Scenario 8: Off-duty Employee Behavior

Reginald Whiplash is a newly promoted manager at FactsMatter, an online newspaper publication with millions of users in the United States. He has seven direct reports who chase down and write stories. Like most online publications, the company has an impressive web page which is updated daily, uses Twitter, Facebook, and a host of other social media applications.

One morning, Whiplash is sent Facebook pictures from an anonymous source about one of his employees, Tom Cruize. Tom Cruize, who has worked for FactsMatter for 6-months, has done an outstanding job. One of the reasons he was hired was because he won several awards for his stories. The second reason was that his stories are always factual and well researched. A third reason is he is working on a book about corporate corruption.

The Facebook pictures show Cruize with two other men who are dressed like women, and Cruize is dressed in drag. They are standing by the bar and behind the bar are mostly nude women on platforms pole dancing.

Whiplash is concerned not so much because of the pictures, but because of what he suspects his boss will do if and when he finds out. His boss, Jerry Fallwellon, an evangelical Christian, is ultra conservative. He knows this because Fallwellon has, on several occasions spoken about his beliefs.

He knows that he must tell Fallwellon but is afraid that he may want to fire Cruize. He suspects this because of a side remark Fallwellon made to his wife when he was talking to her on the phone. Whiplash had just arrived to Fallwellon's office for a meeting and was walking in when he heard Fallwellon tell his wife, "Honey, I am not sure I like working for this company, the policies and procedures need to change. Too many queers and other freaks are allowed to work here." He pretended not to hear by looking around the room while Fallwellon said to his wife, "Bye sweetheart see you soon."

Question 21

What should Whiplash do about the e-mail and pictures?

A

He should delete the e-mail and pictures in hopes that no one else will see them.

B

Call Cruize into his office and ask him for an explanation and what he thinks they should do.

C

Send the e-mail and pictures to the HR department, include a written explanation as to who sent them to him, and keep his mouth shut.

D

Keep them for future reference.

E

Retain the e-mail and pictures and contact the HR department to set up a meeting with himself and the HR Director and/or Employee Relations staff person.

Question 22

Later on, the same day Fallwellon calls Whiplash into his office, shows him the e-mail with the pictures and directs Whiplash to immediately prepare Cruize's termination paperwork.

What should Whiplash do about Fallwellon's directions considering Cruize's and what he knows about Fallwellon's feelings which may result in a civil rights violation if he retaliates against Cruize?

A

Nothing, just complete it and submit it to Fallwellon.

B

His feelings are irrelevant. What is relevant is whether based on state law, the company is not allowed to monitor employee's off duty behavior.

C

Advise Fallwellon that terminating an excellent employee like Cruize could result in legal issues; he has done nothing wrong; he was not at work; you need to check with HR before firing him just based on some Facebook pictures.

D

Both B and C.

E

He should complete the paperwork, put on Fallwellon's desk and advise Cruize that he is going to be fired and why.

Scenario 9: Workforce Needs for Cloud Computing

Adapted From: Fuhrmans, V. (2019, October 28). Workforce retrains itself for cloud. *Wall Street Journal*. Retrieved from http://ezproxy.fau.edu/login?url=http://resolver.ebscohost.com.ezproxy.fau.edu/openurl?url=https://search-proquest-com.ezproxy.fau.edu/docview/2309214760?accountid=10902

MNSP, located in a Midwestern state, is one of the world's largest processors of credit-card and cashless payments. It is in the process of moving away from the mainframes to the cloud. MNSP is not a tech brand (e.g., Apple, Oracle) and has had difficulty recruiting the hundreds of workers it needs skilled in cloud technology. Moreover, the company has an older IT workforce most who have never worked with cloud technology. The CEO does not want to replace its employees with new hires like other companies are doing which will upend 25% of their workforce. He recently read a McKinsey & Co survey that reflected two-thirds of the executives said they would hire mostly new employees.

The CEO, Brett Favre has assigned Mary Watson, MNSP's chief information officer to retrain the workforce. Some of the companies most valuable workers have been with the company for more than 25-years.

Question 23

Which below is/are the **BEST** strategies for retraining the 3,500 IT employees particularly those who are older?

A

Provide incentives to motivate reluctant employees to participate in the retraining.

B

Offer online courses, digital boot camps, meals during training, and weekend training.

C

Pay for related certification courses (e.g., Amazon Web Services solutions architecture).

D

A, B and C.

E

Advise all 3,000 employees that they must opt for retraining or risk being laid off.

Question 24

Based on Mary Watson's strategies, what should the IT Director do to motivate the employees who may be fearful of the training?

A

Allow them to train and partner with younger employees (if they desire) while they learn the new technology; allow the employees a time period to sign up for the retraining and continue to do this in waves so as to reduce the pressure to sign up immediately.

B

Offer bonuses or other incentives to employees; encourage employees to take time to study in groups during work hours; share success stories and brainstorm ideas.

C

Make sure all employees know that the company will provide them with the tools to be retrained but that they need to be committed and put in the time to be retrained.

D

Make sure the retrained engineers have time to do their new jobs (e.g., flex time) while also helping retrain the second and third waves of coworkers behind them; make sure all employees are paid for double duty.

E

All of the above.

CHAPTER 6

Dealing With People/Interpersonal and Emotional Intelligence

OVERVIEW

I am sure you remember reading about some of the research on soft skills in **Chapter 1**. One soft skill is being able to deal with people. Interpersonal skills are considered extremely important as compared to other skills. One of the reasons is the higher a person moves up the management hierarchy the more time they will spend dealing with people from all levels within the organization, and they will also have to deal with a great deal of politics. A word for being good at dealing with politics is "savvy." If a person has good people abilities and demonstrates emotional intelligence (EI) they will be able to survive in their top management position. This statement is not based on any empirical evidence but given my years of experience I know this is true for many people. An example of being politically savvy is telling your boss what he or she wants to hear and being a "yes person." Another reason dealing with people and EI abilities are so important is a person has to put on a happy face, be pleasant, and considerate to people who are very difficult and happen to be members of senior management.

Dealing with people abilities and EI are the subjects of this chapter.

Oral communication, body language, effectiveness when dealing with customers, and being able to work with a team are important aspects of dealing with people skills. However, as you know we all have individual differences and dealing with people may not be one of your current strengths. Also, having to deal with difficult people at work seems to be more common than interacting with people who have strong interpersonal skills. Dealing with people requires energy, much work, tenacity, patience, and interest. The bottom line is dealing with difficult people it is not easy, pleasant, or something any of us look forward to when we go to work. We all want to interact with and deal with people who possess and demonstrate good to excellent interpersonal skills. Subsequently, each of us should strive to develop and demonstrate well above average to excellent interpersonal skills (e.g., a Likert rating scale of 1-5).

As you have already experienced, the main purpose of this book is to help you develop your innate abilities. I know, based on experience that people can improve their interpersonal skills by attending workshops; receiving feedback from supervisors, subordinates, and peers; and through just plain osmosis. When I teach any management and/or human resource (HR) management undergraduate or graduate course, I emphasize the importance of interpersonal skills for success in the workplace. Moreover, if a person desires to move up the management hierarchy in any type of organization, they must possess, develop, and demonstrate at minimum, good to excellent people skills.

But when they are promoted or hired for a top management position, interpersonal skills are, in my opinion and experience, mandatory. Moreover, the higher a person moves up the management hierarchy, the more important their dealing with people skills are. In top management positions, interpersonal skills are sometimes referred to as being "politically savvy." Based on my knowledge and experience, being politically savvy involves being able to engage with people who are difficult, moody, arrogant, and focused on power and control. You must be able to play the game (so to speak) no matter how difficult and stressful it may be to move up the organizational hierarchy.

Riggio and Lee (2007) stated,

> *all too often, in the context of reviewing leader competencies for developmental purposes, managers and other leaders are told that they need to improve their "people skills." What this usually means is that these individuals are having difficulties in the interpersonal aspects of their relationships with supervisors, peers, and perhaps even with superiors. In some cases, it means that the leader is not engaging in enough interpersonal communication to maintain effective work relationships. In other instances, there may be problems at the emotional level—appearing distant and aloof and not "connecting" emotionally with others, or alternatively, engaging in outbursts of negative emotions. The result is that the leader is targeted for development of interpersonal skills, or in more recent years and parlance, told to improve one's "emotional intelligence (EI)," or "EQ" as opposed to "IQ."*

(Riggio & Lee, 2007, p. 418)

Their comments reinforce my views and expand the discussion to leadership development programs and then EI later in this chapter. First, a short history of interpersonal skills and leadership research is provided.

SHORT HISTORY OF INTERPERSONAL SKILLS AND LEADERSHIP

Riggio and Lee (2007) provided a broad summary about developing leader interpersonal skills starting in the mid-1900s to 2007. They reviewed, and I verified the research by Bass (1990), Stogdill (1974), Likert (1961), Stogdill and Coons (1957), Fleishman (1953), Boyatzis (1982), Bass (1985), Bass and Riggio (2006), Avolio (1999, 2005), and London (2002).

The researchers provided evidence that:

- Communication and social skills predict who will emerge as a leader and possess leadership effectiveness.
- Task-oriented and relationship-oriented behaviors are the basis for concepts covered in interpersonal skills training.

- Training programs have been designed to help develop leader's interpersonal skills.
- Interpersonal and communication skills development is very important even though no unified theoretical framework existed, as of 2007.
- Leadership theories such as Leader–Member Exchange and Transformational Leadership emphasize the quality of the relationships between the leaders and their followers of which interpersonal skills are vital.
- Some leadership development programs based on transformational leadership focus on the importance of listening and relationships based on trust.
- Interpersonal skills are almost always included in large corporation leadership development programs.

Regarding leadership development, in every leadership development workshop that I have developed and delivered, most, if not all, of the above points are included in the programs. Moreover, of late, EI has received much attention in the literature, including the development of how to tap into the extent to which a person has or demonstrates EI (Bar-Ons, 1997; Boyatzis, 2001; Boyatzis, Goleman, & Rhee, 2000; Gardner & Stough, 2002; Goleman, 1995, 1998, 2006; Goleman, Boyatzis, & McKee, 2002; Lopes, Cote, & Salovey, 2006; Mayer & Salovey, 1997; Rubin, Munz, & Bommer, 2005; Wong & Law, 2002).

DESCRIPTIONS OF EI

The emotionally intelligent employee needs not just to be a good coper but also a multitasker in juggling diverse sources of demand and setting priorities so as to focus on coping on those demands that are most pressing.

(Zeidner, Roberts, & Matthews, 2009, p. 286)

For example, the leading global car manufacturer—Toyota—has a messaging campaign that implies hiring is not so much cognitive abilities, technical expertise, or skills. Good corporate citizenship is instead what is being sought in new recruits. Companies are now scouting for people who are compassionate, reliable on the job, productive team workers, and care both about their co-workers and their job (i.e., emotionally intelligent individuals).

(Zeidner et al., 2009, p. 253)

The concept of EI has even greater appeal since it is also claimed to be useful when evaluating ongoing functioning and the well-being of employees at critical stages of their careers (i.e., selection, placement, training, and promotion). In addition, as alluded to previously, EI appears valid for gauging the impact and intervention electiveness of organizational change and restructuring.

(see also Bar-On, 1997; Zeidner et al., 2009, p. 260)

EI assists people in "teamwork, in cooperation, and in helping others learn how to work together more effectively" (Goleman, 1998, p. 163). Inside conventional wisdom, because each of these factors is thought to impinge on an organization's success, EI is given great status.

(Zeidner et al., 2009, p. 260)

First, EI is considered by researchers to be important for the working lives of employees, their decision-making, the basis of making good decisions, being able to know, control, and motivate themselves. Moreover, people who are considered EI can approach others in an understanding manner, engage in open and honest communication, and have trusting relationships. A recent meta-analysis by Joseph, Jin, Newman, and O'Boyle (2015) found that other constructs are being measured, that is, conscientiousness, extraversion, self-efficacy, and emotional stability.

Some other research findings about EI are best summarized as:

- EI is considered an ability model.
- The intelligence domain is made up of emotional and mental abilities.
- Mixed model theories group personality, motivation, and social skills into one domain.
- A mixed model by Goleman focused on leaders in the workplace.
- Goleman's mixed model encompasses four dimensions: self-awareness, relationship management, social awareness, and self-management.
- Goleman's model also accentuates motivation and personality traits as well as emotional competence.
- After having adapted Salovey and Mayer's model, Goleman presented a version that he felt would facilitate an understanding of the characteristics that are important for work.

Each of the four dimensions include, what I refer to as, interpersonal skills' subcomponents and are summarized as follows:

- Persons who are *self-aware* of their own feelings, abilities, and limitations are self-confident and have positive self-efficacy.
- Persons who demonstrate *relationship management* abilities have very strong social and communication skills, are able to influence others, inspire others, facilitate change, collaborate well with others, foster teamwork, and manage conflict situations.
- Persons who are *socially aware* are empathetic, focus on serving others, can pick up on other's emotions including political situations.
- Persons who demonstrate *self-management* behaviors can control their emotions, are transparent, tell others what their values, principles, plans, and feelings are. These types of persons are also conscientious, adaptable, proactive, and are motivated and achievement oriented.

(Bar-Ons, 1997; Gardner & Stough, 2002; Goleman, 1998; Goleman, Boyatzis, & McKee, 2002; Lopes, Cote, & Salovey, 2006; Mayer & Salovey, 1997; Rubin, Munz, & Bommer, 2005; Salovey & Mayer, 1990; Wong & Law, 2002).

Riggio and Lee (2007) sum up the relationship between and importance of interpersonal skills and EI,

> *Let us be clear: there is little doubt that the development of skills in interpersonal and emotional communication can make people more effective leaders, and probably more effective employees (and participants in social interactions of all kinds). However, the research directly examining the skill-effectiveness link could be stronger, and evidence for the effectiveness of interpersonal and emotional skill training programs is even less conclusive.*

(p. 422)

Morehouse (2007) provides his definition of EI starting with intrapersonal that according to him and Mandell and Pherwani (2003), pertains to the self-knowledge a person has about themselves as well as their ability to modify their behavior based on their self-knowledge.

Mandell uses the following competencies to describe EI:

- Self-regard
- Emotional self-awareness
- Assertiveness
- Independence
- Self-actualization
- Interpersonal

He included the following subdimensions to define interpersonal:

- Ability to perceive the moods, intentions, and feelings of others and to respond effectively to these.
- Empathy.
- Adaptability (e.g., reality testing, flexibility, and problem-solving).
- Stress management (e.g., manage your own stress, ability to tolerate stress tolerance, manage impulses, general mood, and be happy and optimistic).

Before you read a few in-depth definitions of interpersonal, a few more important research findings about EI follow.

MORE IMPORTANT RESEARCH FINDINGS ABOUT EI

Regarding EI and the workplace, the following findings add to the literature about EI:

- Laabs (1999) found that there are thousands of HR professionals and consultants who strive to improve the social and EI of the employees.
- Schwartz (2000) found that some organizations include EI in active development programs.
- Stein and Book (2000) found that in 1998, the U.S. Department of Defense decided to use measures of EI for personnel who were hired in all branches of the armed services.
- Watkins (2000) emphasized that for the process of HR selection, the success rate of managers in using EI could identify the right candidates at a rate of 90%.
- Since 1982, many researchers have found that EI is a positive predictor of work performance (Barrick, Mount, & Judge, 2001; Chaudhry & Usman, 2011; Chen, Bian, & Hou, 2015; Dulewicz & Higgs, 2004; Hopkins & Bilimoria, 2008; Langhorn, 2004; O'Boyle, Humphrey, Pollack, Hawver, & Story, 2011; Prati, Douglas, Ferris, Ammeter, & Buckley, 2003; Prentice & King, 2013; Vinchur, Schippmann, Switzer, & Roth, 1998).
- Boyatzis (1982) and Huang, Chan, Lam, and Nan (2010) determined that higher self-assessment, self-awareness, self-emotion appraisal, other-emotion appraisal, use of emotion, and regulation of emotion were related to better job performance.

The next section summarizes some research about whether people can be trained to be EI.

CAN EI BE TRAINED?

A Fast Company article describes Google's "insanely popular emotional intelligence course" (Giang, 2015), business blogs attribute corporate performance to the EI of its leaders (e.g., Conley, 2011), and the consulting group TalentSmart claims that 75% of Fortune 500 companies use its EI products or services.

Despite debates over EI as a legitimate construct (see Antonakis, Ashkanasy, & Dasborough, 2009; Locke, 2005; Mayer, Salovey, & Caruso, 2008), HR practitioners spend considerable resources selecting and training a more emotionally intelligent workforce (Fineman, 2004; Nafukho & Muyia, 2014).

A December 2017 web search revealed over 200 vendors providing various forms of EI coaching or training, including those offered by large professional organizations like the American Management Association and the Association for Talent Development. Further, EI training is increasingly being integrated into MBA training, even in prestigious universities such as Yale (Di Meglio, 2013).

With respect to workplace training interventions, researchers often target jobs perceived as high in stress or emotional labor such as police officers, nurses, or managers. In one such study, Slaski Mattingly and Kraiger "identified 58 published and unpublished studies that included an emotional intelligence training program using either a pre-post or treatment control design" (p. 140). They asked the empirical question, "Can EI be trained and answer it by meta-analyzing studies that attempt to increase E via training interventions" (p. 141). Some of the results are summarized best by the authors,

"For the pre-post meta-analysis, a total of 56 samples from 50 studies met the inclusion criteria, for a total sample of 2136. The treatment-control meta-analysis included 28 samples from 26 studies, yielding 2174 participants. Of these 28 samples, 13 used an active (or alternative) treatment group, and 15 used a passive (or no) treatment group. The number of participants in the treatment control sample exceeds the number of participants in the pre-post sample since the former includes control group participants where the latter does not. All studies were completed between 2000 and 2016" (p. 144).

Some other key findings of their meta-analyses were:

- A moderate positive effect for training on EI scores was found: $dc = 0.45$ for treatment control designs and 0.61 for pre-post designs (Mattingly & Kraiger, 2019).
- Trainees should acquire more EI when they can discuss the meaning of the construct and how it applies to them, and they will learn less if they sit and listen (Mattingly & Kraiger, 2019).
- Training must be active (practice) and personal (feedback) (Mattingly & Kraiger, 2019).
- EI scores increase when participants are able to practice examining situations, responding appropriately, and then receiving feedback about their performance (Mattingly & Kraiger, 2019).
- Coaching and homework appear to be positive components of training when they are both used, when training takes place over multiple sessions, and trainees are given assignments to complete (e.g., analyze a case or meet with a coach) between sessions (Mattingly & Kraiger, 2019).

They interpreted their meta-analysis as reflecting that "training improves EI scores, rather than emotional intelligence itself. That is, the demonstrated practical utility of training would have been greater had there been more evidence that either trainees behaved in ways consistent with higher EI (e.g., greater self-awareness and self-management, empathy, and improved interpersonal communication) or that EI training affected other outcomes such as individual job performance or subordinate job satisfaction" (Mattingly & Kraiger, 2019, p. 150).

SOME DEFINITIONS OF DEALING WITH PEOPLE (INTERPERSONAL) SKILLS

Now that you have been introduced to how important interpersonal skills are to leadership development and EI, let's focus on some specific definitions of interpersonal. Throughout your life you have interacted with, been friends with, have had to work with, and encountered people who have very good to excellent dealing with people. Let's review some examples of good to excellent dealing with people behaviors. An individual with above average to excellent interpersonal skills

- Is friendly
- Is approachable
- Makes you feel comfortable
- Makes you feel good about yourself
- Builds another person's self esteem
- Has charisma
- Thanks people
- Shows interest in you
- Listens to you when you are speaking
- Is genuine
- Shows respect for others
- Has a positive reputation
- Compliments others
- Is very easy to talk to
- Acknowledges others
- Gets along well with others
- Smiles
- Respects differences in people

Think about a person whom you have known and respected, as a leader and an individual whom you would wish to emulate. How many of the above interpersonal skills did this person possess? Now let's review a few definitions of dealing with people that I have used in assessment center exercises. You should see a link between the definitions and what you have just learned about the domains of EI.

Dealing With People

- Strives to develop and maintain excellent rapport with personnel under charge and listens to and considers their suggestions and complaints and responds appropriately.

- Adheres to policies in the discharge of duties and responsibilities and ensures the same from personnel under charge.
- Shares knowledge with managers, supervisors, and coworkers for mutual benefit.
- Contributes to maintaining high morale among all employees.
- Develops and maintains cooperative and courteous relationships inter and intradepartmentally, and with external entities such as customers, with whom the position interacts.
- Tactfully and effectively handles requests, suggestions, and complaints to establish and maintain good will.
- Emphasizes the importance of maintaining a positive image.

Interpersonal Skills

- Ability to maintain effective, cooperative, and courteous relationships with employees and the public to maintain good will toward coworkers, peers, superiors, and customers.
- Ability to tactfully and effectively handle requests, suggestions, and complaints.
- Ability to
  - Extend common courtesies to others.
  - Focus on peoples' good qualities rather than their deficiencies.
  - Recognize employees' contributions.
  - Seek feedback from employees.
  - Share information.
  - Show respect for employees' ideas and experience.
  - Show interest in people.
  - Develop effective working relationships with peers.
  - Consider peoples' feelings when making decisions.
  - Relate well to people regardless of their personality or background.
  - Adjust interpersonal style to input/cues from others.
- Ability to emphasize to staff the importance of maintaining a positive image within the company and its customers.
- Ability to refrain from gossiping and reacting to rumors.
- Ability to maintain composure under stress when, confronted with the emergency situations or tight deadlines.

REAL-LIFE EXAMPLES

Ten Scenarios

In the following section you are provided with ten scenarios, which I would like you to carefully read and think about how you would handle each one. The scenarios involve dealing with people/emotional intelligence. The following will take place:

- A scenario is presented.
- You should read and think about the situation described in the scenario.
- Write some notes about how you handle or would handle the situation.
- Think about how you will plan and organize the work to solve the problem or issues.

- Read the rest of the scenarios and go through the same process.
- Take the quiz.

Carefully read and think about what the issues are. When you take the quiz, you will be provided with five possible options.

When reading each scenario, pretend you are at work for the company. Focus only on what is presented. Do not over analyze what is presented. In other words, do not assume things or issues that are not obvious. Also, do not worry about the size of the company, not having an organizational chart, or not knowing the names of the people described in the scenario. In summary, the only information available is what is written. Use this information to demonstrate your dealing with people (aka interpersonal) and emotional intelligence abilities.

- **Bank employee maternity leave and sick child**
- **Coworker tardiness**
- **Subordinate performance problems and father's emergency surgery for cancer diagnosis**
- **Budget cuts and employee issues**
- **Family business closing down due to explosion**
- **Staff meeting about company policy and procedures changes**
- **Incompetent and sabotaging supervisor who provides no coaching**
- **Team member unwilling and unable to express his concerns**
- **Obtaining new client, staff concern, and aggressive vice president (VP)**
- **Performance evaluation training and new pay-for-performance (PFP) system**

When reading each scenario pretend you are at work for the company. Focus only on what is presented. Do not over analyze what is presented. In other words, do not assume things or issues that are not obvious. Also, do not worry about the size of the company, not having an organizational chart or not knowing the names of the people described in the scenario. In summary, the only information available is what is written. Use this to demonstrate your dealing with people (aka interpersonal) and EI abilities.

Scenario 1: Bank Employee Maternity Leave and Sick Child

Assume that you are a Branch Manager in a medium size city of a nationally known bank. Your branch is one of hundreds of around the country. You have been in the position for 2 years and know your staff well. Last week all managers were advised to increase the number of new customers they acquired and their PFP increases would be based partially on the number of new accounts they open each month.

You have an employee who just returned from maternity leave. Prior to going on leave she was one of your top performers. She used all of her allowable family medical leave as provided by the Family Medical Leave Act (1993) and the bank's HR policy. She has been back from leave for only 2 weeks when she receives a call from the baby sitter that her daughter who has spina bifida and colitis, was sick so she just called an ambulance. You tell her to leave work to take care of her daughter.

She is out for 1 week because her daughter has been admitted to the hospital. The employee calls you, is crying and asks you for more time off. She has not accomplished anything at work for the 2 weeks she has been back from maternity leave.

Multiple-Choice Questions: Bank Employee Maternity Leave and Sick Child

Question 1

What do you say to this employee when she asks you for more time off?

A

"You can take a few more days to take care of your family"

B

"We will talk about your need for time off, but your job may be in jeopardy"

C

"You can take today off but as you know you have not accomplished any work since you have been back from maternity leave"

D

"Yes, you can take today off but you must be able to meet your production goals"

E

"Yes, of course, I am very sorry about your daughter. You can take as many off as you need, but we need to discuss how the company can accommodate you during this difficult time"

Question 2

Given that your employee is crying, **WHICH** below is the most appropriate way to handle this situation?

A

I would tell her I am very sorry about her daughter and would offer her any assistance she needs.

B

Nothing, as she is crying, and I cannot make her stop.

C

I would not say or do anything now. Doing so could cause more problems.

D

I will listen to her, interject when I can, tell her I empathize with her situation, and then offer her any assistance she needs.

E

None of the above.

Scenario 2: Coworker Tardiness

You have a coworker, Len, who has continued to arrive late to work. His tardiness is starting to affect your work. For example, when he is late, customers who would be standing at his intake window, move to your window and then a long line forms. You do not know if your supervisor has spoken to him about this and decided at this point, not to report him. Now, you feel it has reached a point where the customers are becoming angry with you and the company (e.g., negative facial expression, "Why is only one window open?" "Why don't they hire more people to help us?").

Len arrives 15 minutes late today and looks awful; for example, his eyes are red, his clothing looks soiled, and his hair looks disheveled. He goes right to work and does not apologize for his tardiness. When you see him in the lunch room, he looks very distraught.

Multiple-Choice Questions: Coworker Tardiness

Question 3

What, if anything, would you say to Len, and why?

A

Nothing because how he looks or why he is late, is none of my business.

B

"Are you feeling alright? This is something that has caused me many problems"

C

"I am going to report your tardiness to our boss"

D

"Len, I hope you are okay. I know you have been late lately, is everything okay with you?"

E

All of the above are acceptable options.

Scenario 3: Subordinate Performance Problems and Father's Emergency Surgery for Cancer Diagnosis

Assume that you are Kevin Kline, a Quality Control Manager of a unit in a chemicals company which has the most employees. The employees deal with quality control issues. There is always a great deal of pressure on everyone to improve quality no matter where they work in the company. One of your employees, Gene's 6-month performance appraisal is due by the end of the month. The company policy is that all reviews must be completed on the day scheduled without fail. In the meeting, you are going to discuss Gene's problems meeting deadlines and making errors in the checking processes.

Today, Gene made a serious error on one report and his 6-month appraisal meeting happens to be scheduled for today at 3 p.m. However, right after lunch Gene approaches you and advises you that his father was admitted to the hospital for emergency surgery based on a cancer diagnosis and asks to leave work immediately.

Multiple-Choice Questions: Subordinate Performance Problems and Emergency Surgery for Cancer Diagnosis

Question 4

Considering Gene's review is scheduled for 3 p.m. today, what should you say to him?

A

"We need to go over your performance and then you can leave"

B

"I am so sorry about your father, leave immediately, and let me know when you will be back to work"

C

"I am concerned about your continued mistakes which we will cover during the review session. Once we are finished feel free to go to the hospital"

D

"You need to leave immediately for the hospital. I am so sorry about this. Your performance evaluation can wait. Family is more important. Let's visit when you return to work"

E

All of the above are acceptable.

Scenario 4: Budget Cuts and Employee Issues

You are a Manager of an Office Products distribution company. Last year, and this year's first quarter revenues are down, and some centers have closed. Senior management has just announced more budget cuts which include; travel and off site or unscheduled training, a freeze on all hiring and promotions, and no company holiday parties. Unfortunately, there are several vacancies in both your division and throughout the company. Also, there are several first line supervisory positions yet to be filled. Your VP calls you into his office and asks you to please meet with your staff to advise them of the changes ASAP. It is not company policy to send out e-mail blasts. Face-to-face meetings are expected.

Another regrettable situation is that your employees are already overworked. They have not had a major PFP increase in over a year, and morale is down despite your best efforts and encouragement.

Multiple-Choice Questions: Budget Cuts and Employee Issues

Question 5

When you advise them of the changes **WHICH** are the most important things to tell them?

A

You are extremely valuable to the company; training opportunities will still be available when possible; we can have parties by sharing the cost; I will chip in the most.

B

As a team we can work through this; take whatever vacation time you need to get some rest, I am sorry that anyone who has applied for a supervisory job will have to wait.

C

If the company does not make the changes, we could all lose our jobs; be patient; you are lucky to have a job; change is not easy.

D

I am sorry that top management made these decisions; but I have no control over them; if anyone needs to talk my door is always open.

E

Both A and B.

Question 6

What behaviors/actions would you demonstrate when interacting with employees to help increase their morale?

A

Tell them that they are extremely valuable to the company and I will do my best to prevent any layoffs. I will also advise them that we can still have after work socials by cost sharing and I will personally chip in most of the costs.

B

Tell them that we are a great team and that I admire their efforts to keep our unit working. I would also indicate that we should discuss rotating days off to get some needed rest.

C

Schedule, fund, and participate in coffee breaks.

D

Walk the talk.

E

All of the above.

Scenario 5: Family Business Closing Down Due to Explosion

Mitchell Clooney is the owner of a 100-year-old family business located in a small town in a state in the northeastern United States. It produces knits and other clothes for the cold weather. Most of Clooney's employees have worked for the company for 20 or more years. The company employs 500 people and is one of the community's largest employers. It is in a strong financial position (e.g., it has a great deal of liquid assets). Mitchell's employees love working for the company and there are several three-generation family workers. Because of the income his employees have earned over the years, many have been able to send their children to the local college.

The company has a well-staffed and knowledgeable HR department. The Benefits department provides medical, dental, and life insurance coverage for all employees. The pay structure uses piece-rate pay for the hourly workers and a well-designed and valued PFP system for exempt employees. Overall, each employee's total compensation package is family friendly, flexible, and includes a rewards and recognition system.

One week, late in the day after most workers had gone home, an explosion occurred in the main factory. Several employees were seriously injured. As a result, the factory would remain closed for at least 6 months for repairs during which time none of his employees would be able to work. The cost of the explosion has been estimated to be in the millions. Mr. Clooney already knows that this will have a major detrimental effect on the business over the short term.

Multiple-Choice Questions: Family Business Closing Down Due to Explosion

Question 7

Because Mr. Clooney must close the factory for a minimum of 6 months, if he is an emotionally intelligent leader what behaviors/actions would he likely demonstrate?

A

Pay employees as much of their standard pay as he can during the time the factory is closed; also make sure that their benefits continue.

B

Tell employees that he will help them collect unemployment payments.

C

Apologize to them for the explosion and assure them that they will be back to work soon. Also advise them that they will be reemployed when the factory reopens.

D

Offer some employees partial pay and encourage others (i.e., the hourly workers) to apply for unemployment compensation.

E

Tell them he appreciates the great work they have done, and he looks forward to seeing them back in 6 months.

Question 8

Considering most of the employees are second or third generation workers and/or have worked for the company for 20 or more years, if Mr. Clooney is emotionally intelligent what is he likely to do for them?

A

Nothing as he should not treat them differently than other employees.

B

Visit their families at home; schedule and pay for a weekly get together for all employees.

C

Provide each family an early bonus checks to assist them with bills while they are not working.

D

B, C, and E.

E

Ensure that all employees are provided with progress reports about the factory repairs.

Question 9

An emotionally intelligent leader would do what, if anything, about his/her injured employees?

A

Ensure that their insurance policy, workers compensation, and Americans with Disabilities benefits are covered.

B

Continue to monitor the recovery process for each employee and their family members.

C

Visit the employee(s) at the hospital and at their homes when and as appropriate.

D

Send flowers, gifts, or meals to each employee on a regular basis.

E

All of the above.

Scenario 6: Staff Meeting About Company Policy and Procedures Changes

Assume you are Julia Danner, VP Human Resources for the ITSEY Corporation, a company which develops web-based software, apps, and other related products. You just left a meeting with the CEO and other senior executives which covered among other issues, the decision to change the PFP policy and procedures. The group decided to change the policy and procedures based on the analytics you provided; i.e., over 70% of nonunion employees received ratings of 4 or 5 for the past 2 years. The CEO considered the amount paid out for the increases was excessive considering 1/2 of the employee's increase is added to their base pay. Moreover, based on the predictive analytics, the correlation between the raises and a variety of metrics was weak at best.

The new PFP system will have three instead of five categories and 64% of employees must be rated a 2. The remaining 46% must be rated a 1 or a 3. You have been charged with the task of rewriting the policy and procedures and providing training to all supervisors. This must take place over the next 6 months.

You are now in your weekly staff meeting and have just delivered the news at which time you immediately notice:

- total silence
- upset and angry looks on every person's face; that is, heads shaking, mouths open, eyes looking down or around, and
- negative body language; that is, armed crossed, pens tapping on the conference table, and a few people nudged each other.

Multiple-Choice Questions: Staff Meeting About Company Policy and Procedures Changes

Question 10

You believe that you possess EI. Therefore, what will you immediately do and/or say to your staff?

A

Ask them to explain their silence and body language to me.

B

Tell them that I understand and empathize with their shocks and concerns (based on their silence and body language) and that we will proceed with a discussion about the changes.

C

Initiate the discussion about the process of rewriting the policy and procedures and starting the training process.

D

Advise them that we must support what top management wants even though we do not agree with it.

E

Tell them that their reaction and body language is unacceptable and then proceed with the meeting.

Scenario 7: Incompetent and Sabotaging Supervisor Who Provides No Coaching

You work as a Cruise Consultant for an internationally renowned cruise line and are approaching 2 full years of employment. You have a degree in Business Administration with a minor in Hospitality. You love your work and your coworkers.

The supervisory reporting structure is a bit unusual because a employee whose job title is Coach is supposed to be available to assist and coach other employees but is not responsible for their performance evaluations. However, the coach is responsible for reporting any performance deficiencies to each employee's Manager. You started work for the cruise line with about 1-year of prior experience working for a competitor line and had an excellent sales record. At this cruise line you have accomplished a lot to include:

- Exceeding your sales goals every month
- Winning several employee of the quarter awards
- Participating as a member of company employee committees
- Engaging in self-development activities after work to sharpen your computer skills
- Continuing to increase your income every year

You have also made several friends at the company but keep your distance at work, remain compliant, avoid socializing, and focus your energies on task completion.

Regardless of the aforementioned, since you first started working for the company, your coach, a long-term employee has provided little if any coaching. He has done just the opposite. He sits with his feet on his desk, is on his cell phone all day and comes and goes as he pleases. When he speaks to you, he is condescending and also eyes you up and down and rolls his eyes. He is arrogant, thinks he knows it all (he was a Cruise Consultant for several years before being promoted to the coach position). He is also very hyper and combative. Moreover, you have heard people gossiping about him and other employees in the break room. Some comment that he is a narcissist and sociopath.

The first example of his behavior, when you initially began your job was when you asked him to help you with a problem a newly booked customer was having with their account. You did not fully understand the policies and procedures. He said he would take care of it. Each time you checked with him he said he took care of it. A week later, you were called to his office via a text message and berated because the customer complained to a higher-level person because their problem was not taken care of. He blamed it on you.

Another example of his incompetent and sabotaging behavior occurred when you asked another coach for assistance. The company policy is that any Cruise Consultant can ask any coach for help at any time. You asked another coach for help because he was unavailable. When he found out about this, he wrote you up for doing this even though you were permitted to do so. Another example was that he wrote you up for not meeting your quota for the month of December. You were on vacation during this time and the company policy is that you must use your vacation time each calendar year, or you will lose it. He penalized you for taking the vacation time which you were entitled to.

A recent example of inappropriate behavior on his part occurred after you returned from a bathroom break. The company requires all hourly employees to clock out for their 8-minute morning and afternoon breaks. He chastised you, in front of other employees, for walking too slowly back to your desk. You were talking with another employee who had asked you a job-related question. As a result of this type of behavior, some employees feel the place is run like a sweat shop, but they retain their employment because of the money they earn which is substantial with cruise bookings.

You have reached the point that you are beginning to fear coming to work and are afraid that you will lose your job because of him. You are becoming afraid of him and his behavior toward you which is starting to affect your mental health.

Question 11

Assuming you are an emotionally intelligent employee, **WHICH** behaviors would you demonstrate to try and establish a better relationship with your coach?

A

Ask him if he would like to have coffee some time so I could receive some coaching from him in a different setting and not on company time.

B

Commend him on his many years of service.

C

Listen, keep a smile on my face, and show no emotion while he admonishes me.

D

Engage in more self-development and share with him what I have done which will help the company and make him look good.

E

All of the above.

Question 12

As a result of his actions you have reached the point where you feel you may not be able to continue working for the company. Therefore, you have decided to speak with someone from the HR department (the company has a confidential Hotline, but employees are allowed to go to the HR department). What is/are the **BEST** ways to share your concerns with whomever you are able to speak with?

A

Share with the HR staff person all of the behaviors he engaged in and what you might have done to upset him to show them you are self-aware.

B

Make sure I compliment him (during the meeting with HR), so I do not come across as a complainer.

C

Explain in a diplomatic, unemotional, self-confident, and facts-only manner what has transpired and seek advice.

D

Tell the HR staff person that you will do whatever is necessary to get on his good side, make sure they understand why you want to do this (e.g., I love my job, am a high producer, and want to retain this status, other).

E

All of the choices are acceptable, but C and D are the best.

Question 13

Assume that your coach calls you into his cubicle and starts the meeting by questioning you about why you worked past your shift (even though the company policy is that if a Consultant is on the phone with a customer when their shift ends they can work overtime) the previous day and starts to raise his voice when you try to explain, **WHICH** behaviors would you demonstrate?

A

Sit down, smile, thank him for calling you into his office, ignore his raised voice, and tell him that you were going to let him know why you worked past your shift the previous day.

B

Ask him to stop raising his voice, tell him that I should not be yelled at, and quote the company policy about working overtime.

C

Listen and smile while he raises his voice and then thank him for bringing this to my attention but then note that I have a legitimate and allowable reason for working overtime.

D

After his voice is lowered and I am seated, calmly and politely tell him why I worked overtime to include what I did for the customer and then thank him for being so conscientious.

E

Both C and D.

Question 14

Let's assume that inappropriate behavior of your coach continues to progress to the point where you think he has made your working conditions very difficult and almost hostile. Your past meeting with the HR department did not result in any improvements. You decide to file an official complaint with the HR department. You prepared and completed the complaint, based on the guidelines provided in the employee handbook and what you learned by going to the EEOC website. Being an emotionally intelligent person, you will do **WHICH** of the following?

A

Submit the complaint only after I have a face-to-face meeting with the appropriate HR staff member.

B

Ask the HR staff member what they can do to resolve this situation before I file the complaint and what we can do together to ensure that I keep my job.

C

Follow all guidelines for preparing an official complaint and hand deliver it to the HR department.

D

Share with the HR staff member that I love my job, the company, and the people but feel that I had no choice but to prepare an official complaint.

E

Both B and D but B is the best.

Question 15

One day your coach comes to your cubicle and asks if he can speak with you. His demeanor seems to have changed; he is less combative, humbler and more laid back. You are not sure if someone from the HR department has spoken to him about the complaint you filed. You ask him to have a seat and he sits down. He starts the interaction by stating, "We need to talk and perhaps we started off on the wrong foot," and then pauses and looks at you.

WHICH is/are the most appropriate ways to respond?

A

Thank him for coming to speak with me.

B

Acknowledge that I agree with him about starting off on the wrong foot and that I am willing to do whatever I can to improve our working relationship.

C

Offer to help him in any way I can so he can be a better coach to me.

D

Tell him that I work very hard to meet the quota, but do not do so to make myself look good but to do great work for the company and him.

E

All of the above.

Note: This scenario was adapted from, Caruso, D., & Salovey, P. (2004). The *Emotionally intelligent manager how to develop and use the four key emotional skills of leadership* (1st ed.). San Francisco, CA: Jossey Bass.

Scenario 8: Team Member Unwilling and Unable to Express His Concerns

Leo was a member of a very successful product development team for a national business which was planning its expansion into at least three countries over the next 2-years. His team had asked for 10 million dollars to pilot test and launch the product but were initially turned down by the senior management team. At that time, Leo had more enthusiasm for the product and its success on the market than the other members, Jerry, June, and Russell. They were ready to move on to another project and suggested that he temper his enthusiasm in the future, given that the CEO was very conservative.

A new VP of Product Development was hired because the former VP took a job with another company. The team met with the VP and lobbied for the money. Once again, Leo had the loudest voice in spite of the fact that:

1. The product development schedule was extremely aggressive.
2. A manufacturer within the United States had yet to be found.
3. Manufacturers were in China, but the CEO wanted all products made in the United States.

The VP provided the team with the $10 million dollars. The opinions of Leo's team members changed, and their support was unanimous. Moreover, a start-up company that could manufacture the product was located in Ohio. Work started during which time Leo determined that he was not satisfied with some of the design specifications. His team members disagreed with him. They were all very excited about the entire project and ignored his concern about the specifications and that their timeline would be difficult to meet and could result in problems with sales. The team worked nights and weekends to finish the design, negotiate with the company in Ohio, conduct beta testing, and push timelines back. A few weeks before the final launch, Leo considered addressing his concerns about one of the specifications but he kept his mouth shut because he wanted to be a team player.

The product was put on the market, but the sales were terrible. The various departments in the company blamed each other instead of trying to fix the problem. During this time, the CEO sold the company to another competitor. Employees found out that this had happened well after the fact during which time some were terminated. All of Leo's teammates were offered jobs with the new owner but he wasn't. He was devastated.

Question 16

Which below **BEST** describes how Leo emotionally handled the situation?

A

He was afraid to convince the team that they were incorrect about their lack of concern with the specifications, aggressive timeline, and so on.

B

Leo was unable to assert himself to the team and was more concerned with what people thought about him than what was best for the team and company.

C

He wanted to avoid any negative consequences.

D

He was afraid of what the team would say or feel about his opinions.

E

A, C, and D are all correct.

Question 17

Regarding Leo's team members which below **BEST** describes how their emotions affected the poor sales of the product?

A

They were not willing to listen to Leo's concerns because they had a blind commitment and emotional attachment to the project once the CEO gave the team 10 million dollars.

B

The team was blind to the problems Leo addressed because they viewed him as a rogue member of the team.

C

They had a blind commitment to the project timeline, so they intentionally ignored his feelings.

D

D is the best answer, but A is also an option.

E

The team was so excited about the project that any negative feelings they may have had were not discussed.

Scenario 9: Obtaining New Client, Staff Concerns, and Aggressive Vice President

Note: This scenario was adapted from, Caruso, D., & Salovey, P. (2004). The *Emotionally intelligent manager how to develop and use the four key emotional skills of leadership* (1st ed.). San Francisco, CA: Jossey Bass.

Melanie and Francisco work for Mercury Jones & Associates, Inc. a nationally renowned ad agency and were preparing for a teleconference meeting with a new client this morning. The VP, Jim Carrey, who is a bit of a micro manager, with a sharp temper and often erratic behavior, wanted to obtain the new client and attended the meeting. He was in the room sitting at the head of the conference table.

The company Dinosaur Resources, Inc. was a referral from one of their long-term accounts. The company produces drug ingredients for the pharmaceutical industry. Francisco was not a proponent of drug companies because both his daughter and cousin died from the side effects of two different drugs that had been released on the market within 1-year of each other. He had previously provided them with some material he obtained from a Google search, which included reputable newspapers and the information about Dinosaur Resources which was not positive. During the interaction, he became somewhat emotional and shed a few tears.

He told Jim and Melanie that he was shocked that they were not concerned about his findings. The company had been sued in the past for a variety of violations and was being investigated by the FDA and other agencies based on the results of a few drug tests for their products published in several scientific journals. The allegations were that some of the results were fake. He asked them if it would be ethical for Mercury Jones & Associates to do work for Dinosaur Resources. Melanie stated, "We should not be concerned about our ethics, we are fine, and we cannot control what our clients do. Your demeanor could cost us this client." Carrey agreed with her and stated to Francisco, "I applaud you for your morals and ethics, but they have nothing to do with who we do business with."

When he reminded Melanie and the VP, Jim Carrey, about the aforementioned, Melanie told him to stop overreacting, Carrey laughed at him and quickly left the room.

Jim Carrey came back a few minutes later with some documents for Melanie and Francisco to review with the Dinosaur Chemicals representatives. He told Francisco in a caustic and stern voice, while rolling his eyes, "Keep your mouth shut and check your opinion and feelings about the company at the door."

The meeting proceeded and the representatives from Dinosaur Resources were pleased with the services the firm was offering. After the meeting ended Francisco stated, "I am sorry if I was against this company. I should have kept my mouth shut."

Question 18

If you were Melanie and Francisco's Manager **WHICH** option below do you think is a better way to have reacted to Francisco's emotions regarding the death of his daughter and cousin?

A

I would have told him I am very sorry for his losses and it is a tragic irony that the company is a drug company.

B

I would offer him the option to not work with this company if we obtain their business.

C

Proceed with the meeting and speak with him later about crying during business meetings at which time we can discuss his losses.

D

I would have told him that I am sorry for his horrible losses, but we must separate business transactions from our emotions, or our judgment will be clouded.

E

Both A and B.

Question 19

If you were a coworker in the meeting with Melanie, Francisco, and Jim, what would you say to Francisco?

A

Nothing because a business meeting is not the time and place for being emotional or dealing with emotions.

B

Nothing, given the VP's personality; I do not want to get yelled at.

C

I would look at him and show him through facial expressions that I support him.

D

I would tell everyone that they are not being very considerate of Francisco's feelings given the deaths in his family which were caused by the company.

E

Both C and D although C is the best option.

Question 20

What do you think is inappropriate, if anything, about Melanie's statement made to Francisco, "We should not be concerned about our ethics, we are fine, and we cannot control what our clients do. Your demeanor could cost us this client."

A

She is not considering Francisco's feelings; does not appear to be concerned that he is discontented with the company; she assumes that Francisco's demeanor will be obvious to the client and she is attacking Francisco.

B

Nothing given that all employees are entitled to state their opinions just like Francisco, even though she could have been more diplomatic when disagreeing with Francisco.

C

She is trying to marginalize Francisco and blame him for something that has not even happened.

D

Nothing because she is just reacting to Francisco's emotional outburst.

E

A–D are good responses although A is the best.

Question 21

What is inappropriate about Jim Carrey's statement made to Francisco, "Keep your mouth shut and check your opinion and feelings about the company at the door."

A

Nothing as this VP is a bully and bullies cannot be controlled.

B

Nothing given Carrey's personality; a leopard does not change its spots.

C

He may be creating a hostile working environment which could cause problems down the road.

D

Telling an employee to shut up and to check his/her opinion at the door, and so on is abusive, and bullying behavior. It is also condescending and could lower morale and employee engagement.

E

C is alright, but D is the most appropriate option.

Scenario 10: Performance Evaluation Training and New Pay-for-Performance System

Assume that you are Marc/Marcie Mulligan, and HR Consultant for HRCares, Inc., a nationally known HR consulting firm. You are on an assignment to deliver 4 days of Performance Evaluation training for 200 employees in groups of 35 to 50 employees. The HR department is in the process of implementing a PFP system. The company is a relatively new start-up (i.e., WeCleanUp, a hazardous waste salvage and overhaul company was founded 6 years ago) and has grown rapidly over the past 2 years.

The majority of employees have a trades background, many have been members of unions in past jobs. However, WeCleanUp is nonunionized. None of the supervisors or managers come from a trades background.

None of the employees or supervisors have received any training on:

- How does a PFP system work?
- Delivering a performance appraisal.
- Documenting employee performance.
- Preparing for the meeting.

and other topics.

The training is somewhat different for each group; the supervisors will receive additional training (e.g., how to document performance, conduct the meeting, and deliver the feedback) but the remainder of the contents will be delivered to everyone. The employees will be provided with training on how to complete their self-evaluation, how the forms are used and the relationship between their job description and the appraisal forms. You were provided with the forms which are divided into different job families; for example, Senior Management, Management, Paraprofessional, Technical, and so on.

Despite having sent several e-mails to your HR contact at the company You were not provided with:

1. The final number of attendees.
2. Any pretraining e-mails disseminated to the employees.
3. Information regarding the type and methods used to increase employee's pay prior to the implementation of a PFP system.

The latter information would have been helpful.

You have arrived early to the training room which has drop-down screens, microphones in the ceiling, white boards, a kitchen area, and other amenities. A clip-on microphone, has also been provided which you immediately affix to your suit collar.

Today's session is comprised of all nonsupervisory and trades employees.

Attendees start to arrive and an HR Representative, Gary Guts is signing them in, and directing them to the breakfast station. He is eating a donut while doing this and you are a bit shocked to see food falling out of his mouth while he is speaking to one person. Then he answers his phone while three people are waiting in line. Additionally, he runs out of the training materials including tent cards for each person to write their name on. You think to yourself, "This is not going to be a good first day of training."

Question 22

Before you start the seminar you notice that 6 people are absent. There are 30 names listed on the roster. You check your cell phone and it is 9:00 a.m. at which point you introduce yourself. Before you finish your second sentence, the six absent employees walk in, get their coffee, at which point you stop speaking and say hello. They ignore you and sit down. One man, says in a caustic and somewhat angry and loud voice, "No one told us that we had to be here. When is lunch and what time does it end? One of his co-worker's nods and says, "You know we do not want to be here."

Guts is sitting in the back of the room and chuckles but does nothing.

What would you say or do about this? (**Note:** Don't forget that 29 people heard the aforementioned).

A

Nothing. I would continue my presentation and ignore him.

B

I would ask them to leave the seminar and ask Guts to escort them out.

C

"Mr . . . (name on tent card), I am sorry you were not informed, lunch is at 12:00 sharp and the class is over at 4:30 PM sharp. Trust me, you will learn a lot and will like being here."

D

I would ask Guts to respond to their concerns.

E

C is the best response although there is nothing wrong with asking Guts to respond.

Question 23

When you start to review the PFP forms with the nonsupervisory group, one employee states,

- "We have not received any significant pay increases the past few years," but before you can answer her question, another employee states,
- "We have had profit sharing, but only certain groups receive anything. Will this training address this?"
- Finally, before the second employee finishes, a third one, stands up and states,
- "We do not understand why we have been required to attend this training because we know management won't pay any of us for our performance."

What do you do/say to him/her and/or what do you do?

A

"I am not aware of any of these issues but based on my knowledge the company is implementing PFP and this training is one of the stages."

B

"Thank you all for your sharing this information and I believe you all understand why you are here."

C

Walk over to Guts, hand him the microphone, and ask him to respond to the employee's questions, and then sit down.

D

"I am sorry, but I cannot answer or address any of your concerns as I was hired to conduct the training."

E

A is the best response, but B is also appropriate.

Question 24

You are delivering the training and come to the section where you are explaining the performance distribution rating system that will be used for all performance evaluations in all job families. The rating scheme is as follows:

1 = **Poor performance**

20% of employees in rating group must be given a 1.

2 = **Average or expected level of performance**

60% of employees in rating must be given a 2.

3 = **Well above average or exemplary performance**

20% of employees in rating group must be given a 3.

The three numbers are not defined other than what is provided above.

You start to explain the rationale behind using only three categories and show a normal distribution bell curve on the screen.

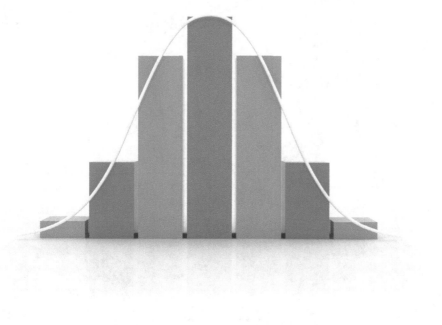

© Ersin Kurtdal/Shutterstock.com

After you have finished, eight employees sitting at different tables raise their hands at the same time. You call on the first person and he states in an angry tone of voice,

"Why are we being rated on a 3-point scale now? In the past, we were rated on a five-point scale. What is going on, it looks like most of us will receive a 2?"

What is the **BEST** way to respond to the questions?

A

I can only advise you that the company made the changes after much evaluation, and I cannot explain what is going on. The HR staff should explain this to you.

B

"I am sorry you are upset about this, but the contents of the workshop do not include why the changes were made and future lower pay increases".

C

This is a good time to take a break during which time you can speak to Mr. Guts.

D

Both A and B.

E

I do not know the reasons the scale changed or anything about the pay increase changes.

OVERVIEW

Blank (2008) determined that one of the reasons executives failed in their careers was related to their poor interpersonal skills. That is not being able to deal with change and/or work well within a team situation. A subcomponent of interpersonal skills is adaptability especially within a corporate or political environment. Being an adaptable person will help you in many ways during your life and career. I am certain that you can document the times when you were adaptable by your choice or because doing so was; (a) the only alternative you had at the time to accomplish your goal(s); (b) you had to deal with a difficult person or situation; or (c) resolve a situation. My life experience has taught me that being too adaptable can also be problematic because other people may use this to their advantage.

This chapter provides a relatively comprehensive overview of adaptability; substantiates that it is a component of emotional intelligence (EI; although defined differently; and provides some research about adaptability and then, like the format of the other chapters several scenarios and questions to answer).

A FEW EXAMPLES

Before we get into the nitty-gritty of this chapter, allow me share with you some of the times I was adaptable by choice or because I had no choice but to be adaptable. The following case summaries reflect my adaptability.

Example 1—Reported to Three Different Bosses: Given the changes in my second job after graduate school, I had to divide my time between two offices in two different locations. I also reported to three different men (even though one was my direct supervisor) who were all very good mentors. Aside from my general responsibilities, I also had to work on a variety of projects. I adapted in the following ways:

- Viewed having two offices and three bosses as an opportunity to learn from the different projects my bosses gave me instead of a burden.
- Made sure I kept each person aware of where I was and what I was working on when applicable.
- Never complained about having to drive back-and-forth between both locations. I used the time to think about how I would accomplish the tasks assigned by each supervisor.

Example 2—Minority Recruiter: I hired the Human Resource (HR) Department's first recruiter. He was an African American male coming from the private to the public sector. I and the interview panel members were very pleased to hire him because one of the goals of my section was to increase the representation of women and minorities in the county. He brought to the job a wealth of experience as a corporate recruiter. Unfortunately, I had to deal with several negative comments made by some of my subordinates as well as other employees who did not report to me. Comments included, "Was he paid above the minimum just because he is a Black male?" I adapted in the following ways:

- Told each person that their comments were inappropriate. It also required me to provide additional training to my subordinates.
- Overly accommodated the recruiter, which worked to my disadvantage.
- Put him on a performance improvement plan and had to monitor his whereabouts and work performance very closely, which was unfair both to me and to him.

Example 3—Terminated 3-Year Contract: I made a decision to terminate a 3-year contract with a client after having reported to the HR director on numerous occasions that one of the project managers was making our work lives very difficult, if not impossible. Before I made the difficult decision to terminate the contract, I adapted in the following ways:

- Communicated with the project manager in a very diplomatic and pleasant manner despite his constant negative comments, which undermined the integrity of my work and the work of my subordinates.
- In my communication with him, I tried, without success to respond to his negative comments, by providing him with factual data, which he ignored.
- Shared the problems with the HR director on a regular basis even though she did not trust what I was telling her, and as a result it increased tension between us, which required me to find ways to negate the bad feelings and further adapt to the situation.

Jeff Boss (2015), a former navy SEAL, principal, and senior advisor at N2 Growth, and author of *Navigating Chaos: How to Find Certainty in Uncertain Situations*, wrote an article for *Forbes Magazine*. He outlined 14 examples of someone who is adaptable, including communication, because doing so provides guidance to others who may be uncertain. His statements reinforce the salience of being adaptable:

> *To adapt you must be open to change, which means you must have the will—emotional tolerance, mental fortitude, spiritual guidance—to not only face uncertainty but smack it in the face and press on.*

> *(Boss, 2015)*

https://www.forbes.com/sites/jeffboss/2015/09/03/14-signs-of-an-adaptable-person/#4e48301616ea

Earlier in this book, you learned some things about soft skills and that one of the soft skills, adaptability, is a component of emotional intelligence (EQ). The following section provides several specific examples of adaptability.

Definitions of Adaptability

The definition I have used to describe adaptability for promotional testing processes is

- Ability to remain flexible and patient in the face of constantly changing needs, to influence events and to execute the required actions to complete cases.
- Ability to modify behavior to accommodate needs and feelings of others.

According to many researchers, the term "adaptability" includes the following definitions:

- Adaptability is a somewhat stable characteristic of a person.
- Being adaptable influences an individual.
- People who are adaptable notice environmental cues.
- Adaptable individuals pay closer attention to things than others.
- Being mindful is part of being adaptable.
- Adaptable individuals may be better able to deal with losing resources as well has acquiring resources in organizations.
- An adaptable individual may be psychologically resourceful.

(Katarzyna, 2016; Van den Heuvel, Demerouti, Bakker, & Schaufeli, 2013; Van den Heuvel, Demerouti, Schreurs, Bakker, & Schaufeli, 2009).

The above mentioned abilities (aka competencies or skills) are also referred by some scholars as soft skills. A citation from Coleman and Argue's (2015) article, "Mediating with Emotional Intelligence: When 'IQ' Just Isn't Enough," is another excellent description of soft skills and their comparison to hard skills.

> Soft skills are the relational skills that allow an individual to excel in relationships with others. A person with excellent "soft skills" may be charismatic, approachable, easy to talk to and someone who can be trusted. Surprisingly, "soft skills" trump "hard skills" when it comes to value to the group. In other words, a person with excellent "hard skills" but low in "soft skills" will be less valuable to the group than a person with mediocre "hard skills" and excellent "soft skills."

> (Coleman & Argue 2015, p. 18)

An example of a hard skill is technical knowledge. A colleague of mine says that soft skills are intrinsic and hard skills are extrinsic. You learn the extrinsic, but you must develop the intrinsic.

Robles (2012) cited research on the importance of soft skills in the workplace from Klaus (2010); Maes, Weldy, and Icenogel (1997); Mitchell, Skinner, and White (2010); Nealy (2005); and Smith (2007). He noted that,

> One study found that 75% of long-term job success depends on people skills, while only 25% is dependent on technical knowledge (Klaus, 2010). As employers are progressively looking for employees who are mature and socially well adjusted, they rate soft skills as number one in importance for entry-level success on the job

> (Wilhelm, 2004, p. 2).

Some Research On Adaptability

Cullen, Edwards, Casper, and Gue (2014) provided some evidence that a person's adaptability is related to job performance, but that organizational support staff are also being adaptable. Shoss, Witt, and Vera (2012) refer to this as adaptive performance, which is dynamic. With respect to adaptive performance, Pulakos, Arad, Donovan, and Plamondon (2000) and Pulakos et al. (2002) conducted a study and proposed eight different ways to examine adaptive performance that pertain to how an individual handles, deals with, or demonstrates certain behaviors in different situations.

The ways include how the individual:

1. Handles emergencies and crisis situations.
2. Handles stress in the workforce.
3. Creatively solves problems.
4. Deals with uncertain and unpredictable work situations.
5. Learns and is able to manipulate new technology, task, and procedures.
6. Demonstrates interpersonal adaptability.
7. Demonstrates cultural adaptability.
8. Demonstrates physically oriented adaptability (Pulakos et al., 2000, 2002).

If you work for an effective manager, are a manager, or want to be promoted to a management position, you should demonstrate competence in the behaviors listed in 1 to 8 above (Pulakos et al., 2000, 2002). Moreover, if you know yourself, you should have an idea as to how adaptable or unadaptable you are. Rate yourself using Pulakos' criteria using the Self-Evaluation rating scale for each behavior. This will provide you with an opportunity to ascertain which intrinsic skills you need to further develop and refine.

In Chapter 6, you learned about dealing with people and emotional quotient (EQ). Please note that EQ and EI are both known as emotional intelligence. Different terms and labels are assigned. I reviewed the literature about the additional components of EQ; for example, self-management and self-control. A person who demonstrates self-management and self-control can keep disruptive emotions and impulses in check and control their impulses (Blank, 2008). Moreover, adaptable individuals can stay calm when pressured, effectively resolve conflict, demonstrate empathy, and show consideration to others when making business decisions (Blank, 2008).

Blank (2008) reviewed Coleman's EI model and its four domains. It is my contention that two of the domains and their subcomponents reflect other ways to define a person's adaptability. This is based on my years of experience with testing and assessment and most notably assessment center methodology. A quick review of two is as follows:

Personal Competence: *these capabilities determine how we manage ourselves.*
1. Self-Awareness

Emotional self-awareness: Reading one's own emotions and recognizing their impact; using 'gut sense' to guide decisions.

Accurate self-assessment: Knowing one's strengths and limits.

Self-confidence: A sound sense of one's self-worth and capabilities.

(Blank, 2008, p. 79)

Social Competence: *These capabilities determine how we manage relationships.*
1. Social Awareness

Empathy: Sensing others' emotions, understanding their perspective, and taking active interest in their concerns.

Organizational awareness: Reading the currents, decision networks, and politics at the organization level.

Service: Recognizing and meeting follower, client, or customer needs.

(Blank, 2008, p. 80)

ADAPTABILITY AND CAREERS

While using "Google" and typing "adaptability," I found many websites on the topic. For example, according to Korn Ferry (2017), a component of being adaptable depends on a person's people skills and whether or not they are socially adjusted. Based on my experience, I totally agree with their contention. Experts at Korn Ferry Institute (2017) recognized that adaptability is important for a person's career and that this innate ability is related to EQ. They noted that an adaptable person does not dwell on problems, but rather moves quickly to find solutions to problems, communicates with their team, and stays focused. Researchers at the Korn Ferry Institute reviewed a study of financial services sales executives and reported some of the findings about adaptability. The study found that the

> *more adaptable the individual, the greater the person's effectiveness is shown by revenue and sales growth. Researchers in India found a positive relationship between emotional intelligence, especially employee adaptability, and how well they did their jobs. American researchers also found that a leader's adaptability predicts better overall team performance.*

> *(https://www.kornferry.com/institute/*
> *adaptability-the-surprisingly-strong-predictor-of-career-success)*

Career advice provided by Roberthalf.com includes a section about adaptability and reinforces what you have already learned about soft skills.

> *"Being adaptable means being a perpetual optimist and exhibiting extraordinary resilience. Adaptability skills can be possessed both in both attitude and action, and one can't exist without the other . . . Learning how to adapt to change is a soft skill that will not only make you a top candidate when applying for roles . . ."*

> *(Roberthalf.com).*

You previously learned that using poor judgment and making bad decisions could cost you your job. Having a stable career is what all of us want. Moreover, the importance of and need for employees who are adaptable is also relevant when companies are hiring or downsizing. The downsizing process results in many problems for the survivors (e.g., guilt, change, loss of coworker relationships) and stress for everyone. According to Coleman and Argue (2015), in response to these changes, 34% of hiring managers said they are placing greater emphasis on emotional intelligence when hiring and promoting employee's postrecession, according to a new

CareerBuilder survey. When asked why emotional intelligence is more important than high IQ, these hiring managers listed the following EI traits (Coleman & Argue, 2015).

- "Employees [with high EI] are more likely to stay calm under pressure;
- Employees know how to resolve conflict effectively;
- Employees are empathetic to their team members and react accordingly;
- Employees lead by example and tend to make more thoughtful business decisions" (p. 18).

SEVEN SCENARIOS

The remainder of this chapter includes nine different scenarios involving adaptability. The following will take place:

- A scenario is presented.
- You should read and think about the situation described in the scenario.
- Write some notes about how you handle or would handle the situation.
- Think about how you will plan and organize the work to solve the problem or issues.
- Read the rest of the scenarios and go through the same process.
- Take the quiz.

Carefully read and think about how you should adapt to each situation. When you take the quiz, you will be provided with five options.

When reading each scenario, pretend you are at work for the company. Focus only on what is presented. Do not over analyze what is presented. In other words, do not assume things or issues that are not obvious. Also, do not worry about the size of the company, not having an organizational chart, or not knowing the names of the people described in the scenario. In summary, the only information available is what is written. Use this information to demonstrate how adaptable you are.

- **Difficult Coworkers and Pay Equity issue**
- **One Difficult Client for a Multidepartment Contract**
- **Your Subordinate Wants Your Job**
- **Power play by peer during staff meeting**
- **Employee morale problem**
- **New boss from outside organization**
- **Brokerage firm trading mistake**

In the next section you are provided with seven scenarios which I would like you to carefully read and think about how you would handle each one. At the end of each scenario, the best way to handle each one is not provided, but when you take the quiz, you are provided with five possible ways to handle each situation. Remember that all the simulation scenarios are intended to help you learn, so play each role.

When reading each scenario, pretend you are at work for the company. Focus only on what is presented. Do not overanalyze what is presented. In other words, do not assume things or issues that are not obvious. Also, do not worry about the size of the company, not having an organizational chart, or not knowing the names of the people described in the scenario.

In summary, the only information available is what is written. Use this to demonstrate your adaptability.

Scenario 1: Difficult Coworkers and Pay Equity Issue

You work as a Staff Associate for an Educational Training Institute. This is your second position after completing graduate school and even though you also applied for the Senior Staff Associate you were offered the entry level position. After you became more acquainted with your boss you decided to ask him why you were not interviewed for the senior position and he told you it was because you lacked the requisite years of experience. You accepted his explanation.

A few months later a woman is hired for the senior position and another woman is hired for an Administrative Assistant position. The latter position is a higher pay grade then both staff positions and you are the lowest paid person. When both start work you are asked by your boss to train them on the testing processes. Your boss informs you that after they are both trained you will be handling the promotional testing processes and they will be handling the entry level processes and other work.

During the training process they become very difficult to work with. They engage in different behaviors to include:

- One files her nails while you talk.
- They start talking to each other while you are training them.
- One shuffles paper while you are talking.
- They roll their eyes while you are providing them with important information.

A few weeks after providing them with thorough training on the different testing and administrative processes (i.e., part of it involves shadowing you while you worked), they continue to ask for your help, leave their work on your desk with notes asking you to complete simple paperwork and when they should be working, are sitting together drinking coffee and gossiping.

Your boss is in another part of the building so he never observes this behavior. Soon they start to become even more difficult to work with because they hand you papers to copy, leave incomplete folders on your desk with notes asking you to check the documents and so on. You feel strongly that their behaviors and actions are inappropriate and out of control. You are particularly concerned because you were told you were not qualified for either of their positions due to your limited years of experience and you are getting paid less.

Multiple-Choice Questions: Difficult Coworkers and Pay Equity Issue

Question 1

What would be your response after your boss informs you that after the two employees are trained you will be handling the promotional testing processes and they will be handling the entry level processes and other work?

A

Ask him if I will be paid more because I will be handling the promotional testing processes.

B

Nothing as his decision requires no response from me.

C

Ask him if he could explain this to me.

D

Smile, thank him for the opportunity and walk out of his office.

E

Ask him why I must train them.

Question 2

How would you react to their behaviors? They start talking to each other while you are talking. One shuffles papers while you are training them. They roll their eyes while you are providing important information?

A

Ignore the behavior.

B

Tell them that they are being rude and inappropriate and direct them to stop.

C

Raise my voice a bit, advise them that I would appreciate their attention and ask them if they are confused about something because they are rolling their eyes while I speak.

D

Walk out whenever they behave this way.

E

Advise them that I will be reporting their behavior to our boss.

Question 3

Considering they are becoming even more difficult to work with (i.e., hand papers to you to copy, leave incomplete folders on your desk, etc.) and you feel strongly that their behaviors and actions are out of control, how would you react?

A

Refer the problem to my boss.

B

Ask them to please stop doing this as I do not work for them.

C

Put a sticky note on each document stating this is their work to do.

D

Ask them if they need more training because they keep giving me their work to do and suggest we meet with our boss about this.

E

A, B, and D are acceptable responses. However, D is the strongest response, if you believe that your boss would be receptive to such a meeting. You can suggest this meeting to them and see how they respond.

Question 4

What would you do, if anything, about being paid less than these two employees even though you had to train them?

A

Nothing.

B

When the time is right, I would ask my boss if something can be done to compensate me.

C

I would carefully and tactically ask my boss why I am getting paid less and how long this will last.

D

I would complain to the HR department.

E

B and C are both acceptable responses.

Scenario 2: One Difficult Client for a Multidepartment Contract

Your management consulting firm has recently entered into a 3-year contract with two different departments. After you signed the contract a meeting was held with HR department representatives and a few of the personnel from the two departments who were managing the project(s) on their end. After the meeting started, one of the Directors who is an older White male, (who was the assigned project manager), stands up and states in a very caustic and agitated manner, "We know your firm has this contract now, but my department wanted to continue using the other vendor. We are not happy that the HR department overruled us. Also, the union is not happy that your firm was selected and will probably be filing grievances and then a lawsuit." Then he sat down.

Shortly thereafter during a question and answer session about the deliverables, he stands up again and states very strongly and in an abrasive manner that his department needed another service but did not want to pay for it. He insisted that it be part of the already signed contract. The HR Director just sat there and did not respond back to him. She looks at you.

Multiple-Choice Questions: One Difficult Client for a Multidepartment Contract
Question 5

How would you respond to the client's comments about wanting a different vendor, and so on?

A

I would not say anything.

B

I would state, "I am sorry you feel that way, but I can assure you that your department will be pleased with our work. We will do our best to exceed your expectations"

C

I would suggest he take it up with the HR department.

D

I would tell him that I do not appreciate being told that grievances will be filed and that there will be a lawsuit and walk out.

E

I would state, "I am sure the other vendor did a great job and my firm will do our best to adhere to the deliverable requirements, collaborate with you and your staff and exceed your expectations."

Question 6

Regarding one of the clients telling you they needed your firm to perform another service but does not want to pay for it, how would you react?

A

I wouldn't.

B

I would tell him another service (which is not a deliverable in the already signed contract) will have to be paid for.

C

Thank him for the information and then state, "We would be glad to perform this service for your department but at an additional cost. We can negotiate a price now if you desire."

D

Advise him to take this up with the HR department.

E

Tell him, "We often want services we do not want to pay for, but this is life. I would be glad to sit down with you in a private meeting to discuss the project and negotiate a price given that my firm already has a signed contract with your department."

Scenario 3: Your Subordinate Wants Your Job

You are an HR Manager and a new hire just started working for you 2-weeks ago. She is 17 years your senior and brings a great deal of knowledge and experience with her to the job. She supervises three other employees who design, develop, validate, and score a variety of employment tests. During one of your first one-on-one conversations with her she thanks you for the opportunity to be in a supervisory position and advises you that she had been passed over for promotion in one company and a governmental agency. Then she tells you about her personal life; for example, she is a divorced mother with no money or assets, is glad she made the move to the state because the climate is more pleasant and wants to move up to a management position as soon as possible.

You go on a 2-week vacation to Europe and when you return your boss, the HR Vice President comes to your office and closes the door. He has a worried look on his face and starts the meeting by telling you, "Do not worry, I am not going to make her a Manager." Then he proceeds to tell you the following (abbreviated sequence of events) wherein she:

- Met with the Compensation Manager and asked him how difficult would it be to create a new section where she would be a Manager.
- Complained to your boss (him) that you are a micro-manager and are incompetent.
- Told me (him) that she wants her own section because the work she and her subordinates perform should be separate from the Recruitment and Selection unit, and she does not want to report to you anymore.

After he finishes telling you the aforementioned, he directs you to do the following:

1. Leave her alone to do her work.
2. Ask her for work samples only when absolutely necessary.
3. Don't tell her that you know that she complained about you.
4. Advise me (him) of any problems.

Multiple-Choice Questions: Your Subordinate Wants Your Job

Question 7

How would you react to her comments (see end of first paragraph)?

A

Demonstrate my concern and interest in the fact that she was not promoted and is a divorced mother. Offer to assist her in any way I can.

B

Tell her I am sorry she was passed over for promotion.

C

Tell her, "I am glad to have you as part of the team and congratulations for being hired for this supervisory position."

D

A and B are acceptable options, but C is really the best choice.

E

Tell her that I am pleased to have offered her the position and would like to discuss why she thinks she was passed over for the promotions.

Question 8

What is the **BEST** way for you to respond to the events that transpired while you were on vacation?

A

I would thank him for deciding to keep her in my section, say that I am not a micro-manager nor am I incompetent.

B

I would ask him why she is permitted to behave this way and what I can do about it.

C

Ask him if he knew that she was meeting with the Compensation Manager.

D

Thank him for his support and for letting me know what transpired. Also ask him for his continued support.

E

Thank him for the information, tell him that I will monitor her less given her perception that I am a micro-manager, and then ask him for his continued support.

Question 9

What is the best way to interact with her going forward?

A

Have as little interaction with her as possible.

B

Be pleasant, review her work as necessary, have minimal interaction with her, do not give her any indication that I know what she did while I was on vacation, and update my boss when advisable.

C

Observe her from afar, document everything and have minimal interaction with her.

D

Tell her that I know what she did, advise her she will keep her job as long as she does not stab me in the back.

E

Meet with her only once a month to review work samples. Ignore her the rest of the time.

Scenario 4: Power Play by Peer During Staff Meeting

Lindsley Woolsey is the HR Director of large county governmental agency. She is participating in a weekly senior executive staff meeting with the Agency head and all department heads. Most of the department heads have been with the agency for more than 25 years, two are nearing retirement, and three are newly hired from other state or federal agencies. All are well educated, and everyone has recently completed a 1-week training session on Total Quality Management.

One department head, Sal Savvy, Director of Operations, is responsible for the majority of the employees working in this department; 700 employees work in the agency and 400 are in his department.

When it is Savvy's turn to provide an update for his department, he indicates that he will not be providing any update but rather he wants the HR department to make the changes he wants. He tells everyone the following:

- I have decided that we need to eliminate the pay grade structure for the clerical positions. All of my managers are in agreement, and we are moving forward with this.
- All applicants should be required to type 100 words per minute. If the skills test needs to change, Lindsley, you and your staff need to expedite this soon.
- We are tired of our clerical staff thinking they have somewhere to go in the organization. A Clerk is a Clerk is a Clerk. There is no career path for them, and we need to stop giving them the idea that they can move up and get paid more.
- Having pay grades is a waste of money.
- We also need to cut the entry pay.
- Moreover, all the clerks care about is moving to the next pay grade and they should be told that it won't happen.

Note: Savvy does not provide any factual evidence or support for his claims.

While he is speaking some eyes are rolling, heads are shaking, pencils are tapping and Dorothy Chaosism, the agency head, smiles. All eyes then were directed at Lindsley. She was taking notes while he was talking.

Chaosism likes it when her Directors formulate new ideas particularly those that save money. She also seems to thrive on conflict and enjoys it when the staff argues with one another. She likes to listen to staff argue and then allows the person who behaves the toughest to have their way.

Lindsley then tactfully states her concerns which included:

1. Shouldn't we have all discussed this before you made a decision?
2. It is not valid or fair to arbitrarily increase the typing score without doing a job analysis;
3. Have you thought about what will happen to the Clerks who are at the next two levels?
4. Why didn't you meet with me before making these decisions?
5. Are you aware of the fact that doing this could violate the Americans with Disabilities act?

After Lindsley finishes speaking, Sal Savvy makes many statements in a caustic, condescending, and berating manner. The statements include:

- Lindsley, you are a typical HR person, you want total control and have to hold onto outdated HR paradigms.
- I have authority to do what I want. You are just the HR Director.
- Our legal counsel will deal with the ADA; you are not the lawyer and it has nothing to do with you.

Immediately, all of the other Directors, some speaking at the same time, indicate that they concur with Lindsley's comments, at which point Chaosism smiles at Savvy and says she likes his ideas.

Then she turns to Lindsley and asks for her response. Before anyone else could respond, Savvy tells Lindsley not to take it personally. Then Chaosism abruptly cancels the meeting and says the issue would be addressed and finalized next week.

Question 10

If you were Lindsley, and were given an opportunity to respond to Savvy's aforementioned statements, which of the options below would be the most appropriate?

A

"Sal, it appears to me that you do not understand the role of HR and that me and my staff collaborate with you and your managers. This topic has nothing to do with control but fairness and job-relatedness and how the changes you want to make could be problematic. Perhaps we could meet to discuss this further?"

B

"I do not appreciate being attacked like this. Moreover, what supporting documentation do you have?"

C

"I am sorry you feel this way, but the HR department has the responsibility for recruitment, testing and selection of staff not your department. Perhaps we can meet to discuss this."

D

"Dorothy, are you going to allow him to talk to me like this in a senior staff meeting?"

E

All of the above are appropriate responses.

Question 11

What other options should Lindsley consider regarding the aforementioned problems?

A

Write a memo outlining the pros and cons of Savvy's plans, edit and then share with him in meeting.

B

Share the above memo with Chaosism and ask for her support. Ask Chaosism to allow everyone to meet to review the memorandum before going forward with Savvy's plans.

C

Emphasize the importance of everyone understanding the pros and cons as well as adverse effects on the ability for agency to recruit applicants if hiring standards change.

D

Make sure Savvy knows that I (Lindsley) understand his concerns but he must give the HR department an opportunity to respond and present their options.

E

All of the above.

Question 12

Assume you have been hired to coach Chaosism. During your first meeting she tells you about the aforementioned situation and emphasized that she is looking forward to observing and deciding which of her Directors are the strongest. What would you advise her?

A

She might want to consider that Savvy's behavior does not reflect good interpersonal skills.

B

Given that all of her senior staff concurred with Lindsley, if she allows Savvy to implement the plans that he appears to have already decided without her (Savvy's approval), then the other Directors may no longer trust her.

C

Chaosism needs to seriously consider the impact of Savvy's plans on the ability of the organization to recruit clerical staff (i.e., starting pay which may be below what the market pays, minimum entrance requirements raised, pay grades eliminated).

D

It would not be in her best interest as the leader of the agency to support one staff person when the majority disagrees. Ask her if she is really being objective or favors Savvy because he is the most assertive of her staff.

E

All of the above although B, C, and D are the best options.

Scenario 5: Employee Morale Problem

Mary Maybe is a newly promoted supervisor for a home healthcare company, WECARE, which has locations in 10 states in the United States. The company provides CNAs, LPNS, and RNs for nursing homes and assisted living facilities. Mary is the Accounts Manager and loves her job. She has four direct reports. One of her employees, Debby Downer, is an Account Representative. She has been with the company for 5 years and loves her work.

Mary feels very lucky because she was promoted to the position even though she has no supervisory experience. She has the required college degree but no credits in management courses. Nevertheless, she thinks her boss, Donna Dizzy made the right decision to promote her.

Debby Downer is working on her college degree, is a single mother of two children one who is a special needs child. Her ex-husband does not provide any child support. She rents her apartment but is considering moving because the landlord is raising the rent again; the second time this year. Despite all of Debby's personal problems Mary thinks Debby is a good worker and has a future with the company. Debby received well above average scores for her last two biannual reviews and a 4% pay increase each year.

Debby is working on her college degree and using the company's tuition reimbursement benefit.

One day Debby does not show up for work and calls in sick at 10:00 a.m. versus the start of the work day. Mary does not speak to Debby as a message was left on her voice mail. The next day, Debby comes to work, and Mary calls her into her office to find out what happened. She advises Debby to feel better, to make sure she calls in at the start of the workday and asks her to complete a sick leave form.

Over the next 2 weeks Mary observes the following about Debby:

- She has her head down at her desk on more than one occasion.
- Weekly end of week customer care reports are 2-days late.
- She is tardy to work twice the first of the 2-weeks.
- She calls in sick again on Thursday of the second week and is out for 3-days the following week.

Mary was unable to take action on any of the above as she was in and out of the office several times each day for meetings and to handle a few crises. She did however, document what she observed.

At the end of the second week Debby returns to work and walks in Mary's office, sits down and starts to cry.

Question 13

If you were Mary how would you handle this?

A

Close the door, put my phone on vibrate, and ask Debby what is wrong.

B

Hand Debby a tissue and wait for her to stop crying.

C

Suggest that Debby go to the lady's room and when she is done crying to come back to my office.

D

Nothing until Debby contains herself.

E

All of the above are not wrong ways to approach Debby but A and B reflect the best adaptability behaviors.

Question 14

After a few minutes Debby stops crying and asks Mary for her help. She says, "Mary I feel like I am losing control and do not know how much longer I can continue like this. I am afraid my work will continue to suffer."

How would you continue the meeting with Debby?

A

I would end the meeting, send her home and tell her before she leaves that I will be scheduling her to go to the EAP tomorrow.

B

Close my office door, ignore all phone calls, ask her why she feels this way, listen to her and offer her any assistance. Commend her for her past performance but agree that of late her problems are starting to affect her work.

C

Both B and C.

D

Ask her if she would like to discuss her problems, tell her that I am there for her and I will ensure that the company provides her with the resources to help her (e.g., counseling).

E

Continue to listen to her and then review all of the documentation from the past 2-weeks. Advise her of the consequences of her working continuing to suffer. Then ask her how she plans to stop losing control.

Question 15

Assume that Debby takes a few days off, during which time Mary plans and schedules a meeting with Debby the day she returns. Which below is the **MOST APPROPRIATE** topic Mary should cover in the meeting?

A

Whether Debby has taken advantage of EAP services and how are things going (only if Debby wants to discuss this).

B

How her college course is going.

C

She might want to ask the EAP for rent payment or other services.

D

To have weekly or bimonthly meetings to discuss her work and how she is doing.

E

All of the above.

Scenario 6: New Boss Transferred to Department

Jack Jerc, Director of Procurement, was just transferred to the Operations department. Jerc has worked for Green Worlds, a 5-year-old company that is currently expediting an Initial Public Offering (IP). Presently the company is offering services in the United States only but has plans for expansion. Top management has been doing a "house cleaning"; that is, many top management staff have been given generous severance packages. Several of them refused the packages and subsequently were offered transfers or demotions. Jack Jerc is one of these individuals.

Although he possesses an M.B.A. from a top school and has many years of managerial experience, he does not have a good reputation.

For example,

- He has a huge ego.
- Rumors reflect that he was moved up the hierarchy not for his work performance but because he "kissed the right butts."
- He holds grudges.
- Staff have to continually follow-up with him.
- Documents have been known to get lost in his office, but it is never his fault.
- He is savvy, articulate and a good b......t artist.
- He is politically connected and plays golf every weekend.
- His family are multi-millionaires!
- He can help a person get ahead but the person has to play the game.

Phillip Hoffman is one of the Operations Managers in the plant and has a meeting scheduled with Jerc. He has yet to meet Jerc but is aware of the aforementioned.

Question 16

Hoffman enters Jerc's office and he is on his cell phone and does not end the call for about 5-minutes. When the conversation ends, Jerc states, "I am doing a walk about and you are my first stop. What do you know about me?"

How should Hoffman react?

A

Smile, welcome him to the department, thank him for being the first person he is meeting with.

B

Tell him I know a few things about him and would like to find out more about him.

C

Commend him on his great leadership abilities and for being transferred to the Operations department.

D

Tell Jerc I only know a few good things about him, am glad to have him as my new boss, and ask him what is the first thing he wants me to do to help acclimate him (Jerc) to the department.

E

Wait for him to continue the conversation and then respond only according to what he thinks Jerc wants to hear.

Question 17

Hoffman submits a required report to Jerc which he is required to sign off on and return to Hoffman. A few days later the report has not been returned. Hoffman must have the report by Monday. He asks Jerc where it is and he says he never received it. His desk is piled high with folders.

It is a Friday afternoon. Jerc starts to walk out of the office and asks Hoffman if he wants to join him on the golf course after 5? Jerc then says, "I am getting an early start."

What should Hoffman do?

A

Ask Jerc if he could look through the folders because he (Hoffman) is sure he submitted it; and tell him he will join Jerc on the golf course and thank him for the invitation.

B

Look through the folders after Jerc leaves and if the report is not there, make another copy, sign it, and bring it with him to the golf course.

C

Walk away and hope that he finds it by tomorrow.

D

Both A and B.

E

Thank him and tell him he (Hoffman) will get another copy.

Scenario 7: Brokerage Firm Trading Mistake

Laura Dern works for a brokerage firm. She loves her position because every day is different, she is never bored, and she learns something new every day. She works in the Operations and Compliance department. In this department, staff complete several tasks that include:

- Write orders, input into the computer.
- Record trade.
- Expedite time written order.
- Manage and process all paperwork.

Today the broker's system used to buy and sell stocks went down which requires the latter tasks to be completed. All trades must be completed before the bell rings signaling the end of the trading day. One of Laura's coworkers, Jennifer Jones, who Laura has been training, answers the phone and took an order. The broker asked her to sell 40,000 shares of a specific stock. The order was made right before the bell rang and the stocks closed. However, even though she was able to process the order she sold 4,000 vs. 40,000 shares. The error was not caught until the next day after the report was printed at which time Laura reviewed it.

Then Laura approaches Jennifer and asks her what happened but instead of answering, Jennifer starts to shake, and then she buckles over and lies on the floor. She starts to cry profusely.

Question 18

What should Laura do?

A

Help her up, and have her sit in a chair; ask her if she is okay and if she needs her to call 911.

B

Remain calm and speak to her in a calm voice.

C

Let her know that mistakes happen and that it will be taken care of.

D

Stay with her until she feels better and if necessary call 911. Check with my supervisor to determine if she should be sent home for the day.

E

All of the above.

Question 19

Right after Laura makes sure Jennifer is okay, one of the receptionists tells her a broker is on the phone and is demanding to speak to her ASAP about the latter trading. She advises the broker about the mistake but does not tell him which employee made the mistake. He starts to raise his voice and states, "How could you let this happen, you need to pay closer attention, you have probably lost me a lot of money and will have to figure out how to recoup my losses!" Next, he raises his voice further and states, "Whomever this person is an idiot and should be fired, I may take my business elsewhere!"

What is the **BEST** way for Laura to respond to the broker?

A

Apologize; calm him down; continue to listen and do not respond back.

B

Ask him if he wants to sell the remaining shares and how soon.

C

Tell him the employee is currently being trained, is a hard worker, and made an honest mistake because of the pressure to expedite the trade as the bell rang.

D

Tell him he should not yell at employees and then hang up on him.

E

A, B, and C are all appropriate.

Question 20

Jennifer was sent home and came back to work the next day. The market opened stronger than the day before and the firm sold the broker's remaining 36,000 shares at a higher rate than the previous day. He was very happy and Laura was extremely relieved.

How should Laura deal with Jennifer's mistake?

A

Meet with her in a private place, ask her how she is feeling; analyze the problem with her; that is, how it happened and how this mistake can be prevented in future; ask her to review all of the steps she took.

B

Remind her that we are all one team; and I am here to assist her whenever she is unsure about something; commend her for her hard work; ask her how she plans to proceed from now on.

C

Advise her to never expedite a trade when the bell is ringing, and tell her the consequences of making a mistake like this again.

D

Both A and B.

E

All of the above.

CHAPTER 8

Workplace Scenarios—How Would You Handle?

OVERVIEW

Now that you have learned about and experienced the application of many universal innate abilities, you will now have another opportunity to practice what you have learned. In this chapter, ten different scenarios are presented. When reading the scenarios you will notice that most of them are longer and more complex than those presented in earlier chapters. The scenarios were designed to cover more issues and more than one ability.

In fact, one or more of these abilities are required to successfully handle the issues covered in each situation. The abilities are planning and organizing, perception and analysis (aka problem analysis), judgment (aka judgment and reasoning), decision-making, dealing with people, and adaptability. Remember that the different abilities are innate to your personality and based on what you know about yourself, some are your strengths and others are your weaknesses. However, as you already know, you can improve your abilities.

Ten Scenarios

Carefully read and think about each scenario and that more than one ability is being measured in each question.

When reading each scenario, pretend you are at work for the company. Focus only on what is presented. Do not over analyze what is presented. In other words, do not assume things or issues that are not obvious. Also, do not worry about the size of the company, not having an organizational chart, or not knowing the names of the people described in the scenario. In summary, the only information available is what is written. Use this information to demonstrate your abilities.

- Ethical dilemma—workplace romance
- Problem employee
- Organizational restructuring
- Policies and procedures

- Inebriated customer at hotel pool bar
- Employee running his own business during work hours
- Hiring process issue
- Handling multiple projects with limited staff
- Workplace bully
- Toxic management colleagues and 360 feedback
- Mini case: Strategic planning

Scenario 1: Ethical Dilemma—Workplace Romance

You are an Accounting Manager and work for ABC Corporation. ABC is an internationally renowned company in the Pharmaceuticals industry. You love working for ABC, your work and coworkers. Your boss, the CFO is the best one you have ever worked for. He has given you a great deal of opportunity to grow in the position. He also allows you to learn on-the-job via on-site training programs and webinars.

One evening you and a few male friends go to a popular restaurant in the city. You happen to look across the room and see your boss hugging and then kissing a woman who is not his wife (you have met his wife before on several occasions). When you take a closer look, you see that the woman is the Vice President's executive assistant.

The next day in the well-stocked and busy company cafeteria you see the two of them across the room sitting together. Then on Friday, as you were walking down the hallway outside your office, you see him by the men's room holding his cell phone and telling her (the executive assistant) what time and which hotel downtown to meet at. He does not know you saw or hear him as his back is to you.

You know that the company has a well-written Code of Ethics. All newly hired employees attend a 4-hour training session and one refresher session annually. In fact, a few years ago the CEO was caught having an affair with the Purchasing Director. They were both married and she filed a sexual harassment charge against him after they broke up. Both were fired. Afterward the Code of Ethics was rewritten and related policies and procedures were changed or added. One of the strict policies is to report unethical behavior within 24-hours of discovery, written communication, the grapevine, and so on.

The following week rumors are spreading about the two of them. You know more than anyone else. You were also advised by a few employees that the HR Director is aware of what is going on.

Multiple-Choice Questions: Ethical Dilemma—Workplace Romance

Question 1

From the choices below, what are the unethical issues?

A

Violation of the code of ethics, rumors being spread, a man and woman hugging and kissing in front of other employees at work.

B

A man dating someone other than his wife, an affair taking place at the workplace, rumors being spread about the affair.

C

An extra marital affair taking place between an executive and a lower level female employee.

D

The code of ethics has been violated and the HR department has not taken any action.

E

Both C and D are correct.

Question 2

What, if anything, is problematic about rumors being disseminated throughout a workplace? Rumors,

A

can lower employee morale.

B

may be true or untrue.

C

can cause major damage to an organization.

D

if continually spread and discussed, create dysfunction.

E

All of the above.

Question 3

Assuming that you are the Accounting Manager, what would you do, if anything, once you were told by other employees that the HR Director knows about your boss' affair?

A

Nothing because I do not want to get my boss fired; he is the best boss I've ever had.

B

Meet with my boss to discuss the situation with him.

C

Tell the employees to mind their own business.

D

Schedule a meeting with the Vice President (my boss' boss) and tell him what I observed.

E

Document everything, tell my boss what I observed and was told, report the situation to the HR department and then follow-up with my boss.

Question 4

Why is having an affair with someone at work unethical especially when both people are married to someone else?

A

It isn't because it is no one's business.

B

It may not be unethical because other employees may be doing the same thing and people are entitled to their own opinion as to what is ethical or unethical.

C

It could be against company policy to date at work, and when the parties are married then this is problematic.

D

If the company does not allow dating, then the employees are violating company policy, cheating on your spouse is unethical, and having an affair with someone at work when you are married violates a company's ethics code.

E

It is not my place to judge what other people do at work or outside of work; live and let live.

Scenario 2: Problem Employee

You work for XYC Corporation as Senior Account Manager. You have been in the position for 2-years and were promoted from within. Prior to your promotion you had never supervised any employees. Fortunately, you were required to complete a 40-hour management development course facilitated by HR training and development staff.

One of your employees who has been with the company 5-years, has been late to work two times this week. You spoke to her about this already and indicated that based on the progressive disciplinary policy, the third time an employee is tardy they will be given a written warning. She was disciplined last year for turning in assignments late and responding to three customers several hours past the required time (i.e., within 24-hours).

Today, she arrives late again. You know this because you just saw her walk in and you could see the clock on the wall. She entered the break room to get a cup of coffee. You ask her to come to your office. When she arrives and sits down, you tell her that we need to discuss her continued tardiness and that she will be disciplined. She states, "I am tired of the managers in this organization going after people of color." The White employees come in late all the time and nothing is done. "I may have to file a complaint with HR." You had no idea that she felt this way.

Multiple-Choice Questions: Problem Employee

Question 5

What plans, if any, would you make to deal with this situation?

A

None because she is just complaining.

B

Schedule a formal meeting with her and prepare the disciplinary paperwork.

C

Schedule another meeting with her to discuss why she feels this way.

D

Pull her personnel file and review in detail before preparing the disciplinary paperwork.

E

C and D are the best planning options.

Question 6

What are the employee's main problems?

A

Her three cases of tardiness.

B

She feels that management goes after people of color.

C

Her belief that there is race discrimination in the organization.

D

A and B are both correct.

E

She does not respond to customers within 24-hours.

Question 7

Considering this employee's past tardiness and problems turning assignments in on time, what developmental plans would you offer her?

A

None, because I will be disciplining her even though she is planning to file a complaint.

B

Schedule her and other employees for a time management seminar and afterward, meet only with her to discuss what she learned.

C

Prepare the disciplinary action, meet with her, discuss goals and objectives with her regarding how she plans to improve and document the meeting.

D

Employee development is the responsibility of the HR department; therefore, I would refer her to one of their staff.

E

All are viable options.

Scenario 3: Organizational Restructuring

Your company has just announced via a video message from the CEO that a reduction in force (RIFF) will be taking place over the next few months. Details as to the exact dates and how this will occur will be forthcoming. You have been with the company for 7 years, just reached your vesting date and hope that your position will not be cut.

Fast forward 1-month later and everyone is advised that the RIFF will take place this Friday. You were told by your boss that your position is safe and that the HR department will be working closely with the various business units on the restructuring process. You do not know what is happening to your coworkers. Your division has 50 employees with 7 in your section. Friday arrives and three of your coworkers are cleaning out their desks, crying and then walking out of the building. Other employees in your division are also leaving. In total about 500 employees have lost their jobs.

The following week the tension in the air is so thick you could cut it with a knife. There are no conversations at the water cooler, no one eating in the lunchroom and very few are in the cafeteria.

Multiple-Choice Questions: Organizational Restructuring

Question 8

Given the loss of three coworkers in your department, which below is/are the **BEST** option(s) to survive because of the changes?

A

Schedule a meeting with my boss and ask what my workload will be given the loss of my coworkers.

B

Ask my boss if my vesting date will be affected by the change.

C

Keep my mouth shut.

D

Find out from other survivors what is going on and share as much information with them and other employees as possible.

E

Do whatever I can to keep my job.

Question 9

Given that the tension is so thick you can cut it with a knife, how will you deal with this?

A

Nothing as this often happens after major changes take place.

B

Stay in good with my boss so I am not the next one to be laid off.

C

Facilitate conversations with other employees at the water cooler and find out how they feel.

D

Do what I can to keep my stress level down so the tension will not affect me.

E

Both A and D.

Scenario 4: Policies and Procedures

When you first started working for company DCE, as part of your on boarding process you were provided with training on many of the most important policies and procedures. Some of the most important ones were Safety, a Zero Tolerance Policy for Harassment, Hostile Work Environment, and Sexual Harassment and Social Media.

You are a Customer Service Representative. It is an entry level position and you were very lucky to be hired given how long it took you to find this job. You love your job, your boss, and your coworkers. You also like and feel very comfortable with how the company is managed and like the open, collegial, and friendly culture.

Over the past week or so, e-mail messages sent to you and other employees, based on your knowledge, violate the Social Media policy and procedures. Based on some of the content, you think that the company may be in jeopardy.

Multiple-Choice Questions: Policies and Procedures

Question 10

What, if any, actions would you take?

A

Send the e-mail trail to my boss but do so anonymously.

B

None as I did not violate the policy and I do not want to "rock the boat."

C

Advise the coworker who is sending the e-mails to take me off the list.

D

Meet with my boss about the policy and procedures violation and show him the e-mail message.

E

Report the problem to the IT department.

Scenario 5: Inebriated Customer at Hotel Pool Bar

You have just started a new job at an upscale hotel and have only recently completed your new employee training. This week you are working at the outside pool bar. You are learning how to bar tend. It is a beautiful sunny afternoon and happy hour at the pool has just started. Your coworker is on his afternoon early dinner break. There is no pool staff around.

A few couples are lounging in the Jacuzzi by the pool, laughing, and splashing water around. One of the men appears to be a bit drunk because he almost stumbles when he walks up the Jacuzzi stairs. He is now walking toward your bar counter. Upon his arrival, he leans on the bar and orders you to immediately mix a Manhattan straight up with cherries. He pounds on the bar, tells you to hurry, proceeds to grab your blouse (or shirt if you are male), and then addresses you with some vulgarities. His words are slurred and you can see that his eyes are very red and bloodshot. When you wait on other customers, he starts to yell at you.

Multiple-Choice Questions: Inebriated Pool Bar Customer

Question 11

How do you handle this situation?

A

Call security.

B

Ignore his behavior as he is a customer.

C

Ask him to please stop yelling at me and grabbing my shirt or I will have to call security.

D

Ask his friends to remove him from the bar.

E

Leave the bar area immediately as he is a threat to me.

Question 12

Considering that he appears to be inebriated, why may this be a problem for the hotel and its guests?

A

He could hurt himself and others.

B

Inebriated and unruly customers can damage the reputation of the hotel.

C

It will only be a problem if the police have to be called.

D

A and B are both problems for the hotel.

E

It may not be a problem because guests at hotels often have too much to drink.

Question 13

What is wrong with the fact that he grabbed your blouse (shirt if you are male) and used vulgar language when addressing you?

A

He may be guilty of assault which is a crime.

B

His behavior may be against the hotel's policies regarding guest behavior.

C

Employees should not be treated this way by guests.

D

Other guests may have observed his behaviors and are offended.

E

All of the above.

Scenario 6: Employee Running His Own Business During Work Hours

Assume you are a Manager working for company EFG and one of your supervisors comes to you with a problem he does not know how to handle. He advises you about the allegations which have been presented to him to include; a plant worker has been running his own business during work hours; some of his coworkers overheard a few of other workers talking about this individual making extra money during working hours; he has bragged to them that he has a good thing going; and this employee has given some of his coworker's equipment that belongs to the company.

Question 14

What are the first things you communicate to this employee?

A

Please provide me with the names of the employees who made the allegations.

B

Nothing now as I need more information.

C

Ask him for more specifics. For example, dates, times, location in plant.

D

Thank him for the information and tell him that I will get back with him.

E

A and B are the most viable options.

Question 15

From the options below, which is/are the **MOST** appropriate future courses of action?

A

Schedule a meeting with each employee who made the allegations and document the information.

B

Organize the material in preparation for a meeting with my boss.

C

Schedule a meeting with the HR director at which time, I will turn over the paperwork to him or her.

D

Make plans to schedule the employee who brought the allegations to my attention for supervisory training.

E

All of the above.

Scenario 7: Hiring Process Issue

The Communications and Public Relations Department has a vacant PR position. The HR Department advertised the position, screened all applications and prepared a referral list. Assume that you are the Director of Communications and your subordinate (the Manager) who must staff the vacant position (i.e., Communications Specialist), indicated that the list of applicants was acceptable and indicated she had scheduled the interviews. However, a few days later she tells you that none of the applicants on the list are qualified for the position after all.

On the same day, you receive a call from the CFO who thanks you for hiring his nephew for the Communications Specialist position.

Question 16

What is wrong with this situation and why?

A

Nothing, because the manager has determined that the applicants are not qualified.

B

The manager told you she had already scheduled the interviews therefore, how could the applicants suddenly become unqualified, and why were unqualified applicants scheduled for interviews?

C

An employee has been offered a job without an interview and is a nephew of a high-level person in the company.

D

Nothing because the departments with the vacant position(s) should have authority to hire who they want.

E

The HR department referred unqualified applicants to my department for interview.

Question 17

What would you say to your manager? I would,

A

advise her that she does not follow the company's hiring procedures (e.g., do not schedule interviews with unqualified job applicants, do not make job offers to candidates before interviewing them).

B

not say anything to her because she has the authority to hire who she wants.

C

ask her to explain the entire situation including the CFO thanking me for hiring his nephew.

D

A and C are viable options.

E

tell her that she will be disciplined for lying to me about the hiring process and making a job offer to the CFO's nephew.

Scenario 8: Handling Multiple Projects With Limited Staff

The Risk Management department is relatively small. The staff is comprised of one full-time administrative coordinator, a part-time clerical person, a Safety Coordinator, and the Director. Everyone processes their paperwork to ensure completion in a timely fashion. The Administrative Coordinator works for the Director but is available at times to assist staff.

You are expected to process your own paperwork. A great deal of time many projects are being worked on simultaneously. At times you must drop what you are doing to handle a crisis.

Question 18

Which options below is/are the **BEST** way(s) to simultaneously deal with multiple projects?

A

Prioritize my work each day by preparing a To Do List; establish due dates and review each day; handle the most pressing project first as the circumstances change.

B

Set due dates for each project and monitor accordingly, skip lunch and all breaks.

C

Ask my boss for help when needed because he or she knows better than I do.

D

Take regular breaks so I will not get stressed out.

Question 19

Regarding handling crises at work, how will you **BEST** adapt to each one?

A

Take a deep breath before dealing with each crisis, do some stretching exercises, stay calm.

B

Ask for assistance from administrative staff, if applicable.

C

Accept crises as a given at work, notify any customers or coworkers that my work is delayed because of a crisis (i.e., depending on what type and how critical the crisis is).

D

Apologize to any customers or coworkers expecting completion of my work and tell them the work will be completed ASAP and specify approximately how long it will take.

E

All of the above.

Scenario 9: Workplace Bully

Adapted from Martin, W., & LaVan, H. (2010). Workplace bullying: A review of the litigated cases. *Employee Responsibilities and Rights Journal, 22,* 175–194.

HIJ is an international corporation that manufactures parts for the automotive industry. Assume that you are newly promoted Manager, Jaycee Johns, and manage 6 direct reports who supervise 45 employees. All of the nonsupervisory employees work in the manufacturing plant and are members of a union. Their job title is *Manufacturing Production Technician* and some of their essential tasks are:

- *Set up and verify the functionality of safety equipment.*
- *Adhere to all applicable regulations, policies, and procedures for health, safety, and environmental compliance.*
- *Calibrate or adjust equipment to ensure quality production, using tools such as calipers, micrometers, height gauges, protractors, or ring gauges.*
- *Monitor and adjust production processes or equipment for quality and productivity.*
- *Troubleshoot problems with equipment, devices, or products.*
- *Set up and operate production equipment in accordance with current good manufacturing practices and standard operating procedures.*

- *Plan and lay out work to meet production and schedule requirements.*
- *Assist engineers in developing, building, or testing prototypes or new products, processes, or procedures.*
- *Measure and record data associated with operating equipment.*
- *Prepare production documents, such as standard operating procedures, manufacturing batch records, inventory reports, or productivity reports.*
- *Provide production, progress, or changeover reports to shift supervisors.*
- *Conduct environmental safety inspections in accordance with standard protocols to ensure that production activities comply with environmental regulations or standards.*

(Reference: https://www.onetonline.org/link/summary/17-3029.09, Manufacturing Production Technician)

You have been a Manager for 6-months. During this time, the company went through downsizing, restructuring, management changes, and cost cutting. Your employees are not happy with the changes.

Employees work in teams of 6 and rotate among the various supervisors for the purpose of job enrichment. In the past, all teams received incentives every quarter for meeting or exceeding their production goals. There is a great deal of healthy internal competition among the teams. However, since the aforementioned changes took place rumors have been circulating that, because the workforce is so stressed out productivity has significantly gone down. The HR Department was going to administer an Employee Opinion Survey, but the CEO wanted to wait until the dust settled from the various changes.

One of your managers, Peter Perfectsion, fills in for all other managers when they are on vacation, medical leave, or when one of them calls in sick. Based on his years working for the company and because of his special knowledge, he knows all of the tasks better than anyone. He also serves as the safety inspector and strictly adheres to all policies and procedures and state and federal Occupational Safety and Health Administration laws.

One day he reports to you that he observed some of the men smoking in restricted areas and a few others were sleeping on the job. You asked for names, but he was reluctant to supply any because he did not want to "get in trouble with the crew." You insisted that he provide the names and told him he should not fear retaliation. He would not give you the names and suggested that you do a "walk about" and will find sufficient evidence.

A few weeks later one of the other managers, Steve Wannabee, comes to your office and reports the following behaviors and actions he observed being taken against Perfectsion:

- Three other managers made verbally aggressive remarks to him;
- One manager pushed Perfectsion and told him that he better keep his mouth shut about the smoking and sleeping on the job, while on three separate occasions two managers told Perfectsion that he was a "closet homosexual" and,
- Several managers are saying that Perfectsion is a company spy.

You start to jot down what he is telling you. He then tells you that he has been hesitant to come forward because he has to work so closely with everyone, fears retaliation and does not want to be socially isolated. Before he gives you an opportunity to respond, he receives a text message, reads it, responds, and then tells you he has to go out on the floor because someone needs assistance troubleshooting some problems with a piece of equipment. Then he walks out of your office.

Multiple Choice Questions

Question 20

What is the **BEST** way for you to deal with Wannabee's hesitancy to come forward because he fears retaliation and social isolation from his coworkers?

A

Nothing, because there is a company policy against retaliation; I cannot do anything about worker's not socializing with one another; and I cannot get involved because they are unionized.

B

Schedule another confidential meeting with Wannabee and find why he fears retaliation; how he would be socially isolated from his coworkers, and how and why will this affect his ability to work (if applicable), and provide him with emotional support.

C

I would refer him to the Employee Assistance Program.

D

I would not do anything because the employees who mistreated Perfectsion will be dealt with when I challenge them in the future.

E

Ask the HR department to conduct a training program on Zero Tolerance for Harassment and Retaliation and another one about Working with Others for all employees.

Question 21

Based on what Wannabee told you about the behaviors and actions taken against Perfectsion; that is,

- Three other managers made verbally aggressive remarks.
- One manager pushed Perfectsion and told him that he needs to keep his mouth shut about the smoking and sleeping on the job, while two managers told Perfectsion that "he is a closet homosexual."
- The rumor being spread by several managers about Perfectsion being a company spy.

What is your **BEST** first and second course of action?

A

Call Wannabee and tell him to report his concerns to the HR department; report the incident to my boss.

B

Make sure I document everything I heard him tell me; call him and ask him to come to my office as soon as he is free today.

C

Call or send an e-mail to Perfectsion advising him that I need to meet with him ASAP; review my notes.

D

Call or send an e-mail to all 6 managers asking them to attend a meeting with me tomorrow at 9:00 a.m. in the conference room.

E

B is the first choice and D is the second choice.

Question 22

If it is found to be **TRUE** that employees are smoking in a restricted area and sleeping on the job, at minimum what should you (Johns) do?

A

Schedule and facilitate a meeting with all employees, advise them of the findings (but keep names confidential) and the consequences if this behavior continues, and schedule all workers for ethics and safety training.

B

All are viable options and should be addressed.

C

Refer the documentation to the HR and Safety Departments for information purposes.

D

Prepare the appropriate progressive disciplinary paperwork for the guilty employees, review with their supervisors and then in private meetings, administer the discipline for each employee.

E

Schedule a meeting with all 6 managers and confidentially discuss their issues with each other.

Question 23

What is wrong with an employee being called a closet homosexual by another employee especially in front of other coworkers?

A

It is mean, offensive, and inappropriate behavior that could be creating a hostile work environment.

B

Nothing, considering union workers are known for being a bit rough around the edges, and hazing each other.

C

It probably violates sections of the Employee Handbook, the company Code of Ethics and possibly federal and state employment laws.

D

A and C only.

E

Nothing, unless the employee files a formal complaint with his/her boss and/or the HR department.

Question 24

If the manager who pushed Perfectsion and told him that he better keep his mouth shut about the smoking and sleeping on the job, while two managers told Perfectsion that he was a closet homosexual, is verified as being **TRUE**, what course of action(s) would you (Jones) take?

A

Review the Employee Handbook and related policies and procedures to determine what disciplinary action(s) can be taken; prepare documents according to each violation as appropriate.

B

Prepare the disciplinary paperwork for each person and submit to my boss for review.

C

Refer the documentation to the HR department and immediately suspend each person pending the outcome of HR's decisions.

D

At this time, A and B are the immediate courses of action.

E

Prepare each person's termination paperwork after having reviewed the contents of their personnel files.

Scenario 10: Toxic Management Colleagues and 360 Degree Feedback

Adapted from: Groysberg, B., & Baden, K. C. (2019). Case study: When two leaders on the senior team hate each other. *Harvard Business Review, 97*(1), 145–149. Retrieved from http://search. ebscohost.com.ezproxy.fau.edu/login.aspx?direct=true&AuthType=ip,cookie,url,uid&db=buh&A N=133608397&site=eds-live&scope=site

Overview

Assume that you are Mike Miracle, V.P. of Sales for Marvel Sports, an international corporation. You were promoted into the position and have held it for 1-year. The company has experienced significant growth; over the past 2-years sales have increased 30% to over $150 million annually.

The company has an open and collaborative culture. The employee surveys results for the past 2-years reflect an overall 55% employee satisfaction rate although the percentages are lower or exceed the figure based on the criteria being measured.

The Sales and Finance departments have been sometimes at odds but since Miracle started working for Marvel Sports he worked to fix the problems. However, you did not realize just how bad things were between two employees; Controlle and Jones.

Controlle and Jones' Past Problems

Both Controlle and Jones are conscientious, task oriented, and dedicated employees. You rereviewed your notes about their past problems which revolve around their different and strong personalities. For example, Controlle dislikes the length of time it takes Jones to approve financial transactions and has told him, "You are a bean counter." Jones has walked out of meetings they have had because Controlle continually interrupts him and raises his voice. Controlle is a multitasker but Jones isn't, and Jones hates it when Controlle answers his cell, and works on other things during meetings. Jones has also complained to his boss about Controlle's condescending demeanor and his love of power although he has never been able to describe what he means by "love of power."

You have counseled Controlle on the latter and he has assured you he would work to improve his relationship with Jones but only if Jones agrees to do the same. A meeting was held in the HR conference room 3-months ago. You, Jones' boss, James Woods, CFO, Controlle and Jones were in attendance. After a lengthy discussion it was decided that Controlle and Jones would attend a Leadership Development program together. However, they didn't because (a) the program was cancelled by the company; (b) Jones was on vacation during the time the company was conducting the program in another city in the state and; (c) Controlle was on FMLA for the birth of his son at that time. To date, nothing has been done to reschedule them for the training.

360 Degree Feedback

The HR department which is well respected recently administered the annual 360 Degree Feedback survey. Each person's feedback report is marked confidential by the HR department but sometimes people share information with one another. The HR Director, Suzy Savvie, calls you and asks if she could meet with you ASAP about one report. It is for Karl Controlle, Manager of Sales. You tell her to come to your office.

She gives you a copy and shares some of the open-ended comments made about him as well as the average scores. Then she states, "His average scores are the lowest in the company. I am very concerned."

Like all 360 reports the open-ended comments are anonymous so no comments can be traced back to a subordinate, peer, or customer. Twelve individuals responded to each person's, 360 Degree questionnaire. Savvie reviewed the most negative comments about Controlle:

- "He is the most controlling and dictatorial person I have ever had to work with"
- "He makes decisions without ever consulting others"
- "He piles too much work on everyone with no explanation and unreasonable due dates"
- "I hate working with him"
- "He picks fights with other peers who he has to work with"
- "He loves power and sometimes uses it in a punitive way"
- "The lack of trust between Controlle and his peers (especially Jones) has an adverse effect on me and other employees"
- "He abuses his power by continually trying to undermine the financial controls"

After Savvie and Miracle reread the comments, Savvie states, "I think we should discuss what to do about this." Controlle nods and puts his copy of the documents on his desk.

However, Savvie notes, "We also need to review Jones' report because his in no angel." She then asks you, "When will they be rescheduled to attend the leadership training together?"

Question 25

Which below is/are the **BEST** statements you will make to Savvie?

A

"Do you think Controlle should be fired, and is the documentation a justifiable reason?"

B

"When will Controlle receive his report and do you agree that I should schedule a meeting with him to review the comments?"

C

B is the best response although D and E are okay.

D

"Thank you for sharing Controlle's report with me, I will get back with you once I decide what to do."

E

"When will I receive a copy of Jones' report?; I want to review his before I decide what to do"

Question 26

From the interventions listed below, **WHICH** ones would you select to help resolve Controlle's problems?

A

Schedule him to meet with a coach.

B

Prepare the paperwork to place Controlle on a Performance Improvement Plan.

C

Schedule one-on-one meetings with Controlle after he has a chance to review the report.

D

Both A and C.

E

Refer him to the EAP department because he may have some type of mental illness.

Question 27

What do you think is problematic about the comments made about Controlle regarding his use/abuse of power?

A

The comments are not specific enough to determine if he has a problem with power.

B

If he is treating people in a punitive manner and also undermines the Finance department, and this behavior continues, more problems may ensue (e.g., turnover, decreased morale, and productivity).

C

There may not be problem because the comments are anonymous and may have been made by disgruntled employees; abuse of power is based on a person's perception, not reality.

D

It all depends on which employee made the comments and what the context was.

Question 28

What action/actions below is/are the **BEST** to deal with Jones and Controlle?

A

Meet with Jones' boss and suggest that Jones and Controlle meet to resolve their problems; and monitor their progress.

B

Discuss Controlle's feedback with him and ask him for specifics about problems he has had with Jones and ask him how he plans to improve their relationship.

C

Make sure any involvement I have with both Jones and Controlle, includes keeping Jones' boss in the communication loop.

D

Provide Controlle with on-going support while he works to improve his relationship with Jones.

E

All of the above.

Strategic Planning

Adapted from Mersino, A. C. (2007). *Emotional Intelligence for Project Managers : The People Skills You Need to Achieve Outstanding Results*. New York: AMACOM. Retrieved from http://search. ebscohost.com.ezproxy.fau.edu/login.aspx?direct=true&AuthType=ip,cookie,url,uid&db=nlebk& AN=214576&site=eds-live&scope=site

Overview

Seaworthy, Inc. is a multinational corporation that ships containers to and from the U.S to China, Malaysia, and Vietnam. William Bligh is a newly hired Manager, Manufacturing and Production. He was employed by a Chinese competitor for the past 10 years. Based on his resume he worked on many strategic planning projects and was successful in accomplishing some major goals and objectives.

His predecessor, James Brutus, retired after working for Seaworthy for 25-years. According to information Bligh was provided by his boss, John Ahab, V.P. of Operations, Brutus became ineffective. For example, he was not handling pressure very well; e.g., he would lose his temper at least once a week, and was counseled several times over the past two years for not effectively dealing with team issues. He was not put on a performance improvement program or formally disciplined. Brutus' boss decided to let him continue to work because Brutus had carefully planned his retirement date with the HR department.

Bligh has been with Seaworthy for 1-month. During this time, the company has gone through downsizing and restructuring to include some changes in management personnel and several cost cutting measures. Bligh's employees told him that they are not happy with the changes.

Bligh has 6 direct reports who supervise 35 *Tank Car, Truck and Ship Loaders*. Employees work in teams of 6 and rotate amongst the various supervisors for the purpose of job enrichment. In the past, all teams received incentives on a quarterly basis for meeting or exceeding their production goals. There is a great deal of healthy internal competition among the teams.

Although Bligh is a Manager, many of his job tasks are hands-on which has been the standard operating procedure at Seaworthy.

Essential Job Duties

Some of Bligh's essential job duties are:

- Plan work assignments and equipment allocations to meet transportation, operations or production goals.
- Direct workers in transportation or related services, such as pumping, moving, storing, or loading or unloading of materials or people.
- Review orders, production schedules, blueprints, or shipping or receiving notices to determine work sequences and material shipping dates, types, volumes, or destinations.
- Inspect or test materials, containers, stock, vehicles, equipment, or facilities to ensure that they are safe, free of defects, and consistent with specifications.
- Confer with customers, supervisors, contractors, or other personnel to exchange information or to resolve problems.
- Monitor field work to ensure proper performance and use of materials.
- Plan and establish ground and sea transportation routes.
- Resolve worker problems or collaborate with employees to assist in problem resolution.
- Recommend or implement personnel actions, such as employee selection, evaluation, rewards, or disciplinary actions.
- Explain and demonstrate work tasks to new workers or assign training tasks to experienced workers.
- Recommend and implement measures to improve worker motivation, equipment performance, work methods, or customer services.
- Assist workers in tasks, such as coupling railroad cars or loading vehicles.

The context in which his work is performed includes:

- **Time Pressure**
- **Responsible for Others' Health and Safety**
- **Work with Work Group or Team**
- **Coordinate or Lead Others**
- **Importance of Being Exact or Accurate**

(Reference: https://www.onetonline.org/link/summary/53-1031.00, First Line Supervisors of Transportation and Materials Moving and Vehicle Operators)

All non-supervisory employees working in the manufacturing plant are members of the union. Their job title is *Tank Car, Truck and Ship Loaders*.

Some of the Loader's essential tasks are:

- Verify tank car, barge, or truck load numbers to ensure car placement accuracy based on written or verbal instructions.
- Check conditions and weights of vessels to ensure cleanliness and compliance with loading procedures.
- Monitor product movement to and from storage tanks, coordinating activities with other workers to ensure constant product flow.
- Operate ship loading and unloading equipment, conveyors, hoists, and other specialized material handling equipment such as railroad tank car unloading equipment.
- Record operating data such as products and quantities pumped, gauge readings, and operating times, manually or using computers.
- Test vessels for leaks, damage, and defects, and repair or replace defective parts as necessary.
- Unload cars containing liquids by connecting hoses to outlet plugs and pumping compressed air into cars to force liquids into storage tanks.
- Perform general warehouse activities, such as opening containers and crates, filling warehouse orders, assisting in taking inventory, and weighing and checking materials.

(Reference: https://www.onetonline.org/link/summary/53-7121.00, Tank, Car, Truck and Ship Leaders)

Strategic Plan

As noted previously, Bligh has had extensive past experience with strategic planning. Each level in the company's organizational structure (i.e., executive, operational, tactical) has a strategic plan. The company is comprised of divisions, departments and units. Three of Bligh's most important goals in the strategic plan for his division are:

Goal #1: Review, modify, reallocate and streamline work assignments, work methods, production schedules, and work sequences to reduce processing and shipping time, inconsistencies in specifications, defects, and employee accidents.

Goal #2: Improve process of dealing with and resolving worker problems and problem resolution in order to increase motivation, productivity and customer service ratings.

Goal #3: Evaluate new employee training program(s) in order to accomplish objectives 1 & 2.

The above goals align with his and the Loader's job duties. Their essential tasks which align with the strategic plan. For example:

- Monitor product movement to and from storage tanks, coordinating activities with other workers to ensure constant product flow.
- Operate ship loading and unloading equipment, conveyors, hoists, and other specialized material handling equipment such as railroad tank car unloading equipment.
- Test vessels for leaks, damage, and defects, and repair or replace defective parts as necessary.

Multiple Choice Questions

Question 29

Let's assume that Bligh's workers have not been provided with the goals from the strategic plan that will affect them. If you were Bligh what would you do about this?

A

Schedule one or more meetings with the workers and their supervisors; conduct meetings with everyone and outline how important their contributions are in meeting the established goals.

B

Ensure each person receives a copy of the strategic plan.

C

Provide direction and assistance to the supervisors regarding any or all work to be completed to accomplish goals, including weekly meetings.

D

Delegate execution of all strategic planning matters to the supervisors.

E

A, B, and C only.

Question 30

As noted in the case the **Loaders** perform several essential job tasks that are part of (i.e., aligned with) the strategic plan.

Assume that Bligh held a meeting with all of the supervisors to review the essential tasks and to share data with them about the tasks which substantiates why?

Goal: "Review, modify, reallocate and streamline work assignments, work methods, production schedules, and work sequences to reduce processing and shipping time, inconsistencies in specifications, defects, and employee accidents," is a primary goal in the strategic plan.

What kind of data do you think Bligh should obtain and share with them?

A

Accuracy rates of car, truck, or barge rates; bottlenecks which have prevented constant product flow; specific problems with loading and unloading of equipment; type, number of leaks; damage and repair problems of vessels and containers; number, type, and cost of employee accidents, and past trend data for all tasks.

B

Annual reports.

C

Written reports on work methods, production schedules, processing and shipping time, defects, and accidents.

D

A and C are the most appropriate although an audit report (choice E) may be helpful depending on its contents.

E

Internal audit reports which include statistics in all relevant categories.

Question 31

Considering Bligh does not directly supervise the **Loaders**, which is/are the **BEST** ways he can ensure that the strategic plan goals are executed?

A

Assist the supervisors and Loaders whenever necessary to solve problems which may occur in accomplishing any of the goals; maintain control of the goals but do not make rash decisions without conferring with the supervisors.

B

Demonstrate concern and interest when problems do occur that may slow down goal accomplishment; reward everyone when milestones are met.

C

Maintain regular open lines of communication with everyone; provide feedback when needed or requested; participate with the teams, as appropriate.

D

A, B, and C.

E

Meet with the supervisors as needed to check on the status of all goals.

Question 32

Regarding strategic plan. **Goal #1**. The reviewing, modifying, reallocating and streamlining work assignments, and so on, several supervisors advise Bligh in writing, that the employees feel that there are "*too many parts of their jobs to improve at one* time."

If you were Bligh which would be your priority courses of action?

A

Meet with all supervisors and obtain more specific detail about this; review the Loader's job tasks that are directly aligned with the goals to ensure that the supervisors understand how all of the tasks are intertwined; facilitate a discussion about how the tasks relate to the goal.

B

Advise the supervisors that the strategic plan has been finalized, the employees are part of the process and that they need to be committed to accomplishing their goals.

C

Ask the supervisors to review the problems associated with each of the tasks (poor coordination, too many defects, delays, other) and then share with Loaders so they understand how and why their job tasks are intertwined.

D

Schedule follow-up meetings to determine if employee's concerns have been addressed.

E

A, C, and D.

Question 33

Bligh is in his office finishing reading a report. Two of the most engaged and committed supervisors come to his office for a prescheduled meeting about some problem employees. The employees are strong union supporters and usually the first ones to file grievances. The supervisors tell Bligh the following and ask for his help.

A few of the workers have engaged in what they consider to be obstructionist behavior, while others show up late for meetings or make statements like, "I do not like working on goals," "They are setting us up to fail."

If you were Bligh what would you do and/or say to the two supervisors?

A

Ask them how they dealt with the workers when this occurred and if the behavior continues, tell them I am sorry that this is happening; make sure that they determine if the behavior is serious enough to initiate some sort of action (as outlined in the union contract); find out if the behavior is having an adverse effect on morale and productivity.

B

Ask them to provide me with the names and dates of the incidents as well as the type of grievances they have filed in the past.

C

Offer them any assistance and support they need; thank them for bringing this to my attention.

D

A is the best option, but C is also important, and E may give you more information and if necessary, Bligh should ascertain (on his own) information concerning previous grievances.

E

Ask them to provide, in writing, more specifics about who, when, and why they do not like working on goals and feel they are being set up to fail, and to make preparations for counseling meetings.

CHAPTER 9

A Subordinate Counseling Exercise
Corporation/Organization
Supervisor/Manager
Subordinate Counseling and Written Exercise

CANDIDATE INSTRUCTIONS

In this exercise, you will be asked to use written information about one of your employees to develop a plan of action. You will have 30 minutes to read, evaluate, and write your responses to the written material (i.e., Leslie Stahl's personnel file) about the situations/problems. This packet includes some of the most recent material from Stahl's personnel file.

Assume that you are at work in your office and completing paper work. The materials include the written background material about the issues that you will review. After you review this material, complete the quiz questions. You may write on any or all the pages in this packet of materials to prepare for the quiz.

You will be evaluated on the following skill dimensions (aka, abilities):

- **Problem Analysis /Problem Solving**
- **Judgment/Decision-Making**
- **Planning and Organizing**
- **Interpersonal Relations**
- **Written Communication**

Take no more than 30 minutes to prepare for the quiz. This is because, if you were actually going through a promotional testing process for a supervisory or management position with a company or organization, you would not be allowed to take more time than what is provided in the instructions.

Written Questions

When you are preparing for the quiz you may want to write down your answers to the following four questions. However, this is NOT mandatory. If you write down your answers do it on a piece of paper not here. If you were actually participating in a promotional testing process you might be asked to provide your answers to these questions in a verbal format.

Free Response:

Question 1

What information is indicative of any problem areas that need to be addressed? Be specific.

Question 2

What immediate actions will you take to deal with the problems/issues?

Question 3

How would you conduct/handle a meeting with Ms. Stahl?

Question 4

What actions would you take to implement your plans?

SCENARIO

You are to assume that you are Account Representative, Supervisor Eddy/Edie (if a female) Smith with X Corporation/Organization. You were recently promoted to the position and are looking forward to the challenge.

You are now assigned to the Customer Service Department on the day shift. It is Monday afternoon, May 15 20XX and you have completed two work task logs from the past 2-days.

You are still getting to know your staff even though you have only worked in the Packaging department. Your new immediate supervisor is Ryan Gossling. He left this packet of information about Ms. Stahl for you to review with her and handle based on your problem analysis and judgment and decision-making.

Your predecessor Chris Hemsworth, recently retired and left many things undone including meeting with Ms. Stahl about the latter and other items in this packet of information. Assume that you will need to meet with her to address these issues before you go out of town for company training about the new processing system.

Leslie Stahl has been with the company since March 20XX and only recently finished her new employee orientation (aka on-boarding process) and 3-months of on-the-job training (OJT). However, several sessions were cancelled by the trainers and were never rescheduled

E-mail Message

To: Leslie Stahl

Date: April 8, 20XX

From: Chris Hemsworth, Supervisor

Through: Ryan Gossling

Subject: <u>**Customer Compliments**</u>

We are very pleased to advise you that you will be receiving two written compliments from two customers you helped.

Thank you,

Chris Hemsworth

E-mail Message

To: Chris Hemsworth, Supervisor

Date: April 19, 20XX

From: Leslie Stahl

Subject: <u>Need Your Help</u>

As you know, I recently completed my training, but I am still confused about a few policies and procedures and what to do and when. Could we meet ASAP before I have any problems?

The ones I need help on understanding pertain to customer returns and reimbursements.

Also, from what I have been told by a few other Account Representatives, mentoring of employees is sorely lacking in our department. Please do not think I am complaining but being one of the few women, I want to make sure I meet your and the department's expectations.

When I asked a few of the more senior people for assistance they said they were too busy and that I should figure it out myself.

Thank you.

LS

E-mail Message

To: Chris Hemsworth, Supervisor

From: Robert Menendez

              Denzel Washington

Date: May 12, 20XX

Subject: <u>**What Are You Going to Do About Leslie Stahl?**</u>

We need to speak with you ASAP. It is about Leslie Stahl. We do not think she is up to the task of being an Account Representative, at least not with this company. She does not seem to know nor fully understand some of our policies and procedures.

When we offer her assistance, she says she is okay.

RM

DW

E-mail Message

To:	Chris Hemsworth, Supervisor
From:	Suzy Blunt, Account Rep
	Debbie Dufus, Account Rep
Date:	April 15, 20XX
Subject:	<u>**Leslie Stahl**</u>

We would like to meet with you ASAP to advise you of what we observed in the lunchroom yesterday.

While we were eating lunch, Stahl walks in, looks at us, looks at her watch and sits down. She already finished her lunch hour. Why is she allowed more time than we are to have lunch? This is not fair.

Blunt and Dufus

<h2 style="text-align:center">E-mail Message</h2>

To: Leslie Stahl

Date: April 16, 20XX

From: Chris Hemsworth, Supervisor

Subject: <u>**Missing Reports**</u>

The Records staff notified me that they are missing two reports from you. This is a reminder that I need them ASAP as I had previously asked you for them. When you told me you were very busy, I advised you this is unacceptable. Please submit the reports at the end of your shift today.

Thank you.

cc: Employee notes file

Employee Performance Notes

Note by	Date	Comment
Hemsworth	3/31/20XX	Leslie Stahl completed her OJT and was told that she will be closely monitored because she seems a bit unsure of herself. She recently returned from maternity leave and had to take a few days off.
Hemsworth	4/9/20XX	Leslie Stahl is a valued member of her team and maintains a professional appearance and provides excellent customer service. She does, however, need to more carefully complete her work reports.
Hemsworth	4/18/20XX	Leslie Stahl seems to be confused about some of our policies and procedures. More training may be needed.
Hemsworth	5/4/20XX	Leslie Stahl is never late for work. In fact, she comes in early, stays late sometimes, and never asks for OT.

E-mail Message

To: Kevin Hemsworth, Supervisor

From: Leslie Stahl

Date: May 12, 20XX

Subject: **Request for Personal Leave**

It would be greatly appreciated if you would approve a week of vacation time starting next week. I am going through a very tumultuous divorce and next week I must go to court. My husband has filed for full custody of my older son. He never notified me in advance of the court date. I am totally beside myself to say the least.

I am very stressed out and I have not had a full nights' sleep for the past 7-days. Moreover, as you know, my mother recently died of a horrible cancer and I have been the primary care giver for my father.

LS

SUBORDINATE COUNSELING EXERCISE

Multiple-Choice Questions

Perception and Analysis/Problem Analysis

Question 5

What is your initial perception of Leslie Stahl's major problems?

A

Leslie needs more training on policies and procedures, did not turn in two reports, and is going through a divorce.

B

She does not get along with her coworkers.

C

Leslie misses a lot of work.

D

She is having trouble with her boss.

E

She received two compliments on April 12th.

Perception and Analysis/Problem Analysis

Question 6

Which points below are relevant about Chris Hemsworth?

A

Based on the documents it appears that he did not assist or guide Leslie.

B

Hemsworth complimented Stahl in his employee performance notes.

C

There are no documents reflecting that he has met with her to deal with her problems.

D

There is no indication that he responded to her April 19th plea for help.

E

All of the above.

Judgment/Decision-Making and Planning and Organizing

Question 7

Given you are told to assume that you are Stahl's supervisor, what would be your first actions? I would

A

schedule a meeting with her.

B

meet with my Director and ask for his assistance.

C

meet with the employees who complained about her.

D

prepare disciplinary paperwork and have Gossling approve it.

E

check to determine if paperwork had been submitted on her personal leave.

Perception and Analysis/Problem Analysis and Judgment/Decision-Making

Question 8

What are the problems/issues with Blunt and Dufus sending an e-mail to Hemsworth about Stahl?

A

How do they know how long she took for her lunch hour?

B

Why are they paying attention to how much time an employee takes for their lunch?

C

Why are they complaining about this?

D

Are these employees possible trouble makers?

E

All of the above.

Judgment/Decision-Making

Question 9

As Stahl's new supervisor, what responsibility do you have regarding the fact that she does not fully understand some policies and procedures?

A

None, the person(s) who conducted her OJT are responsible and should be held accountable.

B

Total responsibility because I am her boss and must ensure that she understands all of our policies and procedures.

C

Some responsibility even though I did not train her.

D

All of the above are plausible.

E

None because the HR department referred an unqualified person.

Judgment/Decision-Making and Dealing With People/Interpersonal

Question 10

When you meet with Ms. Stahl, how will you start the meeting?

A

Ask her how she is feeling and let her know I will support her and help her deal with her personal problems.

B

Advise her about the complaints from other employees about her.

C

Ask her why she takes more time for lunch then allowed.

D

Tell her that her performance problems are serious and may result in termination.

E

Ask her what she thinks about there being so few women Account Representatives.

Judgment/Decision-Making and Dealing With People/Interpersonal

Question 11

Assuming no one is immediately available to provide Stahl with some more OJT, what would you do?

A

I would meet with her and explain how to handle customer returns and reimbursements.

B

I would ask her which policies and procedures she does not understand and review them with her.

C

I would schedule her for the OJT as soon as possible.

D

I would ask my boss what to do.

E

Both A and B.

Organizing

Question 12

In preparation for your meeting with Leslie Stahl, how would you organize the documents?

A

I would put them in date order, then group them by topic, and then note which are the most serious and the least serious.

B

There is no need to organize the documents because some were sent to me by Stahl and others (e-mails from coworkers) she does not know about.

C

I would tell her how I am going to respond to each complaint.

D

I would show her that there are many more complaints than compliments.

E

Both C and D.

Planning and Organizing, Perception and Analysis/Problem Analysis, and Judgment/Decision-Making

Question 13

What would you do about Blunt and Dufus?

A

Nothing. Just deal with Stahl about this issue.

B

Schedule a meeting with them to obtain more information about their concerns.

C

Ask around to find out if anyone else is having any problems with Stahl or with Blunt and/or Dufus.

D

Advise them that they should not be monitoring coworkers' lunch time.

E

Ask my supervisor but first check their personnel files to ascertain if this is typical behavior.

Perception and Analysis/Problem Analysis and Judgment/Decision-Making Dealing With People

Question 14

How would you deal with Stahl's e-mail dated May 12, 20XX?

A

Tell her that I cannot approve her vacation time.

B

Meet with her to discuss her request during which time I would tell her that I understand that she needs to address her personal problems.

C

Defer this to my supervisor because she has so many problems.

D

Give her the time off just to go to court and find a facility for her father.

E

Refer her to the EAP.

Perception and Analysis/Problem Analysis and Judgment/Decision-Making

Question 15

Which below is/are the **BEST** options for conducting a meeting with Leslie Stahl?

A

Identify each of the problems with her and ask her how she plans on or what she is going to do solve them.

B

Share my concerns with her, with the knowledge that she has been trying by coming in early and staying late. Ask her for input and tell her that together we will brainstorm ways of dealing with each issue and finding viable options.

C

Telling her that I recognize the compliments she received in April and then ask her if her problems on the job are the result of the issues that women have after giving birth accompanied by the fact that she is going through a divorce.

D

Accept her request for time off so she can deal with the issues of having to provide for her father and deal with a divorce. Arrange for a meeting with her upon her return to work, so that we can work together to address the issues and arrive at an acceptable conclusion.

E

Depending upon your perception of the situation, both B and/or D are the **BEST** options.

Question 16

As her new supervisor, when do you think that Leslie's problems began?

A

On March 31, after she returned from taking a few days off after the baby was born.

B

On April 9th, when Hemsworth noted that she would, "need to more carefully complete her work."

C

On April 19th, when she asked Hemsworth for help and then on April 18 he wrote, "more training may be needed."

D

On May 12, when Menendez and Washington wrote their e-mail.

E

Actually, there is no starting date as it is all cumulative.

Question 17

When you have a meeting with Leslie Stahl, what would you actually do?

A

Suggest that she seek assistance from the EAP Coordinator in the Human Resources department, regarding assisting her in dealing with her personal problems.

B

Share with her the company policies about understanding all of the standard operating procedures (SOPS) and (e.g., policies and procedures) for Account Representatives by the end of training and encourage her to reread them during her time off.

C

Schedule a time, after her return, to meet with her on an on-going basis in order to mentor her and answer her questions about the policy and procedures (Note: It is not appropriate to indicate that, at this time, you expect her to understand the policies and procedures within a specific time period).

D

Find out why she spends extra time in the lunch room and why she believes that female employees are ignored. Ask her what she would suggest that you do with the female employees to make them feel that they are part of the team.

E

Both A and C are applicable.

Assessor Guide for Subordinate Counseling Exercise

On the next few pages is an Assessor Guide that would be used to evaluate your verbal responses if you were actually participating in a promotional testing process for a manager position. After your preparation time is over, you would be escorted into a room where you would make a verbal presentation to the assessor panel, during which time you would answer the questions and cover any other details. Your verbal answers may be made to live assessors or you may speak while being recorded. If you were completing this exercise live you would be required to write a memo about your meeting with Stahl. The written communication ability is included as the last page of the Assessor Guide.

The process would occur as follows:

1. The panel welcomes you.
2. Someone on the panel asks you whether you are ready to begin.
3. When ready, the time starts, and a test administrator monitors your time with a stop watch.
4. You make your presentation.
5. No questions are asked by the assessors.
6. You may not ask the assessors any questions.
7. The assessors take notes while you are speaking.
8. The assessors document your statements.
9. The assessors do not write down conclusions (e.g., he did a great job) but observations (e.g., "Good morning ladies and gentlemen, I will be covering . . . ").
10. Time is called by the test administrator.
11. The test administrator collects your documents and escorts out of the room.
12. The assessors review their notes and complete the check list before the next candidate arrives.

X CORPORATION/ORGANIZATION
SUPERVISOR/MANAGER
SUBORDINATE COUNSELING
ASSESSOR GUIDE

Candidate # _____   Assessor # _____   Date _____

Rating Dimension	Tentative Score	Final Score
Perception and Analysis/Problem Analysis		
Judgment/Decision-Making		
Planning and Organizing		
Dealing with People/Interpersonal		
Oral Communication		
Written Communication		

PROBLEM ANALYSIS/PROBLEM SOLVING: The ability to quickly identify a problem and to analyze it; to notice details or phenomena; to sort out pertinent information; to foresee the consequences of various alternatives. To what extent can the individual obtain relevant information from available information and screen out less essential details? Does the individual misinterpret information? To what extent does the individual demonstrate perceptions of an interaction between various aspects of the problem and between various actions taken or available to be taken. To what extent can the individual use data and related information to evaluate a problem? To what extent does the individual logically interpret information to solve problems?

Most Appropriate/Problem Analysis/Problem Solving Behaviors/Actions	✓
1. Recognizes importance of Stahl's past good performance (i.e., employee performance notes); and that she received a Certificate of Appreciation.	❏❏
2. Perceives importance of addressing Stahl's past good performance during a confidential meeting with her.	❏❏
3. Perceives that the divorce she is going through may be related to her current problems.	❏❏
4. Recognizes that Stahl's work problems may be related to her personal problems.	❏❏
5. Demonstrates awareness of importance/significance of confidential note from Menendez and Washington; and may comment on the issues they addressed (e.g., that she is not up to the task).	❏❏❏ ❏❏❏
6. Recognizes that before counseling or disciplining Stahl, a thorough investigation needs to be first completed and/or he or she needs to observe Stahl at work.	❏
7. Perceives that Stahl may need some training on time management because of the missing reports.	❏
8. Perceives that Stahl needs coaching from him or her.	❏
9. Recognizes that Stahl may need counseling and/or referral to EAP.	❏❏
10. Other behaviors/actions not listed above (each behavior must be documented).	❏

Problem Analysis/Problem Solving Rating
❏

JUDGMENT/DECISION-MAKING: The ability to make sound decisions promptly on difficult problems; the exercise of judgment and consideration of available information; the willingness to make a decision when required. Does not overly delegate; does not delay action on important items; takes firm position and makes position clear. Evaluates situation to determine action to be taken; assigns tasks to subordinates when nature of the incident requires coordinated efforts of several subordinates. Basically, to what extent does the individual use all information to take the most appropriate action and exhibit a willingness to make decisions when necessary?

Most Appropriate Judgment/Decision-Making Behaviors/Actions	✓
1. Would commend Stahl on her past good performance and certificate of appreciation.	❑❑
2. Would outline Stahl's recent problems in a confidential meeting with her.	❑
3. Indicates he or she would offer Stahl any assistance she needs; that his or her door is always open to her.	❑❑ ❑
4. Would schedule a confidential meeting with Stahl.	❑
5. Would advise Stahl of the consequences of the problems continuing (e.g., disciplinary action).	❑
6. Will ask Stahl for her input regarding why she has had some problems and would give her the opportunity to discuss her personal problems.	❑❑
7. Would schedule a follow-up meeting with Stahl during which time he or she would coach her.	❑
8. Other behaviors/actions not listed above (each behavior must be documented).	❑

Judgment/Decision-Making Rating
❑

PLANNING AND ORGANIZING: Ability to plan and organize daily work routine; establish priorities for the completion of work in accordance with sound time-management methodology. Ability to avoid duplication of effort, estimate expected time of completion of work elements, and establish a personal schedule accordingly. Ability to know and understand expectations regarding such activities and works to ensure such expectations are met and in a timely manner. Develops and formulates ways, means, and timing to achieve established goals and objectives. Ability to effectively and efficiently utilize resources to achieve such goals and objectives. Ability to break work down into subtasks and prioritize these subtasks so it can be done effectively; to anticipate problems before they come up; to prepare effective plans to control difficulties and problems; to set objectives, priorities, and so on.

Most Appropriate Planning and Organizing Behaviors/Actions	✓
1. Would ensure that Stahl knows what is expected of her (i.e., reread the policies and procedures, ask her about her lunch hour, turn reports in on time).	❑❑❑ ❑
2. Uses information provided to him or her to run an effective and efficient presentation (e.g., referred to notes and documents).	❑❑❑
3. Lists very specific details on how he or she plans to approach the problems when he or she meets with Stahl.	❑
4. Provides an introduction to presentation, covers the main points, and summarizes the key points within 10 minutes.	❑
5. Identifies a time line during which time Stahl is expected to improve (e.g., or progressive discipline will follow).	❑
6. Covers all problems/issues within 10-minute period (i.e., time was not called before he or she was summarizing key points).	❑
7. Indicates he or she will make plans to observe Stahl on the job once or twice or week or when applicable.	❑
8. Discusses issues in an organized manner (e.g., did not repeat same points; did not go back and forth and was not tangential).	❑❑❑
9. Other behaviors/actions not listed above (each behavior must be documented).	❑

Planning and Organizing Rating
❑

DEALING WITH PEOPLE/INTERPERSONAL: Ability to establish, integrate, and maintain effective and harmonious working relationships with other employees, other agencies, and citizens; work as a member of team, respect and encourage working cooperatively with subordinates and coworkers and others without regard to their gender, age, race, beliefs, or cultural background. Ability to deal with people beyond giving and receiving instructions. Respects ideas of others, praises subordinates for good and outstanding performance, investigates disputes, and complaints against subordinates.

Most Appropriate Dealing with People/Interpersonal Behaviors/Actions	✓
1. Shows concern for Stahl's personal problems (e.g., going through a divorce, mother's recent death, husband filing for custody of children).	❏❏
2. Would give Stahl an opportunity to vent/discuss her divorce, and in confidence.	❏❏
3. Would commend Stahl on her past good performance (i.e., employee performance notes; customer compliments).	❏
4. Would ensure that Stahl knows that he or she is there for her; that she is a valuable employee; and he or she wants to help bring her performance up.	❏❏❏
5. Would ask Stahl whether there is anything he or she can do to assist her while she is going through a difficult time.	❏
6. Offers to refer her to the EAP.	❏
7. Indicates that he or she would reassure Stahl that the EAP information will remain confidential.	❏
8. Indicates that he or she would offer Stahl more time off (if applicable) to deal with divorce situation.	❏❏
9. Would offer to coach Stahl on how to coach and mentor her subordinates.	❏❏
10. Other behaviors/actions not listed above (each behavior must be documented).	❏

Dealing with People/Interpersonal Relations Rating
❏

WRITTEN COMMUNICATION: Ability to recognize and use correct English grammar, punctuation, and spelling; communicate information in a succinct and organized manner; and produce written information, which may include technical material, which is appropriate for the intended audience.

Most Appropriate Written Communication Behaviors/Actions	✓
1. Used correct English grammar.	❏
2. Used appropriate spelling.	❏
3. Used appropriate sentence construction (e.g., not too long or too short, used paragraphs, did not over use bullet points or lists).	❏
4. Used appropriate punctuation.	❏
5. Writing was clear and succinct vs. tangential and confusing.	❏
6. Writing was well organized (i.e., had a beginning, middle, end, etc.).	❏
7. Wrote for the appropriate audience.	❏
8. Prepared memo in appropriate format.	❏
9. Other behaviors/actions not listed above (each behavior must be documented and consider answers to other questions in other domains).	❏

Written Communication Rating
❏

CHAPTER 10

Generic Management In-Basket Exercise
Supervisor/Manager
In-Basket Exercise
Pre/instructions for the In-Basket Exercise

OVERVIEW

The in-basket (IB) exercise is commonly used to assess a person's management abilities; that is, planning and organizing, problem analysis/problem-solving, judgment and decision-making, and dealing with people. Written communication is also measured in all IBs, but in this case, it is not because multiple-choice questions are used to assess your skills.

IB exercises are used widely throughout the world as one exercise for a management selection process. In this case, the exercise is being used for developmental purposes: yours. Therefore, your approach to the exercise will be different. For example, you do not have to worry as to whether you are going to be promoted. However, by reviewing the 11 items in the exercise, you will be exposed to what might be found in your IB at your place of employment.

When reading the instructions, assume that you are the supervisor or manager. If you are not currently in a supervisory or management position, then think about how you would handle each item. If you are currently a supervisor or manager, view this as an opportunity to develop your skills.

When reading each item, take notes about what issues are presented. For example:

- **Human resources (HR; people) problems**
- **Employee performance appraisal documents or observation reports**
- **HR policies and procedures**
- **Customer complaints**
- **Meetings to schedule and attend**
- **Reports to read and comment on**

A few other points to consider as you are reading the items:

- Even though this is a developmental exercise, you may pretend that you are taking a promotional exam.

Because you are pretending some of the instructions do not apply.
- For example, you are not expected to hand write anything.
- Written communication cannot be measured in a multiple-choice question.
- Do not be concerned about the 20XX dates.
- Pay attention to the months and days.
- Read the instructions very carefully.
- The instructions are not designed to trick you.
- The items in the IB have actually occurred in a work setting, but the names, dates, and some other components have been changed to ensure anonymity.
- Read through the entire IB before you start working on completing any items.
- Prioritize the items into a rank order list.
- No one group of subject matter experts (SMEs) will ever totally agree on the exact order of the items.
- Many of the items in the exercise were interrelated.
- You should be able to identify and sort the related items into one pile.
- You can write several memos if the topic is not one where you would normally copy other individuals in your department.
- You can write one memo to cover many topics.
- *Do not* forget to consider what interpersonal behaviors/actions are necessary.
- Very few people receive perfect scores (i.e., a 5 on a 1–5 point rating scale) in IB exercises.
- *Do not* think that the exercise was structured to trick you.
- Remember that more than one assessor and preferably three assessors will be scoring each IB.

To reiterate in this IB exercise, you do not have to respond by writing memos because your performance will be measured by answering multiple-choice questions. Now take a deep breath and start the exercise.

INSTRUCTIONS FOR IB EXERCISE

This test is commonly known as an IB exercise.

Although the situation in this exercise is artificial with some unrealistic restrictions on the time allowed you, the methods and activities you can employ in communicating with others and the problems you will deal with are real. The experiences and problems have been obtained and adapted from actual situations that supervisors and/or managers working at their jobs encounter in everyday situations.

The purpose of this exercise is to evaluate your ability to perform certain critical management functions and also give you an opportunity to display your style and approach to handling various types of common situations supervisors and/or managers working at any company or organization may encounter. You are not able, therefore, to get in contact with anyone. You must decide what action to take and take some form of appropriate action on matters without additional information or without discussing the issue with anyone.

This exercise is set in a hypothetical X Corporation/Organization in X City, United States.

You are not allowed to handle an item by "discussing" it with someone or by "learning" something not in the exercise to allow you to decide that issue is no longer valid, or that you have obtained some sort of agreement that allows you to not take any action. That is, you cannot make up things that permit you to avoid having to make a decision and choose some form of action.

DO NOT assume that just because you would do something in your company or organization that it is "right" or the only way to do something in this exercise. By the same token, just because you would not do something in your company or organization, do not assume that it is "wrong" to do it in this exercise. In this exercise, you are expected to use **YOUR OWN BEST JUDGMENT** in handling the items. This exercise is designed to test your management and supervisory abilities in certain defined areas and not your knowledge of the procedures or operations of the division or department where you currently work.

There are 11 items (a few items have two pages and are marked as such), some of which are more than one page in length. Be sure to review each document carefully to make sure that you have read it completely. All items have an **ITEM NUMBER** at the bottom of each page of the item. You **MUST** handle **EVERY** item in the exercise in some manner. "Handling" an item may mean nothing more than reviewing it and holding it for future action, or it may require some immediate action of some sort. You should dispose of each item according to your best judgment. In an actual situation, you may desire more information before deciding on a course of action. In this case, however, you are limited to the information at hand and must make a decision **BASED ON THE AVAILABLE INFORMATION**.

NOTE: If these were actually participating in hiring or promotional testing process, the following statement would apply. It is your choice whether you want to follow all of these instructions. However, you should adhere to the time constraints.

So that we know how you handle the material, **WRITE DOWN EVERYTHING THAT YOU DO OR DECIDE TO DO. WRITE IT EXACTLY HOW YOU WOULD WRITE IT IN AN ACTUAL SITUATION**.

You have been provided with paper, sticky notes, and other materials needed to complete the exercise. You may write on any items or mark them up in any manner that you see fit. If you want to, you may write on the item any comments, directions, and so on, that you want to make in lieu of making such comments on a separate piece of paper.

For this IB exercise, you will be evaluated on the following skills: *Problem Analysis/Problem-Solving, Judgment/Decision-Making, Planning and Organizing, Interpersonal Relations, and Written Communication*.

You have 1½ hours to handle all 11 items.

Note: Because this is only a practice exercise and there is no test administrator to start and end the exercise, be honest and do not go over 1½ hours.

SCENARIO AND ITEMS

Assume that you are Russell Crowe (or Rossie Crowe is you are female). For the purposes of this developmental exercise, you can assume that Russell is a male or female name. If you are a woman, assume that your name is Rossie.

You have recently applied for the promotion position to supervisor/manager and were just promoted. Your predecessor, Kevin Costner, took a job with another company. You are starting your new job on May 21, but wanted to come to the administration office today, Sunday, May 20, to get a head start. When you got there, you found some documents in your IB. As you already know, the person in this position handles a great deal of administrative issues and paperwork.

Your boss, Mitchell Muscell, left some documents in your IB to review and handle. Two reports were also left for you to review and decide what to do with each one. Another document is a general order (GO) [aka Policy and procedure(s)], which you need to handle, and some other items.

In disposing of the items in the IB, your **SOLE** means of communicating with anyone is in writing. Therefore, any messages, direction, or information that you relay must be clear, concise, and complete.

REMEMBER

1. THIS IS SUNDAY AFTERNOON, MAY 20, 20XX.
2. YOU ARE SUPERVISOR/MANAGER RUSSELL OR ROSSIE CROWE.
3. YOU CANNOT REACH ANYONE BY TELEPHONE, COMPUTER, OR IN PERSON.
4. FILES AND RECORDS ARE NOT AVAILABLE TO YOU. YOU MUST WORK WITH THE INFORMATION AT HAND.
5. **YOU HAVE 1½ HOURS TO HANDLE THE 11 ITEMS.**
6. YOU SHOULD TAKE ANY ACTION TO SET UP ACTIVITIES FOR YOUR RETURN PRIOR TO LEAVING THE OFFICE, EVEN IF SUCH ACTIVITIES ARE NOT A SPECIFIC IB ITEM. YOU WANT THE OFFICE TO RUN AS SMOOTHLY AS POSSIBLE IN YOUR ABSENCE.
7. BE SURE TO MAKE IT CLEAR WHAT YOU DID OR HAVE MADE PLANS TO DO FOR EACH OF THE 11 ITEMS IN THE EXERCISE.
8. YOU MAY WRITE ON THE ITEMS OR ATTACH MEMOS OR NOTES TO THEM. WRITE YOUR NOTES AND MEMOS EXACTLY HOW YOU WOULD WRITE THEM IN AN ACTUAL SITUATION.

Memorandum

To:	All Supervisors/Managers
From:	Dudley Dogbert, VP HR
Date:	May 14, 20XX
Re:	<u>**Suggestions for Code of Ethics Policies and Procedures Manual**</u>

We are working on writing a code of ethics policies and procedures for the company manual and are soliciting your important suggestions. Attached on the next few pages are a few sections from Google's code of ethics. We obtained from Alphabet, Google's parent company, online for free. The link is https://abc.xyz/investor/other/google-code-of-conduct.html

Kindly provide feedback on what else you think should be added as well as some of the examples from Google, where applicable.

Also, we are developing a training program on ethics and will be including some examples of ethical issues. If possible please provide us with an example of an unethical situation that occurred at one of your past places of unemployment. Do not include the name of the company, or real names.

When done, submit your notes and description of your actions to your boss and he or she will review your draft but transmit up the chain of command without changing the document.

Please have this completed and submitted by May 24, 20XX.

Dudley Dogbert

Google Code of Conduct

The Google Code of Conduct is one of the ways we put Google's values into practice. It's built around the recognition that everything we do in connection with our work at Google will be, and should be, measured against the highest possible standards of ethical business conduct. We set the bar that high for practical as well as aspirational reasons: Our commitment to the highest standards helps us hire great people, build great products, and attract loyal users. Respect for our users, for the opportunity, and for each other are foundational to our success, and are something we need to support every day.

So please do read the Code and Google's values, and follow both in spirit and letter, always bearing in mind that each of us has a personal responsibility to incorporate and to encourage other Googlers to incorporate, the principles of the Code and values into our work. And if you have a question or ever think that one of your fellow Googlers or the company as a whole may be falling short of our commitment, don't be silent. We want—and need—to hear from you.

Who Must Follow Our Code?

We expect all of our employees and Board members to know and follow the Code. Failure to do so can result in disciplinary action, including termination of employment. Moreover, while the Code is specifically written for Google employees and Board members, we expect Google contractors, consultants, and others who may be temporarily assigned to perform work or services for Google to follow the Code in connection with their work for us. Failure of a Google contractor, consultant, or other covered service provider to follow the Code can result in termination of their relationship with Google.

What If I Have a Code-Related Question or Concern?

If you have a question or concern, don't just sit there. You can contact your manager, your HR representative, or Ethics & Compliance. You can also submit a question or raise a concern of a suspected violation of our Code or any other Google policy through the Ethics & Compliance Helpline. Finally, if you believe a violation of law has occurred, you can always raise that through the Ethics & Compliance Helpline or with a government agency.

I. No Retaliation

Google prohibits retaliation against any worker here at Google who reports or participates in an investigation of a possible violation of our Code, policies, or the law. If you believe you are being retaliated against, please contact Ethics & Compliance.

I. Serve Our Users

Our users value Google not only because we deliver great products and services, but also because we hold ourselves to a higher standard in how we treat users and operate more generally. Keeping the following principles in mind will help us to maintain that high standard:

1. Integrity

Our reputation as a company that our users can trust is our most valuable asset, and it is up to all of us to make sure that we continually earn that trust. All of our communications and other interactions with our users should increase their trust in us.

2. Usefulness

Our products, features, and services should make Google more useful for all our users. We have many different types of users, from individuals to large businesses, but one guiding principle: "Is what we are offering useful?"

3. Privacy, Security, and Freedom of Expression

Always remember that we are asking users to trust us with their personal information. Preserving that trust requires that each of us respect and protect the privacy and security of that information. Our security procedures strictly limit access to and use of users' personal information, and require that each of us take measures to protect user data from unauthorized access. Know your responsibilities under these procedures, and collect, use, and access user personal information only as authorized by our security policies, our privacy policies, and applicable data protection laws.

Google is committed to advancing privacy and freedom of expression for our users around the world. Where user privacy and freedom of expression face government challenges, we seek to implement internationally recognized standards that respect those rights as we develop products, do business in diverse markets, and respond to government requests to access user information or remove user content. Contact Legal or Ethics & Compliance if you have questions on implementing these standards in connection with what you do at Google.

1. **Equal Opportunity Employment**

   Employment here is based solely upon individual merit and qualifications directly related to professional competence. We strictly prohibit unlawful discrimination or harassment on the basis of race, color, religion, veteran status, national origin, ancestry, pregnancy status, sex, gender identity or expression, age, marital status, mental or physical disability, medical condition, sexual orientation, or any other characteristics protected by law. We also make all reasonable accommodations to meet our obligations under laws protecting the rights of the disabled.

2. **Harassment, Discrimination, and Bullying**

   Google prohibits discrimination, harassment, and bullying in any form—verbal, physical, or visual, as discussed more fully in our Policy Against Discrimination, Harassment, and Retaliation. If you believe you've been bullied or harassed by anyone at Google, or by a Google partner or vendor, we strongly encourage you to immediately report the incident to your supervisor, HR, or both. Similarly, supervisors and managers who learn of any such incident should immediately report it to HR. HR will promptly and thoroughly investigate any complaints and take appropriate action.

II. Conflicts of Interest

1. **Drugs and Alcohols**

    Our position on substance abuse is simple: It is incompatible with the health and safety of our employees, and we don't permit it. Consumption of alcohol is not banned at our offices, but use good judgment and never drink in a way that leads to impaired performance or inappropriate behavior, endangers the safety of others, or violates the law. Illegal drugs in our offices or at sponsored events are strictly prohibited. If a manager has reasonable suspicion to believe that an employee's use of drugs and/or alcohol may adversely affect the employee's job performance or the safety of the employee or others in the workplace, the manager may request an alcohol and/or drug screening. A reasonable suspicion may be based on objective symptoms such as employee's appearance, behavior, or speech.

2. **Safe Workplace**

    We are committed to a violence-free work environment, and we will not tolerate any level of violence or the threat of violence in the workplace. Under no circumstances should anyone bring a weapon to work. If you become aware of a violation of this policy, you should report it to HR immediately. In case of potential violence, contact Google security.

3. **Dog Policy**

    Google's affection for our canine friends is an integral facet of our corporate culture. We like cats, but we're a dog company, so as a general rule we feel cats visiting our offices would be fairly stressed out. However, before bringing your canine companion to the office, please make sure you review our Dog Policy.

III. Avoid Conflicts of Interest

When you are in a situation in which competing loyalties could cause you to pursue a personal benefit for you, your friends, or your family at the expense of Google or our users, you may be faced with a conflict of interest. All of us should avoid conflicts of interest and circumstances that reasonably present the appearance of a conflict.

When considering a course of action, ask yourself whether the action you're considering could create an incentive for you; or appear to others to create an incentive for you, to benefit yourself, your friends, or family; or an associated business at the expense of Google. If the answer is "yes," the action you're considering is likely to create a conflict of interest situation, and you should avoid it.

Guidance in seven areas where conflicts of interest often arise is provided as follows:

- Personal investments
- Outside employment, advisory roles, board seats, and starting your own business
- Business opportunities found through work
- Inventions
- Friends and relatives; coworker relationships
- Accepting gifts, entertainment, and other business courtesies
- Use of Google products and services

In each of these situations, the rule is the same—if you are considering entering into a business situation that creates a conflict of interest, don't. If you are in a business situation that may create a conflict of interest, or the appearance of a conflict of interest, review the situation with your manager and Ethics & Compliance. Finally, it's important to understand that as circumstances change, a situation that previously didn't present a conflict of interest may present one.

1. **Personal Investments**

   Avoid making personal investments in companies that are Google competitors or business partners when the investment might cause, or appear to cause, you to act in a way that could harm Google.

   When determining whether a personal investment creates a conflict of interest, consider the relationship between the business of the outside company, Google's business, and what you do at Google, including whether the company has a business relationship with Google that you can influence and the extent to which the company competes with Google.

You should also consider (a) any overlap between your specific role at Google and the company's business, (b) the significance of the investment, including the size of the investment in relation to your net worth, (c) whether the investment is in a public or private company, (d) your ownership percentage of the company, and (e) the extent to which the investment gives you the ability to manage and control the company.

Investments in venture capital or other similar funds that invest in a broad cross section of companies that may include Google competitors or business partners generally do not create conflicts of interest. However, a conflict of interest may exist if you control the fund's investment activity.

1. **Outside Employment, Advisory Roles, Board Seats, and Starting Your Own**
   Developing or helping to develop outside inventions that (a) relate to Google's existing or reasonably anticipated products and services, (b) relate to your position at Google, or (c) are developed using Google corporate resources may create conflicts of interest and be subject to the provisions of Google's Confidential Information and Invention Assignment Agreement and other employment agreements. If you have any questions about potential conflicts or intellectual property ownership involving an outside invention or other intellectual property, consult Ethics & Compliance or Legal.

2. **Friends and Relatives; Coworker Relationships**
   Avoid participating in management or decision-making regarding potential or existing Google business relationships that involve your relatives, spouse or significant other, or close friends. This includes being the hiring manager for a position for which your relative or close friend is being considered or being a relationship manager for a company associated with your spouse or significant other.

   To be clear, just because a relative, spouse or significant other, or close friend works at Google or becomes a Google competitor or business partner doesn't mean there is a conflict of interest. However, if you are also involved in that Google business relationship, it can be very sensitive. The right thing to do in that situation is to discuss the relationship with your manager and Ethics & Compliance.

ITEM 1—PAGE 187

Finally, romantic relationships between coworkers can, depending on the work roles and respective positions of the coworkers involved, create an actual or apparent conflict of interest. If a romantic relationship does create an actual or apparent conflict, it may require changes to work arrangements or even the termination of employment of either one or both individuals involved. Consult Google's Employee Handbook for additional guidance on this issue.

1. **Accepting Gifts, Entertainment, and Other Business Courtesies**

   Accepting gifts, entertainment, and other business courtesies from a Google competitor or business partner can easily create the appearance of a conflict of interest, especially if the value of the item is significant. Google's Non-Government Related Gifts & Client Entertainment Policy provides specific guidance on when it is appropriate for Googlers to accept gifts, entertainment, or any other business courtesy (including discounts or benefits that are not made available to all Googlers) from any of our competitors or business partners.

   Generally, acceptance of inexpensive "token" noncash gifts is permissible. In addition, infrequent and moderate business meals and entertainment with clients and infrequent invitations to attend local sporting events and celebratory meals with clients can be appropriate aspects of many Google business relationships, provided that they aren't excessive and don't create the appearance of impropriety. Before accepting any gift or courtesy, consult the Non-Government Related Gifts & Client Entertainment Policy, and be aware that you may need to obtain manager approval.

   Contact Ethics & Compliance if you have any questions. See the discussion of Anti-Bribery Laws in Section VII(d) for guidance on when it is appropriate to give gifts and business courtesies in the course of doing Google business.

III. Google Partners

Just as you are careful not to disclose confidential Google information, it's equally important not to disclose any confidential information from our partners. Don't accept confidential information from other companies without first having all parties sign an appropriate nondisclosure agreement approved by Legal. Even after the agreement is signed, try only to accept as much information as you need to accomplish your business objectives.

1. Intellectual Property

Google's intellectual property rights (our trademarks, logos, copyrights, trade secrets, "know-how," and patents) are among our most valuable assets. Unauthorized use can lead to their loss or serious loss of value. You must respect all copyright and other intellectual property laws, including laws governing the fair use of copyrights, trademarks, and brands. You must never use Google's (or its affiliated entities') logos, marks, or other protected information or property for any business or commercial venture without preclearance from the Marketing team. We strongly encourage you to report any suspected misuse of trademarks, logos, or other Google intellectual property to Legal.

Likewise, respect the intellectual property rights of others. Inappropriate use of others' intellectual property may expose Google and you to criminal and civil fines and penalties. Please seek advice from Legal before you solicit, accept, or use proprietary information from individuals outside the company or let them use or have access to Google proprietary information. You should also check with Legal if developing a product that uses content not belonging to Google.

A word about open source—Google is committed to open-source software development. Consistent with our policy of respecting the valid intellectual property rights of others, we strictly comply with the license requirements under which open-source software is distributed. Failing to do so may lead to legal claims against Google, as well as significant damage to the company's reputation and its standing in the open-source community. Please seek guidance from Legal and the Open Source Programs Office before incorporating open-source code into any Google product, service, or internal project.

ITEM 1—PAGE 189

IV. Obey the Law

Google takes its responsibilities to comply with laws and regulations very seriously and each of us is expected to comply with applicable legal requirements and prohibitions. While it's impossible for anyone to know all aspects of every applicable law, you should understand the major laws and regulations that apply to your work. Take advantage of Legal and Ethics & Compliance to assist you here. A few specific laws are easy to violate unintentionally and so are worth pointing out here:

Certain conduct is absolutely prohibited under these laws, and could result in your imprisonment, not to mention severe penalties for Google.

Examples of prohibited conduct include

- Agreeing with competitors about prices
- Agreeing with competitors to rig bids or to allocate customers or markets
- Agreeing with competitors to boycott a supplier or customer
  Other activities can also be illegal, unfair, or create the appearance of impropriety. Such activities include
- Sharing competitively sensitive information (e.g., prices, costs, market distribution) with competitors
- Entering into a business arrangement or pursuing a strategy with the sole purpose of harming a competitor
- Using Google's size or strength to gain an unfair competitive advantage

Although the spirit of these laws is straightforward, their application to particular situations can be quite complex.

Google is committed to competing fair and square, so please contact Ethics & Compliance if you have any questions about the antitrust laws and how they apply to you. Any personnel found to have violated Google's Antitrust Policies will, subject to local laws, be disciplined, up to and including termination of employment. If you suspect that anyone at the company is violating the competition laws, notify Ethics & Compliance immediately.

Antibribery Laws

Like all businesses, Google is subject to lots of laws, both United States and non-United States, that prohibit bribery in virtually every kind of commercial setting. The rule for us at Google is simple—don't bribe anybody, anytime, for any reason.

Dealing With Government Officials

The United States also has strict rules that severely limit the ability of a company or its employees to give gifts and business courtesies to a U.S. government official and also limit the official's ability to accept such gifts. The Honest Leadership and Open Government Act prohibits giving any gifts, including travel and other courtesies, to members, officers, and employees of the U.S. Senate and House of Representatives unless they fit within one of a number of specific exceptions. Gifts to employees of the U.S. executive branch are also regulated and subject to limits. Finally, state and local government officials in the United States are also subject to additional legal restrictions. Consult Google's Anti-Bribery and Government Ethics Policy before giving any such gifts or business courtesies and obtain all required preapprovals. In sum, before offering any gifts or business courtesies to an U.S. or other government official, you should consult Google's Anti-Bribery and Government Ethics Policy. Carefully follow the limits and prohibitions described there, and obtain any required preapprovals. If after consulting the Policy you aren't sure what to do, ask Ethics & Compliance.

ITEM 1—PAGE 191

Memorandum

To: Russell Crowe, Supervisor/Manager

From: Mitchell Muscell, Director

Date: May 18, 20XX

Re: <u>**Congratulations on Your Promotion and Review of Job Tasks**</u>

As part of your orientation to your new position and so we get off to the right start, following is a list of tasks our supervisors/managers typically handle. Some days there is so much going on at one time that new supervisors/managers become overwhelmed. I want to be able to coach and mentor you on things you need help with ASAP.

Please write a memo indicating what your course of action would be in handling the following situations. Also, assume they are happening simultaneously. Have this memo ready for my review by May 23, 20XX. Then we will meet to discuss it and move forward.

- When you arrive to work you are told that two key staff called in sick.
- You find 10 e-mail messages in outlook.
- Your performance activity monthly report is due today.
- Payroll happens to be due today (whichever day you work on this).
- Overtime sheets for two employees need to be completed.
- Your spouse calls you from work with an emergency and leaves a message on your cell phone.
- Your newly hired administrative assistant is standing by your door and needs help. She looks worried.
- A department manager is on hold for you and according to the receptionist, he is angry.
- A new hire calls and asks for help dealing a shipping issue.

Memorandum

To: Gerard Butler, Account Representative

From: Supervisor/Manager, Kevin Costner

Date: May 9, 20XX

Subject: Letter of Counseling

On 2 days, April 30 and May 7, 20XX, you arrived late to work and on Tuesday (May 8, 20XX) the very next day you left work early without authorization. This is unacceptable behavior because of staffing coverage issues.

We need to meet to discuss this.

In the meantime, this is a letter of counseling, which will go in your personnel file. You are in violation of **Consistency**—reliability, predictability, and good judgment, **Tardiness** (work, court, off duty)—**Leaving assignment without authorization** Category A is the lowest level of discipline. Repetition of similar misconduct or first offenses of a more serious misconduct may lead to progressively higher penalty ranges in Categories B, C, and culminating in Category D, which includes termination of employment.

Your actions are in violation of the corporation's general orders and any further violations of the general orders will lead to progressive discipline up to and including termination.

_____	_____
Gerard Butler	Date

_____	_____
Kevin Costner	Date

E-mail Message

To: All Newly Promoted Supervisors/Managers

From: Mitchell Muscell

Date: May 15, 20XX

Re: **Mentoring and Coaching Employees**

As you all know; mentoring subordinates is of utmost importance to me. I am well aware that many employees do not feel that their supervisors know how to mentor or coach them OR that they do not take the time to do so. Given that you are newly promoted supervisor/manager in a first-line supervisory position, I want your ideas on ways you think your supervisor should coach and mentor you.

Please submit your list of ideas to your director who will review them and submit to me. I will be compiling a report, which will contain many of your ideas.

This is due on May 23, 20XX.

Thank you.

Mitchell Muscell

Cc: Henry Hubris, VP Operations

Phone Message

To: Kevin Costner, Supervisor/Manager

From: Suzy Que, Receptionist

Date: May 11, 20XX

Re: <u>**Called in Sick Will Be Out Several Days/Family Problems**</u>

Gerard Butler called in sick and will be out for the next few days. He must deal with some family problems. He sounded very upset.

Handwritten Note in Taped Envelope Addressed to Kevin Costner

May 10, 20XX

Mr. Costner, we did not want to email, put on voice mail or send a txt message. We do not want to get in trouble. But we feel this situation needed to be brought to your attention immediately. We are writing this to you because we know Edward Norton will continue this behavior if we do not report it.

We were in the break room last night and we heard Edward Norton speaking to another staff person, Robert Downey about one of our new employees. He made a sexist comment about Tammy Teeze. He said, "She is the best-looking female ever to work here, she is stacked, has a great butt and will be fun to tease, get it TEEZE." Then he walked off laughing.

X Corporation/Organization Observation Report

NAME: Javier Bardem			**Job Title:** Senior Account Representative	
DIVISION:	**SHIFT:** DAY		**DATE:** April 20, 20XX	
ACTIVITY OBSERVED:	Exemplary:	■	Unsatisfactory: ❏	
I. KNOWLEDGE				
A. Rules, Policies, Procedures		■		❏
B. Techniques of Assignment		■		❏
II. CARE OF EQUIPMENT AND PERSONAL APPEARANCE				
A. Vehicle and Equipment		■		❏
B. Business Attire and Personal Equipment		■		❏
C. Appearance and Grooming				■
D. Other Equipment		■		❏
III. WORK EFFECTIVENESS				
A. Planning and Organization		■		❏
B. Handling Stressful Situations		■		❏
C. Judgment and Decision-Making		■		❏
D. Coaching and Mentoring People				■
E. Volume of Work				■
F. Quality of Work				
IV. ABILITY TO COMMUNICATE				
A. Spoken Communication		■		❏
B. Written Communication		■		❏
V. PERSONAL FACTORS				
A. Conduct		■		❏
B. Attitude		■		❏
C. Dependability		■		❏
D. Cooperativeness		■		❏
E. Initiative		■		❏

ADDITIONAL COMMENTS/FACTS ON REVERSE SIDE: THE SUBJECT OF THIS REPORT HAS SIGNED AND RECEIVED A COPY

Javier is an outstanding employee who works quite well with all of his subordinates. He is punctual and often remains on the job after his shift to assist his employees. He will not, however, spend time mentoring them. He also acts like a "know-it-all" and brags about his experience working for other companies.

Discounting these factors, he is a good manager with a lot of knowledge to share.

SUBMITTED BY: Kevin Costner   **DATE:** April 23, 20XX

SUBMITTED TO: Mitchell Muscell   **DATE:** April 23, 20XX

Facts/Narrative

By signing this I am acknowledging that I have read it, discussed it with the supervisor, and will receive a copy once signed. I understand that I may respond, in writing, within 5 calendar days of receipt.

Date: <u>April 26, 20XX</u>   Signed: _____

Javier Bardem

Cc: files

E-mail Message

From: Javier Bardem

Sent: May 10, 20XX

To: Kevin Costner

Subject: Dwayne Johnson's **Low Morale and Negative Attitude**

I am having significant morale problems with Dwayne Johnson. All he does is complain. He also keeps talking about retirement and since he started talking about it, his attitude has become very negative. He complains about having the shortage of staff, that he has already retired once. His low morale and negative attitude can bring down the morale of my team. I wonder if this has to do with his age. Maybe he should retire.

Can we meet as soon possible to discuss this and for you to give me management tips. Thanks.

Javier Bardem

Memorandum

To: All Supervisors and Managers

From: Mitchell Muscell

Date: April 26, 20XX

Re: **Mandatory Effective Communications Training**

As you all know, communication is the greatest asset we have as an organization. In this regard, we budgeted for a consultant who is a national expert on communications. She and her team have provided training to thousands of employees from corporations around the world.

Given the cost of this 8-hour training program, everyone must attend. On a date, which has yet to be finalized, training will also be provided to all subordinate staff.

The date and time is: May 26, 2018.

Henri Hubris

E-mail Message

TO: ALL DEPARTMENT HEADS

DATE: May 17, 20XX

FROM: Peter Perfectionius, Annual Blood Drive Chairman

SUBJECT: **ANNUAL BLOOD DRIVE**

We are approaching the time for preparations for the biannual employees' blood drive. As you know, twice a year someone in each department has taken on the responsibility of recruiting donors. Traditionally, I have requested assistance at the supervisor and worker level of the organization for the donor recruiters. I believe after 6-years and approximately 12 blood drives, I am encountering some obvious obstacles that are affecting the effectiveness of the drives.

I attribute the dwindling numbers of units to two main reasons:

1. Stagnation of the recruiters, because those who are willing to volunteer their efforts has boiled down to a small nucleus of people whom I have had to repeatedly return to.

2. Although management has supported our efforts from a distance, there has never been a concerted thrust from management to show support for the program. I believe that a visible effort from the "management team" would enhance the program overall in a couple of ways. First, it would give the traditional volunteers a needed break. Second, it would display that this program is not an employee association, rah rah, but rather a genuine effort of all corporate employees to fulfill a genuine and increasingly more critical community need. That being more and more resistance to participate in donations and the subsequent shortages of supply available to the Red Cross.

    I regret that this last obstacle is something that will thwart your efforts if you choose to participate as a recruiter, because for the most part it conceals a more real fear of needles, which is a reality we have to live with; however, I'll trust your innovative minds to create the spirit of giving.

    I will need a recruiter from each department and remote facility location. Please advise ASAP as there is a recruitment meeting scheduled for May 28, 20XX, at 1:00 p.m.

Thank you.

E-mail Message

From: Edward Norton

Sent: May 11, 20XX

To: Kevin Costner

Subject: **Vacation Request**

I know this is short notice, but I would like to request vacation time for May 12 to 16.

However, it is not urgent and if you do need me to come in, leave word on my answering machine since I will be away those days. If I don't hear from you (knowing how busy you are), I will assume that it's okay.

Again, sorry for the short notice, but my entire family is excited about this opportunity.

Edward Norton

April 20XX				
Mon	**Tue**	**Wed**	**Thu**	**Fri**
2	3	4	5	6
9	10	11	12	13
16	17	18	19	20
23	24	25	26	27
30				

May 20XX						June
Sun	**Mon**	**Tue**	**Wed**	**Thu**	**Fri**	**Sat**
		1	2	3	4	5
6	7	8	9	10	11	12
13	14	15	16	17	18	19
20	21	22	23	24	25	26
27	28	29	30	31		

GENERIC MANAGEMENT IB MULTIPLE-CHOICE QUESTIONS

Problem Analysis/Problem-Solving and Judgment/Decision-Making

Question 1

What are the key issues addressed in the IB exercise?

A

Vacation requests, blood drive, and completion of an employee's performance appraisal.

B

Human Resources problems, policies and procedures input, and scheduling of training.

C

Employee problems and documents to complete, sexual harassment complaint, and review of work tasks to complete.

D

Blood drive, vacation leave request, employee called out sick for several days, mentoring and coaching of employees.

E

All of the above.

Question 2

Which item numbers below is/are the most important in terms of criticality and risk to the company?

A

3, 5, and 7

B

6

C

2, 8

D

1

E

All are critical and potential risks for the company

Planning and Organizing

Question 3

From a planning and organizing perspective, which item(s) would you complete first?

A

2 and 6

B

3, 5, and 7

C

3, 5, 7, and 8

D

1 and 4

E

All of the above

Judgment/Decision-Making

Question 4

Which employees are having problems?

A

Kevin Costner, Robert Downey

B

Javier Bardem, Edward Norton

C

Gerard Butler, Javier Bardem, Edward Norton

D

Suzy Que, Mitchell Muscell

E

Dudley Dogbert, Peter Perfectionius

Question 5

According to the items, which employee appears to be having the most problems?

A

Kevin Costner

B

Suzy Que

C

Edward Norton

D

Javier Bardem

E

Gerard Butler

Problem Analysis/Problem-Solving and Judgment/ Decision-Making

Question 6

From the following list, what was reported about Edward Norton? He

A

Allegedly embezzled money.

B

Is inconsistent and unreliable.

C

Called in sick for several days.

D

Made a sexist comment about a female employee.

E

None of the above.

Question 7

Which employee is displaying a negative attitude and can reduce the morale of other employees?

A

Javier Bardem

B

Dwayne Johnson

C

Edward Norton

D

Robert Downey

E

Tyler Reis

Question 8

Who is Tammy Teeze? She

A

Is the woman whom Edward Norton made a sexist comment about.

B

Is the VP of HR.

C

Is a receptionist.

D

Works with Dwayne Johnson and is also very negative.

E

All of the above.

Judgment and Decision-Making

Question 9

What is the problem with Edward Norton allegedly stating, "She is the best-looking female ever to work here, she is stacked, has a great butt and will be fun to tease, get it TEEZE."

A

Nothing, Norton was only kidding about her to another male.

B

Nothing, because it is not a proven fact.

C

It probably violates policies and procedures and is unwanted behavior. If Tammy Teeze was in the room at the time, it may have been a violation of Title VII.

D

It creates a hostile work environment.

E

Both C and D.

Question 10

What actions would you take against Edward Norton?

A

I would prepare the paperwork for his termination.

B

Nothing because the person who wrote the note could be lying.

C

If what he said is proven to be true, I would follow standard operating procedures regarding this kind of situation.

D

I would call him in to my office and ask him for his side of the story.

E

I would call him and Robert Downey in to my office and discuss the seriousness of their behavior.

Planning and Organizing, Problem Analysis/Problem-Solving, and Judgment and Decision-Making

Question 11

Regarding Item 2, which of the following actions from the bulleted list would you complete first?

A

Call my wife back; tell my administrative assistant to tell the manager I will call him later; return the new hire's phone call.

B

Check which e-mails are the most important; call my wife back; find out who called in sick.

C

Ask my new administrative assistant what she needs; help the new hire with the shipping issue; call my wife back.

D

Call my wife back; tell the receptionist I will speak with department manager as soon as I find out what the emergency my wife has; motion to my administrative assistant to hold on.

E

Have my administrative assistant to call some staff in on their day off; speak to the department manager; call my wife back.

Problem Analysis/Problem-Solving and Judgment and Decision-Making

Question 12

What is significant about Item 4?

A

The due date.

B

Some employees do not mentor or coach their employees.

C

That Director Muscell thinks that mentoring and coaching employees is important to him.

D

Muscell wants each employee to submit their list of ideas.

E

Both B and C.

Dealing With People and Judgment and Decision-Making

Question 13

What actions would you take regarding Gerard Butler after he returns from sick leave (Item 5)?

A

None, because employees are entitled to call in sick.

B

Find out why he was out sick for so many days.

C

Meet with him to find out if he is okay (because of family problems and he was upset) and offer him any assistance I can.

D

Schedule a meeting with him and ask him what he was upset about.

E

All of the above.

Dealing With People and Judgment and Decision-Making

Question 14

Regarding Javier Bardem, how would you handle a meeting with him?

A

Ask him to rereview the report, ask for his comments, have him sign it.

B

Review the contents with him, ask for his input, commend him on his strengths, coach him on the need to mentor his employees, and tell him he should not act like a "know it all," and why.

C

Tell him that I am sorry that Costner did not have a meeting with him and then ask him to sign the document.

D

Schedule him for training on how to better deal with subordinates, and then meet with him.

E

Both A and D.

Judgment and Decision-Making

Question 15

Regarding Dwayne Johnson's low morale and negative attitude, what is problematic about the e-mail message Javier Bardem sent to Kevin Costner?

A

Javier Bardem made a comment about his age and "that maybe he should retire" which could be a violation of company policies and procedures.

B

Bardem's comment about Johnson's age could result in a hostile work environment for him (Note: Managers should not disseminate e-mails sent to them from their employees to other people in the organization).

C

Nothing, because employees who have negative attitudes can cause morale problems for other employees.

D

An older employee talks about retiring at work when there is a staff shortage.

E

Dwayne Johnson should not be telling everyone he plans to retire.

Problem Analysis and Decision-Making

Question 16

What is the significance about Dudley Dogbert's memo asking for input about the writing of the company Code of Ethics?

A

The company does not have a Code of Ethics and needs one.

B

It is from the VP of HR who is soliciting input and reflects a collaborative approach to improving company operations.

C

The sample policy and procedures were free and came from Google.

D

Both A and C.

E

Case examples from employees will be included and used in a future training program.

Dealing With People and Judgment and Decision-Making

Question 17

Regarding Edward Norton's sexist comment about Tammy Teeze, what is/are the best initial actions to take?

A

Set up a meeting with Robert Downey to reverify this.

B

Refer the issue to the HR Department.

C

Meet with Tammy Teeze and assure her that this behavior will not be tolerated and apologize to her.

D

Nothing until the situation is investigated by the HR Department.

E

Prepare disciplinary paperwork for Edward Norton, meet with Mitchell Muscell, and then schedule a meeting with him.

Planning and Organizing and Judgment and Decision-Making

Question 18

If you were actually required to handle all 11 items by writing e-mails or memos about the items, which five items would you complete first?

A

3, 5, 6, 7, 8

B

2, 6, 11, 1, 4

C

4, 9, 10, 11, 2

D

1, 2, 3, 4, 5

E

1, 4, 6, 5, 3

Planning and Organizing

Question 19

There are dates for many of the IB items. How can/should the dates be used?

A

To schedule important meetings.

B

Establish a chronology of events about an employee or issue.

C

To ensure that assignments from superiors are completed on time.

D

To ensure that tasks assigned to subordinates are completed on time.

E

All of the above.

Question 20

Which items should be completed last?

A

1, 2, 4, 5, 9

B

5, 9, 10, 11

C

3, 5, 10, 11

D

1, 3, 5, 7

E

2, 4, 6, 8, 10

Judgment and Decision-Making

Question 21

What should be done about Edward Norton's e-mail message sent to Kevin Costner, and why?

A

Nothing, because the date has already passed.

B

Find out if Costner approved it.

C

Nothing, because Norton stated that his vacation request was not urgent.

D

All of the above are plausible.

E

Nothing, because Costner no longer works for the company.

CHAPTER 11
Problem Analysis Cases

OVERVIEW

This chapter has four problem analysis cases dealing with a variety of different issues. The cases are longer than the scenarios that you experienced in previous chapters and more things are occurring or have occurred.

Even though the title of this chapter references *problem analysis*, other innate abilities are measured in many of the questions.

In general, with a problem analysis case the candidates are given a set of instructions including a time limit on preparing the case. The case instructions may require the candidate to prepare an oral or written report and/or both. Because the cases in this chapter are longer than the ones you previously dealt with, you will need to read each one more thoroughly before answering the multiple choice questions.

Do not assume things that are not written, do not make anything up, and pretend that you are at work. Moreover, even though there may be other ways to handle the different situations presented in each case other than the options provided in A–E, select the answer you feel is the most appropriate.

The idea for the first case about strategic planning was obtained from a book which is cited at the beginning of the case. My ideas for three other cases were adapted from Harvard Business Review case studies. The reference citations are included at the beginning of the case. If you bought the eBook, you can access the case studies on line.

CASES

- **Hospital complaint about peer, work schedule, communication, and patient experience scores**
- **Which candidate should be promoted?**

- Toxic workplace
- Falsified sales reports

Case 1: Hospital Complaint About Peer, Work Schedule Communication, and Patient Experience Scores

Skills Measured: Planning and Organizing, Problem Analysis/Problem-Solving, Judgment, Decision-Making, and Emotional Intelligence Constructs

Gerry Gemstone is a Nurse Manager of a large regional hospital company. She works in the geriatric unit. She was promoted to the position 6-months ago. She was recently awarded a master's degree in nursing management, which was one of the criteria for obtaining a management position. One of her more difficult tasks as a Manager of the unit is the use of improvement to the electronic work schedule including honoring time off requests. She is still learning how to use the electronic scheduling system. The system is relatively new and still has some bugs.

Gerry replaced a Clinical Manager who worked in the unit for 6-years and retired. One of the many standard operating procedures (SOP) is a safety huddle with all staff at 7:00 a.m. and again at 7:00 p.m. All staff are required to be present at the huddle when they start their shift (i.e., 7:00 a.m. or 7:00 p.m.).

The hospital has comprehensive and well-written policies and procedures that are regularly updated and disseminated by the HR department. Additionally, whenever a policy is in the process of being changed, hospital management staff may participate by providing input. Team collaboration is part of the culture of the hospital. Managers are also permitted, where applicable, to modify a procedure to accommodate staff needs. There are clear policies and procedures for attendance and paid time off, which includes paid vacation and sick time and advance scheduling of holidays.

Complaint About Nurse Peer

One Sunday afternoon Gerry receives a text message from one of her nurses, Reese Withering who asks to speak to her. Gerry immediately calls Reese and she advises Gerry that she is having a difficult time working with a particular nurse, Jeremy Remer. Gerry listens to her concerns and asks Reese to send her a detailed email. Within a week after receiving the email, the next week Gerry receives more office visits and reports from her charge nurses about the same employee. The verbal reports indicate that he arrives late and leaves abruptly before the shift change and without completing his reports. Moreover, at least once a week he also causes problems with the schedule. Gerry wonders why this problem is only now being reported to her.

Over the new 2-days, three nurses individually come to her and complain about Jeremy's poor communication skills and unprofessional behavior but do not provide any specific examples. They claim it is his general attitude and behavior as well as lack of empathy for the patients. They state their complaints and then rush off to take care of their patients. Based on the three nurse's tone of voice, facial expressions, and overall demeanor, Gerry knows that they are upset.

Electronic Work Schedule

Gerry's predecessor was a whiz at managing the electronic schedule, but even after 6-months she is still learning how to use it. Every week she has to make several last-minute scheduling changes because some staff call in sick or have an emergency, and so on. The procedure requires staff to request their days off on paper form which she has to approve and sign and then make the change(s) in the online system. Jerry does her best to ensure all of her staff are happy with their schedules, particularly days off for holidays, which each employee having a preference.

However, she notices that everyone wants Christmas and New Year's Eve off. She has to make some tough decisions and deny some staff these days off. They are not happy and come to her office to complain.

Patient Experience Scores

Every Monday morning Gerry receives a report of the Hospital Consumer Assessment of Healthcare Providers and Systems (HCAHPS) scores, which reflect her unit's Patient Experience. The HCAHPS survey ask patients who are discharged home many questions about their recent hospital stay, which includes communication with nurses and doctors, the responsiveness of hospital staff, cleanliness, and communication about medicines. The same week after Gerry receives the new verbal complaint about Jeremy, she happens to be reading the HCAHPS scores and it is apparent that the unit has to work on responsiveness regarding the "Call Bell." Patients have reported that it was taking too long to have someone answer the call bell and then to come to the room for assistance. Moreover the scores have declined compared to the last three reports.

Question 6

Regarding the complaints about Remer which is/are the **MOST APPROPRIATE** actions that Gerry should take?

A

Review Remer's personnel file and all attendance records; document in writing complaints made against him (but exclude complainant's names); review his past record; prepare materials to cover in meeting with him.

B

Meet with her supervisor to review past and present complaints and her plan of action and then meet with Remer.

C

Review progressive disciplinary policy and determine what if any, action(s) should be taken against Remer; develop a personal improvement plan (PIP), to map out how he could improve his communication skills with his peers, physicians, and patients.

D

Prepare Remer's termination paperwork; review with supervisor and HR department; schedule termination date.

E

A and B are the most appropriate but C can be done later.

Question 7

Gerry finds out that Remer is actually the only person who does not respond to the call bell in a timely manner. What should she do about this?

A

Validate the number of times Remer was late responding to the call bell.

B

Document the dates and times Remer did not respond to the call bell.

C

Meet with Remer and present the data to him; ask for his input as to why he was late.

D

In a meeting with Remer, ask him how he plans to correct this deficiency; explain the consequences of him continuing to not respond to the call bell in a timely manner; obtain his commitment; document what transpires in the meeting.

E

All of the above.

Question 8

How should Gerry deal with the nurses who complained about Remer?

A

Meet with each nurse individually and then in a group find out more about what ways is Remer being unprofessional; discuss and document. Also open the conversation in order to identify any other of their concerns.

B

Nothing because they already complained about Remer.

C

Thank each nurse for their feedback.

D

A and E are the most appropriate.

E

Ask them to make sure they immediately document in writing (date, time, etc.).

Question 9

What should Gerry do about the problems with the continual scheduling changes and unhappy nurses?

A

Conduct a review and analysis of the number of and reasons for changes; note which ones are outside standard policy and procedures; rewrite the policy and procedures; ensure changes work with online system.

B

Meet with each nurse and ask him/her why they are unhappy; document; ensure them that she will attempt to make changes based on everyone's input and then conduct focus group meetings with all nurses and brainstorm ways to change system. Tell them their input is essential.

C

Refer problems to the HR and IT departments so they can make the changes.

D

Hold each nurse accountable who has violated the policy and procedures on scheduling; make sure every nurse knows that they cannot always have holidays off.

E

Both A and B.

Question 10

Which below is/are the **BEST** ways for Gerry to deal with the unacceptable HCAHPS scores?

A

Schedule a staff meeting to discuss patient experience scores and the whys behind the procedures; obtain their input on how to resolve the problem.

B

Ask them to document on a time log how long it takes to respond and submit the log to her.

C

Review and analyze current and past scores and then determine what to do.

D

Refer the problem to her boss for resolution; dealing with HCAHPS scores are above her pay grade.

E

Contact neighboring hospitals and try to obtain their scores; speak to other nursing professionals for their suggestions.

Case 2: Which Candidate Should Be Promoted?

Adapted from Polzer, J. T. (2018, May–June). Case study trust the algorithm or your gut? A VP decides which candidate to promote. *Harvard Business Review*, pp. 147–151.

Skills Measured: Planning and Organizing, Problem Analysis/Problem-Solving, Judgment, Decision-Making

Overview

Candace Bergen is a VP of Marketing for a global beauty products company. She has a vacancy for a marketing manager whose responsibilities would include managing a portfolio of 56 beauty products. One candidate is a white female, Sally Struthers, a brand manager for the skin care line.

Another candidate is a Chinese male, Wang Wei, who is considered by his previous supervisor to be one of the sharpest, motivated and creative talents. He is the brand manager for the men's skin care lines. Wang's resume was forwarded to Candace by the HR department because Wei was not included in the list of internal candidates who were notified of the opening to apply. This was because he was only recently hired by the company and his credentials had not been entered into the Human Resources Information System (HRIS). The third candidate is a Hispanic female, Gabriela Abrego, a brand manager for women's specialty spa products.

Candidates and Algorithm Data

Based on the analytics screening tool, which is part of the HRIS system, the HR Director, William Macey suggested Wei because he was a 95% match for the position. Struthers's match was 89% and Abrego's was 90%.

According to Macey, for several of the recent internal promotions and three or more external hires, the analytics tool has been a very good predictor. Although Bergen is impressed with Wei's credentials, she does not like that the HR department is using an analytics tool as the primary basis for referring candidates. Although Wei's prediction index was higher than both females, his other recent accomplishments were similar to those of Struthers and Abrego.

Based on their credentials, all three candidates were equal in respect to years of marketing and supervisory experience. In addition, both possessed MBA degrees from high-ranking schools.

One of Macey's staff prepared a matrix that compared each candidate's abilities based on HR's initial interviews. A 1 to 5 rating scale was used where a 5 is excellent. After reviewing the matrix on the next page. Bergen could not make up her mind as to which person to promote. Subsequently Macey strongly suggested that she conduct a structured interview with each candidates and summarized in an email to her, some of the most important components:

1. More valid than an unstructured interview and has better predictability.
2. Questions are job related.
3. The questions can tap into abilities that are important for job success (e.g., dealing with people).
4. All candidates are asked the same questions; given the same amount of time to answer the questions, are treated the same in the interview, and so on.
5. A panel of trained raters are used whose training includes how to record the candidate's responses.
6. Each question has response standards.
7. A well-defined rating scale is used.
8. Can help to reduce internal biases.

After having reviewed the scores, credentials and other related data, Bergen tells Macey that she knows a great deal about each candidate and thinks that her judgment is the most important criteria; she should just promote the person who she believes to be the best candidate.

Matrix: Candidate Characteristics and Abilities

Name	Personality Characteristics, Languages Spoken, Most Recent Accomplishments	Planning and Organizing	Working as a Team	Judgment/ Decision-Making	Dealing With People
Sally Struthers	Outgoing, talkative, conscientious, fast thinker, analytical, energetic, articulate, provides clear and fast responses to questions **Languages spoken:** English, Spanish, and some German **Most recent accomplishments:** Designed and implemented new subscription service and newsletter	Well above average	Above average	Very good	Excellent
Wang Wei	Analytical, conscientious, reserved, soft spoken, very patient, articulate, thinks a few seconds before answering questions, avoids eye contact, but when providing answers smiles at panel members **Most recent accomplishments:** Updated and reintroduced old product line, which was a huge success; sales increased by 70% **Languages spoken:** Mandarin Chinese, English, some Japanese, and Spanish	Excellent	Well above average	Very good	Well above average
Gabriela Abrego	Very animated, smiles a lot, conscientious, very talkative, a bit tangential when answering questions but answers a specific, energetic **Recent accomplishments:** Expanded international network by 35% **Languages spoken:** Spanish, English, and understands some Arabic				

ADDITIONAL ALGORITHM DATA INFORMATION AND BERGEN'S THOUGHTS

Macey sends Bergen a few facts about algorithms for Bergen to consider:

- Some people are averse to algorithms because they prefer their own intuitive judgment.
- According to Pew Research, a majority of Americans (75%) would not apply for a job that relied solely on an algorithm.
- As more data is fed into the system, algorithms should be more reliable.
- Algorithms may not be able to predict how well a person can work on a team.

A week later Bergen is in her office drinking her second cup of coffee and thinking about whom to promote. The thoughts that go through her mind, back and forth, back and forth then she writes down and reviews each statement.

- The algorithm is brand new and is only one predictor of success.
- I do not believe that the data will prevent me from being biased; I want to promote who I feel the most comfortable with.
- Do I prefer Sally over Wei and Gabriela because I know her the best, but what would happen if Sally were passed over?
- The algorithm is not a substitute for my judgment that I think is the best, but I need to be able to justify who I promote.
- They can all do the job but I like Sally the most.
- I need to own my decision.
- I do not want morale to suffer.
- Is it really true that hiring managers make their decision on who to select in just 30 seconds? Have I done this?

A few more days go by and not only does Macey call her and ask her what she is going to do, but Bergen's immediate supervisor sends her an email asking for a time-certain update on the promotion.

Question 11

Which are the **MOST IMPORTANT** reasons for Bergen to conduct a structured interview with each candidate? To,

A

follow best practices for promoting internal candidates (e.g., multiple predictors); eliminate bias, ensure fairness, own her decision and have the documentation to support it other than the algorithm percentages and data in matrix.

B

keep morale up and prevent attrition.

C

support the HR Director's expert advice and to maintain a good relationship with him.

D

defend her promotional decision, prevent a lawsuit and turnover.

E

All of the above.

Question 12

Assume that the company has strong diversity hiring and promotional goals and policies and procedures. Also assume that there is an underrepresentation of Asians throughout the company. Moreover, Bergen has not yet decided whether she will conduct a structured interview with each candidate.

Given the information presented about Wei, which below is Bergen's **BEST** option?

A

Promote Wei to support the diversity goals and avoid a lawsuit.

B

Recommend that the vacancy be put on hold or eliminated from the budget.

C

Ask Macey to make the decision so he owns it.

D

Conduct the structured interviews, review all of the data, and promote based on who is the top-ranked candidate.

E

All of the above are viable options.

Question 13

Assume that Bergen and a panel of three other internal management peers conduct a structured interview process with the three candidates. A staff person from the recruitment and selection unit developed the interview questions and response standards and conducted training for the four raters. The result of the process is that Wei ranks number one. A consensus process was conducted and the rater's individual scores for each question were within one point. The end result is that Wei's final overall score on a 100 point scale is 10 points higher than Struthers or Abrego.

Based on your analysis of the case material, who would you recommend Bergen promote, why and what else would you do?

A

Struthers, because Bergen feels the most comfortable with her, and Bergen can promote whom she wants, and she does not feel comfortable with the algorithm process.

B

Wei, because he is the top candidate and also received the highest algorithm percentage.

C

No one because there was probably bias in the scores because the raters probably scored Wei the highest because of the company's diversity goals, and he is Asian.

D

Due to possible contamination in the scoring process, decertify the entire process, start from scratch, do not use the algorithm percentages, and have the HR department handle the entire selection process.

E

B is the most appropriate option but A may also be acceptable to top management and the HR department.

Question 14

If you were Bergen, what would you say to Struthers and Abrego?

A

Tell them that they did well, but Wei scored higher.

B

That you value them as employees and would without any guarantees, encourage them to apply for the next marketing manager position that is posted as an internal promotion.

C

Nothing because both really know that Wei is the better candidate.

D

That you appreciate them and you will give them special treatment when necessary.

E

A and B above.

Case 3: Toxic Workplace

Adapted from Ginoe, F. (2018, November–December). Case study can you fix a toxic culture without firing people? A CFO wonders how to turn around a struggling division. *Harvard Business Review*, pp. 143–147.

Skills Measured: Planning and Organizing, Problem Analysis/Problem-Solving, Judgment, Decision-Making, Emotional Intelligence Constructs

Overview

Kevin Bacon is the CFO for a company that manufactures climate control systems for homes. The Company, ClimControl, Inc. is a division of a large holding company and has been its worst performing unit for over 6-years. The turnaround expert was hired to recommend some budget cuts, which only helped a little. Give the reduction in some costs, the company is now slowly moving toward stability. The HR Director, Laurence Fishburne has expressed his concerns on numerous occasions to Bacon, the VP, Jason Thorn and CEO, Michael Milliken to deaf ears. Bacon is attending one of many financial review meetings. When he arrives, only one of eight invited to participate is there. The first person, Dudley Doozey looks at Bacon and states, *"What am I doing here. Not only have I never attended one of these meetings but I have no clue what will be covered."* He shuffles in his chair and then Marty Sulky walks in and they greet one another. Sulky takes a seat and immediately says, *"I suspect no one else will be attending the meeting. No one cares about the financials, what difference do they make? Besides, the people I have talked to lately are threatening to quit,"* after which the HR Director, Fishburne walks in and takes a seat.

Doozey and Sulky roll their eyes at him and say nothing. Bacon greats him and once Fishburne takes a seat and places his papers on the table, Doozey says, *"When I walked into the plant today, there was total silence, no one looked at or greeted me. People hate coming to work here. My buddies just clock in, work, take their breaks, eat lunch, and leave. It really does suck working here. What do you think Laurence?"* Fishburne responds, *"You know what I think, I have voiced my concerns on several occasions verbally and in writing to top management."* *"Yeah,"* says Doozey, *"this used to be a fun place to work, we used to have company picnics, Friday night parties, on-site lunches, bonuses, but making a living wage of $15 an hour isn't cutting it. I do not trust anyone"* Sulky responds, *"Well what do you expect, the culture sucks and what is referred to?, I think some say it is a toxic place workplace. If I were 10 years younger I would leave."* Ten minutes pass and no one else arrives so Bacon suggests that the meeting be terminated. He removes his cell phone from his pants pocket and as everyone walks out of the room he walks slowly to his office shaking his head.

When he returns to his office, he calls VP Thorn's office and speaks to his administrative assistant. She advises him that Thorn is on vacation, will be back tomorrow and she will have Thorn call him. The next day Thorn comes to Bacon's office and he fills him in on what transpired the day before. The essence of what Thorn told Bacon during the meeting includes:

- The company should do some house cleaning; that is, fire all of the negative employees regardless of the number.
- Select them partially based on interviews with their coworkers; and whomever is the least preferred based on their negativity should be included on the termination list.
- Make an announcement that layoffs will take place soon.
- We have a ton of over 40 workers who have been with the company a long time, but some of them should also fired.
- Values are important and we need employees who embrace our values and can act/behave in a positive manner.

After his meeting with Thorn, Bacon knows that he must act ASAP.

Question 15

What is problematic about firing a large number of long-term employees?

A

It reduces the morale of the survivors.

B

Age discrimination.

C

Reduced productivity.

D

Some or many of the remaining employees may quit.

E

All of the above.

Question 16

Which below is/are the **BEST** option(s) for fixing the toxic culture?

A

Mandated culture change training for all employees.

B

Based upon manager input, terminate only the worst performers and those who are the most negative.

C

Administer, score, and disseminate an employee engagement survey.

D

Top managers should meet with all employees, in small groups and brainstorm with them options to deal with the issues.

E

B, C, and D are viable options with D being the first step before a reduction in force (RIF) program is initiated.

Question 17

What are the benefits of retaining most of the employees who are not problems?

A

They have institutional knowledge.

B

They can help to improve the culture.

C

Less likelihood of lawsuits.

D

A and B only.

E

Reduced training costs for hiring new staff.

Question 18

What can Bacon and Fishburne do instead of acting on Thorn's recommendations?

A

Make sure via personal interviews that the employees who are not fired are the right ones to help rebuild the culture.

B

Advise the employees exactly where the company is, what the culture problems are and that they are needed to help make the improvements.

C

Empower the interested and eager employees to serve as unofficial change leaders and work with the HR department on the initiative.

D

Communicate with all employees how vital and important they are to the company and that management will listen to their concerns and suggestions, and do something about them.

E

B, C, and D with D being the initial step.

Case 4: Falsified Sales Report

Adapted from Pure, S. (2019, September–October). Case study your star salesperson lied. Should he get a second chance? *Harvard Business Review*, pp. 156–161.

Skills Measured: Planning and Organizing, Problem Analysis/Problem-Solving, Judgment, Decision-Making

Overview

Assume that you are Don Johnson, the Sales Director for Full Bodied, a company that designs, manufacturers, and distributes custom-made athletic clothing for all ages. You are not a big user of social media but use it because you have to.

You attended the university with Joe Pesci who was hired by the company through the normal process. You referred him for a few openings and he was offered a position in your division. During his tenure, you have done your best to keep your long-term friendship with him private and outside of work. Pesci was one of the company's top sales people and always met or exceeded his sales goals. In fact he was in the top 50% for the past 4-quarters. He brought in over $350,000 in sales a year. Pesci is also well respected by his colleagues, is a great consensus builder and receives outstanding customer evaluations.

What Pesci Did

You log onto the company site and go to his page. It is the time of the month when you review the end of the month sales reports. Based on your preliminary review of the report, it appears that he falsified some of his entries. You know this because he was on leave when he recorded calls with customers. Moreover, a few weeks before his vacation he called in sick for a few days because he said he was sick with the flu. You check out his tweet feed and find out that he was watching a ball game with a friend at home when he was supposed to be sick in bed with a bad flu. Based on this data, you contact your boss, the VP of Sales, Yusef Siddhartha and advise him of your findings.

The company has a Code of Ethics that includes a zero-tolerance policy for ethics violations. Siddhartha reviews the data and agrees that Pesci falsified the report. You call the VP of HR, Katie Holmes, and advise her of the findings. She comes to your office and reviews the data. You decide to start the process of dealing with Pesci's falsified entries by calling him for a one-on-one meeting during which time you will document what he tells you. You tell them that once the meeting is over you will report back to back to Siddhartha and Holmes.

Meeting With Pesci

During the meeting, Pesci is very open with you about the false entries. He admits falsifying the report and justifies his actions based on the following:

- Sales are poor because of competition from South Korea.
- His wife needs a great deal of assistance with their new baby.
- He made the calls to the customers but on different days.
- He was afraid that he would not meet his sales goals and didn't know what to do.
- He knows he used poor judgment and decision-making but was under great pressure and stress.

During the meeting, Pesci also pleads with you to not fire him and references your long-term relationship. He also notes that based on his memory, a few other employees violated the ethics code and kept their jobs. For example, another employee falsified a time sheet and she kept her job.

Question 19

Instead of firing Pesci which below are the **BEST** alternatives?

A

Place him on probation for a period of 90-days during which time all of his work will be closely reviewed.

B

Require that he attend a refresher ethics workshop.

C

Make him pay back his most recent pay increase via payroll deductions.

D

Write a legal agreement that stipulates if he has any other infractions he will reevaluated and may be fired, may lose his sales incentives, and his retirement benefits.

E

All are viable options but A and B are the least harsh.

Question 20

Which are the **MOST APPROPRIATE** reason(s) for terminating Pesci's employment with the company?

A

He may put the company at risk with the customers.

B

The company has a zero-tolerance policy for ethics violations.

C

It will demonstrate that the leaders in the company walk-the-talk.

D

To prevent him from suing the company.

E

A, B, and C.

Question 21

As his supervisor and friend what would you suggest he do?

A

Look for another job and you will give him a great reference.

B

Meet with an Employee Assistance counselor to help him deal with his personal problems.

C

Meet with him on an ongoing basis to help him get back on track.

D

Nothing, since he already signed the legal agreement.

E

Both B and C are essential and immediate.

Question 22

Assume a few of your peers do not agree that firing Pesci is the best decision. Considering this what are the problems with firing a top performer who has never had problems in the past?

A

They could go to work for a competitor (if they are not required to sign a noncompete agreement).

B

The employee could take some of their customers with them.

C

They could post negative comments about the company on social media sites.

D

Not being empathetic about the employee's personal problems; not having faith in him/her, being unwilling to coach him/her.

E

All of the above but D should be the priority.

GENERAL COMMENTS

I really appreciated Dr. Willis' willingness to share some personal experiences from her life. Some of her scenarios really hit home with me but most of all, I liked how she expounded on "who you know." I have heard that so many times in my life and I feel that many times people are saying networking is more important than pursuing education and credentials. I don't know which is more important, but it almost seems too broad a statement. It reminds me of the aforementioned use of "common sense." I agree with Dr. Willis. Make your way and work for what you want and in doing that, be open to new people in your life.

Don't rush to judgment: The text describes individuals who do things in a hurry as hasty and rushing is not the best action to take when making decision because it can lead to a person making a poor decision. Instead the text describes that the best components of judgment include identifying core issues, implementing decisions based on effective policies, and even seeking expert advice. I agree with these points because the best decisions I've made were when I did research, asked for advice, and made a well-thought-out decision even when under pressure.

Made me think about real-world scenarios in the workplace.

It was real-world information that will definitely be used later on in life.

Being able to apply your innate abilities to your career can be the difference between a successful and unsuccessful career. Developing skills that will help you progress in your career is ideal to show your complex skills to whoever you're working for and show them that they need someone with your skills.

Dr. Willis (2017) provides an exhaustive list of innate abilities in her book *Developing Your Innate Abilities by Experiencing Assessment Center Exercises*, which are broken down into the categories of perception and analysis, judgment/decision-making, dealing with people, adaptability, and planning and organizing. I use these daily, the better I am at all these aspects of my job function, the better my career outlook becomes.

The information in this book was a reinforcement of what I try and do every day. In my job, I often get customer complaints about how my operations team is in reviewing their files. The most common complaint is that an item we are asking for is not necessary. When one of my customers calls to complain about a condition they feel is unnecessary, rather than immediately come to a conclusion, I investigate the file to determine whether we are correct or not and then follow up accordingly.

I strongly believe that I can benefit from what I have learned in **Chapters 4** and **5** professionally. I plan on working on my judgment and decision-making skills within the workplace. It is important to understand the costs and benefits of my judgment calls. I will choose to think of all alternatives before decision-making and not assume that every situation could be handled through "common sense." I will also try my best to provide good judgment calls in order to have beneficial decision-making outcomes for the company I work for.

Developing and expanding on my innate abilities such as communication skills, team work skills, and problem-solving abilities will be essential to survive and be successful in any work environment.

According to the text, ". . . when a subordinate observes their manager behaving unethically and even immorally, the subordinate may mirror the behavior." I did not realize the effects of unethical decisions being made by leaders and how they could be transferred onto subordinate staff. After reading that section, I was able to identify these same effects in my workplace. I have managers that don't make the best leadership decisions in terms of having effective and influential communication. In turn, this has created an environment of hostile staff who disrespect and speak condescendingly to each other, as it has been translated through management that this behavior is okay.

I really enjoyed reading Dr. Willis' examples of good and bad decisions she's made throughout her career and the resulting outcomes. Whether we make excellent decisions, bad decisions, good decisions based on good judgment, or a poor decision that had a desirable outcome and became a good decision, there are lessons to learn from them all.

CHAPTER 2

Planning and organizing is crucial for long-term success in any position. As a manager, you must be able to multitask and ensure completion of projects, tasks, and responsibilities, not only by yourself but by your team. Management is a multifaceted position. By having a thorough understanding of how to use one's innate abilities as well as plan and organize, a manager will ultimately lower the stress level of the position.

A lot of times when I plan the list of things I need to get done I usually just try to make a list of everything I need to get done. However, in **Chapter 2** of the book I read, "As you might already know, planning and organizing is not as easy as you think. It does not happen by just snapping your fingers, looking at a piece of paper or the computer screen or scheduling an impromptu meeting with staff, etc. It takes time . . ." (Willis, 2017). After reading this, I realize that I do not spend enough time and effort into planning out what I need to do.

CHAPTER 3

Identifying the actual problems of a case has always been a challenge for me, but the perception and analysis questions listed **in Chapter 3** helped guide me through. I started off by listing the problems as I read the case the second time and then summarizing my findings. It gave me direction and a set of goals to accomplish. I also found through the MindTools survey, that I have a hit or miss style of problem-solving and need to work on my consistency when problem-solving.

Chapter 3 helped me come up with a new thought process when it comes to problem-solving. I now have a new understanding in how our thought process works and how to improve it. I really enjoyed the idea that the factors associated with problem-solving are individually based. That's a great point because everyone's thought process is not the same, and we shouldn't think there is one way to go about analyzing problems. My favorite tip was to "Describe the problem as simply as possible." I love that idea because sometimes I get overworked trying to explain the problem. By putting it into simple terms, it becomes less overwhelming.

Chapter 3 helped me to understand how people process and interpret their environment whether socially or professionally. I also learned how important quality leadership and effective communication can prevent boundaries and workplace conflicts.

Reading **Chapter 3** gave me the right mindset when dealing with an issue within a business organization. In order to fix a problem, you need to identify the issue, form possibilities that could create an alternative, and develop that new system moving forward.

CHAPTER 4

The text does a great job in **Chapter 4** and especially **Chapter 5**, demonstrating and explaining how judgment and decision making are interrelated. For example, **Chapter 5** asks us to use "practical judgment" and "decision-making skills" to answer the quiz questions. This is a clear indicator of the relation between both decision-making and judgment. The text in **Chapter 4** cites many examples of how judgment and decision-making are interrelated; for example, "a person's judgment impacts their decision-making" and "judgment is also involved in decision-making."

The information helped me to realize the importance of developing my judgment and decision-making skills. As a manager, I will eventually be called on to lead members of the organization. At times I may need to respond to customer or subordinate issues, ethical and moral issues, and perhaps team problems. By using the four factors listed earlier, that is, identify the issues, diagnose the problem, implement decisions, and seek guidance and research, I can ensure that I use sound judgments to make decisions.

In **Chapter 4**, I learned about other types of judgment that include moral and ethical. I learned specifically what these types of judgments focus on and how important it is to be able to make these decisions. I learned how excessive unethical and moral behavior is in organizations over "almost 40-years." The examples provided by Dr. Willis regarding personal experiences with poor judgment, unethical, and immoral behavior allowed me to grasp actual instances where poor judgment led to poor decision-making.

In **Chapter 4, Scenario 7: "Problem Employee with a Negative Personality"** helped me out a lot about how to deal with other people in a workplace just because I have a very strong personality and can get clouded by my judgment but sometimes working with that other person even if you don't want to deal with their personality doesn't mean ignoring them is the best thing, if they have an issue following the proper protocol, helping them fix their problem can benefit both parties. For example, even though they have a bad attitude by you showing them that doesn't faze you, can make them realize they need to improve their workplace attitude and then reflects good on you and shows you know how to handle a situation.

Not only did **Chapter 4** show me what poor judgment skills are, it also covered **how to exercise analytical judgment, which can help judgment skills**. I will be using this exercise at work: Seeking expert or experienced advice where appropriate, and researching issues, situations and alternatives before exercising judgment. While working with a doctor who is constantly seeing patients all day, it is tough to ask him advice on decisions. For example, while the doctor is doing his rounds with patients in the office, we can have a patient who goes to the emergency room (ER) and the hospital calls wanting to speak to our doctor. With doctor not being available, I then can ask my manager on her perspective of what she would do. As I use my daily judgment on how to make decisions, and if I run into an obstacle, I now know that it is possible to seek help from others to improve my judgment skills.

In **Chapter 4**, I also learned about how critical poor judgment can be in a workplace and how it could result in an individual losing their job. Having judgment that is flawed, clouded, impulsive, or immoral can all be factors in the severity of losing a job. At my most recent job, one of the new workers always acted on impulse and made decisions that required little thought. It eventually caught up to him because other employees noticed and began to get fed up with his behavior and actions. They ended up reporting it to our manager and he eventually lost the position as a result of his spontaneous and careless decisions.

There are many things I would like to implement in my workplace that I have learned from reading **Chapters 4 and 5**. I would certainly like to change my thought process from realistic to optimistic. I think being realistic is just as dangerous as being optimistic may be. There are certain situations at work that I believe I could take my time to evaluate what's going on and take my time to fully understand a situation prior to making a final decision, rather than hoping for the best using bad judgment.

While reading **Chapter 4**, I learned about how making ethical and moral decisions is vital to succeed. If a leader acts unethically, it can start a domino effect if a subordinate begins to mirror the leader's unethical acts. I have already seen this happen in my own workplace with an assistant manager being rude toward guests; a fellow coworker started acting like them and acted rude toward guests, as well. To make sure this will never happen for me, I have to always think what the best ethical option is and then act upon it.

In **Chapter 4**, it states that leader's ethical decisions don't just affect certain people, it affects the entire company. There is a chain reaction in the business world especially when leaders make unethical decisions. Everything starts with leadership and it is important that they set a good example and show their subordinates the ethical and moral way of going about their business. When leaders make unethical decisions, it not only can give the company a bad reputation, but it also affects the subordinates and how much they value ethical behavior when their leader shows that ethics are on the back burner.

CHAPTER 5

Some of the examples from **Chapter 5** are very insightful and great for me to bring to my own workplace. Decision-making was definitely a favorite read for me, understanding the positive outcomes in either a negative or a positive situation. Good judgment can lead you to good decision-making, and this doesn't make you a perfect employee, but it does show that you understand your own thought process and take the necessary time to cast a decision.

Reading both **Chapters 4 and 5** opened my eyes to how much judgment and decision-making are interrelated. While reading the scenarios and answering them, I was more aware of first the judgment I was making about the situation and then how this judgment had affected what my final decision was in answering the problem. After reading the chapters, I am now able to look back at some of the difficult decisions I have had to make and can see now that my judgment in those situations had a big effect on the outcome of my decision. Looking forward to decision-making, I will definitely strive to first make sure I am using good judgment and then, as a result, I will be making better decisions.

Chapter 5, Scenario 4: "Employee Drinking Problem": I took this section a bit personally but also as a learning experience because I have been in a situation when I have had a coworker I was very good friends with and I knew she was coming into work drunk and drinking on the job, but since she was a good friend of mine I didn't do anything about it and kept my mouth shut. This scenario taught me how to handle such a situation if I was ever in it again. In Question 1 "considering you are not his supervisor, what would be your decision," my "common sense" (using that word again) at that time was to keep my mouth shut but this made me realize that advising your boss as soon as possible that someone might have a drinking problem is the right step to take in this situation.

I found the examples from **Chapter 5** to be very helpful for my understanding of decision-making in the workplace. I specifically enjoyed reading the one about good decisions based on good judgment. I think I liked this one because ideally everyone would like to make good decisions based on their good judgment. Good judgment shows that a person can portray critical thinking in the workplace.

Chapter 5 discusses very in-depth research about the different aspects and results of decision-making. I found it really interesting, that according to Fitzgerald, 50% of management decisions fail. I would think a fair amount of decisions made by management would lead to failure but not half of them. I shouldn't be surprised because I've seen plenty of business decisions implemented hastily, which ultimately failed.

Chapter 5 is all about decision-making and the first point that stood out to me was the amount of research that had been done on decision-making in the workplace. This research was done on many different sizes of organizations and one finding "50% of senior management decisions fail" (Fitzgerald, 2002). For example, in my workplace, there have been many changes in the past year and many of these changes have not been successful. This just shows that not all decisions made are ideal.

The Decision-Making Model: Introduced by Miller and Byrnes in 2001. "A person who is able to self-regulate his or her decision-making, is also a person who is able to self-regulate him or herself" (Byrnes, Miller, & Reynolds, 1999, Byrnes, 2013). They considered many different aspects and styles of decision-making and looked at it from many different perspectives. What I learned from this was that everyone makes decisions in different ways and that is determined by the information they have as well as how mindful they are of the consequences and their own knowledge.

In **Chapter 5**, I learned a very interesting statistic. It is very interesting that "50% of senior management decisions fail" due to reasons such as hubris and unfair treatment of others. Many people think senior management rarely make mistakes. I also think hubris is a very interesting topic when it comes talking about management. I have definitely been in situations where senior management did not want to even consider what I had to say. Many of them thought that they are more experienced and knew exactly what needs to be done. This resulted in unfortunate results at certain times and could have been avoided by weighing all opinions.

"It is very interesting that '50% of senior management decisions fail' due to reasons such as hubris and unfair treatment of others." This definitely resonated with me. I have witnessed senior members of a company make decisions that heavily affect the success of a company and were made because of their ego and pride. I am a firm believer that experience is a teacher but sometimes employers have to realize when they need to let go of some leaders.

In Chapter 5, I also learned how to make decisions when dealing with other coworkers. They used an example about an employee having a drinking problem. I also had a similar experience when I bartended, where someone was not only drinking on the job but drinking the company's liquor. I wasn't sure how to handle that kind of situation but now I do.

In **Chapter 5**, I also learned about **ethics and morals** and how they apply to the workplace. An example they gave in the book was someone who used a sick day when they were not sick. I have had a personal experience when someone called in sick when they just wanted to spend the day with their boyfriend, which resulted in the company being understaffed for that day. This put a lot of extra work on all the other employees, which was not appreciated.

CHAPTER 10

Real work world: I thought this in-basket exercise was very cool and helped us all grasp some knowledge about what the real-world workplace will be like. The situations in this exercise were useful in guiding us regarding what decisions to make for certain employees and the issues that the organization was going through.

Critical thinking: I thought the questions about ranking certain items and pointing out specific employees were the toughest because they required the most critical thinking. Critical thinking is very important in the workplace because it helps shape the organization and leads it to success by the decisions that are made.

Applied theories: I thought the in-basket (IB) exercise provided a valuable learning experience that simulated real work environment scenarios and decisions. I felt that the exercise allowed us to apply the theories and strategies we have worked through and learned in this course to the IB assignment. As far as issues or concerns, I pretty much was able to complete the exercise without any issues or confusions. I thought this exercise was by far the most beneficial assignment over the course of the entire semester.

Learning tool: The IB exercise overall was pretty good as a learning tool. It reminded me of the predictive index (PI) employers are using now which it is used as a personality test for the hiring process.

I was a bit frustrated with myself doing the exercise because I got a couple of silly questions wrong, which were a bit tricky.

It was very interesting analyzing the IB exercise, with instances that were presented happening every day in different businesses around the world. The exercise showed not only positive and negative situations for the company, but also how to solve them in the most efficient way.

Prioritizing tasks: The IB exercise provided some valuable real-life office scenarios. I agree that learning how to prioritize tasks is an essential skill. The question about prioritizing the tasks that involved the family emergency I felt was the hardest.

The memos: An observation from the memos is that this particular company seems to have a learning environment as they are making training and mentoring a priority from the beginning. I wish more companies would recognize how important it is to develop their employees.

Handling situations in a timely manner: Another insight I gained is how one situation can escalate if not properly addressed in a timely manner or how sometimes there are reasons for employee behaviors we are not aware of unless we take the time to counsel them as with Gerard Butler and Javier Bardem.

Priority lists: I actually enjoyed doing this exercise and would have to say it was my favorite one. I know that in management you have to deal with certain issues that are similar to what was discussed in the exercise, so it was good way to get you thinking. One thing that stood out to me from the exercise was Item 4. I think it's a great idea to ask newly promoted supervisors/managers to make a list of what they need from their supervisors in terms of mentoring/coaching them. Many don't receive the proper training which I think many issues could be avoided if they did, so they can succeed in their new roles.

READER'S WORKPLACE EXPERIENCES

Considering two job offers: Years ago, I was in a situation where I had two job offers, I was considering. One paid about $10,000 more per year but I would have been working for a leader that had a reputation of being a bit tyrannical and over bearing where I would have little room for independent thinking and decision-making. The position would allow me much more autonomy in my role with a great leadership team. I decided to take the latter and wound up staying with the company for more than 10-years. Even though I left money on the table, it was a great environment to work in and happiness is more important than money.

Shipment for a project: When a poor decision becomes a good decision. I sent out a shipment for a project without the customer signing the addendum that was issued, which the customer had to sign. I scheduled a contractor to be at the site to begin the project. The project administrator told me the customer refused to sign the addendum, so I began to panic because the goods were arriving any day now. The customer signed the day the goods arrived, and the contractor was able to install right away, and the customer couldn't have been any more pleased with how quick the turnaround process was so smooth. I was praised for this, but I swore it was a horrible idea after the goods left the building.

Referring the wrong person for a position: One of my ex-coworkers was referred to my director by his mother, who has worked as a nurse for the hospital for many years. He was hired shortly after applying but after a few months he started to show his true work ethic. For example, people would catch him sleeping at his desk, he would lie about simple things, catch an attitude when he didn't want to do something, and so on. Well one day he caught an attitude with the wrong person, one of the charge nurses of a floor, and it spiraled from there. I think he felt he was untouchable since his mother referred him but that was not the case. They had compiled a list of complaints and this was just the icing on the cake, so he was terminated, which many of us felt was long overdue. Two instances of poor judgment and bad decision-making were used, one was my director who hired him because he was referred to her. The other was him for thinking he could get away with things because of his mother.

Alleged sexual harassment: About a year ago, I had to deal with a situation of alleged sexual harassment in our company. A female employee complained that a male coworker from another department was what she described as, "too touchy-feely," but she didn't want him to be fired over it. As I probed deeper, she said he would hug her and sometimes kiss her on the cheek as a greeting, he would also make comments about her appearance that made her uncomfortable. As I began the investigation, I approached his supervisor and advised him of the situation and asked whether he had observed anything. In response, I was told that the female employee would often come into the department and I interviewed the accused employee and he again restated that she had always been open to hugs and was not aware it was a problem.

Sexual harassment is a serious accusation with grave implications. A decision had to be made; do we follow the company's disciplinary policy beginning with a warning, or do we formally charge him with sexual harassment and terminate him? After careful consideration, research, and seeking advice from other managers, we decided to give a verbal warning to the offending employee.

I had a conversation with the accuser and explained our determination and asked her to inform me if the behavior did not cease immediately, I also asked that she limit interactions to what is necessary and professional. I thanked her for reporting the inappropriate behavior and assured her that if a problem occurred again, we would formally charge him with sexual harassment and terminate him. She expressed feeling grateful for our actions and happy with our decision to give him second chance.

Then, I had a conversation with the male employee and his supervisor. I explained how his actions made her feel uncomfortable and thus made the behavior inappropriate. We discussed cultural differences and appropriate business etiquette. He was very apologetic as it was not his intent to offend her, he was also grateful to be given a second chance.

This situation occurred almost a year ago, both employees are still with the company and excelling in their respective departments.

Employees using the "slip and fall" bit: I don't understand how anyone could think that feigning an on the job injury is in any way acceptable, let alone funny. It is a prime example of inappropriate, unethical, and immoral behavior. I have actually experienced this in a past job. There was an employee who complained that they had something like a shelf, or a ladder fall on them during their shift, and had to be treated at a hospital. Unfortunately, there was no documentation of the incident, no witnesses to back up their story, nor any medical records of their claimed injuries. They attempted to sue the company, but due to the lack of evidence, the case was thrown out. In the end, when the scandal broke, the employee had to leave the company due to the shift in the work environment's atmosphere.

Scamming money from foreigner's credit cards: The first thing I learned regarding judgment and decision-making is exactly how intertwined they are. I suppose I had never given it much thought before but when I take the time to separate them, I can certainly see why one rarely comes up without the other when searching Google. More specifically, the impact of moral and ethical judgment on not only my career but also those who I work with. The micro example that Dr. Willis used, where if a subordinate sees their manager behaving unethically or immorally, might be the most effective one I can think of. I have personally seen this happen before. I worked as a guest services manager at a hotel and one of the front desk supervisors figured out a way to scam money from foreigners' credit cards. He was close friends with a subordinate of his and the bad judgment rubbed off. Both were fired.

Boss having affair with another employee: Poor judgment can be a liability to the company and can result in a lawsuit against the company. At first, I didn't realize that poor judgment can led to lawsuits and liability for whom you work for. After reading the chapter and the examples, I realized that individuals who used poor judgment cause lots of problems. Employees using poor judgment showed other employees the wrong way to do things. If employees make bad judgment decisions, it could lead to the company being sued. For example, in one of my previous job, my boss was having an affair with another employee. This led to the two people (my boss and the other person) taking 2- to 3-hour lunches every day and it led other employees to making bad decisions. I actually had someone I worked with say the boss is having an affair and abusing workplace time, so why can't I do the same. So, this led to other employees doing personal things on company time and not caring.

Death in workplace: In a typical day, there are many judgment and decisions that managers have to make. These are critical to the success of many businesses and employees have to trust that managers will make the correct judgment. What stood out to me in this section was the cases of death in the workplace, many of which had been caused by bad judgment. This is an extremely real-life issue and if not taken seriously can have terrible consequences.

Unethical behavior about monthly sales numbers: Moral and ethical judgments are very important factors in the work environment. According to the book, leaders of organizations or countries who have engaged in unethical and immoral behavior can bring the organization down. I have seen this happen firsthand. The beginning of last year at my current employer, we had a chief operating officer (COO) who was very unethical with the sales numbers for every month. Once the investors began to dig into the projects and more into our system, many unforeseen situations came to the light. Within a couple of months, she was suspended and then fired. My boss was put in a terrible situation in result of her being unethical behavior.

Golf team: My personal workplace is technically not a job, but as the captain of my golf team I am looked up to by the younger players on my team that I am surrounded by. Making good decisions will help me be a good leader to my teammates along with paving a path for these guys and for their future. I will be able to help them with the mental aspect of the game and also help these guys realize that we are out here playing a sport and in the end it is not do or die. We just need to go out there and try our best to play as smart as we can to post a good number.

Friend at work being rude to a customer: I also learned how having bad judgment can cost you your job. If your judgment is clouded, flawed, or not ethically sound, you will make bad decisions. Judgment is directly related to the decisions a person makes. One day at work an employee was being rude to a customer. I immediately reported it to my boss, even though it was my friend. If I had bad judgment, I would have ignored the misconduct.

COMMENTS ABOUT SOME OF THE SCENARIOS

Rumor about one's coworkers: One of the scenarios provided in the book revolves around decision-making when presented with a rumor about one's coworkers. This is a very good scenario as everyone will, at one time or another, be faced with a situation where rumors are being spread about someone. A person who utilizes poor judgment is likely to spread the rumor rather than attempt to gather the facts. As a personal note, this is something I have witnessed all too often on Facebook. I have seen friends and family of mine post "news reports" about something that is not accurate (truly "fake news"). They were simply taken in by the story and didn't bother to consider whether there was any truth to it.

The sunk costs example: This also made me think about my own career. I work in residential real estate sales and there are times when holding onto a particular client needs to be revisited. These are some of the hardest decisions in my business. I have to try separate business and emotion to make the best decision. There are times when I can look at all I have put into a listing that just won't sell, both time-wise and financially, and convince myself to just hold on for a little longer when I may know deep down that it is time to cut ties. It is a difficult thing in business to figure out when you should wave the white flag.

An unethical situation observed or experienced in the workplace and how the latter abilities were misused by the unethical person: In my last position, we would always hire 10 to 15 employees for holiday season. There were certain rules for seasonal employees that were different than part-time and full-time employees. They could work more than 29 hours in a week, they couldn't be seasonal for more than 3-months, they had a lower pay rate, and they didn't go through as much training. When scheduling people, we had to make sure we still gave enough hours to our part-time employees so they didn't feel undervalued and received their regular work hours. We couldn't make the seasonal people do anything different than the part-time or full-time employees just because they were temporary. At the end of the "season," we could choose to keep certain employees that performed well and kept track of this throughout their time with us so we have data to back up our decisions. We could choose to keep no one or keep everyone but the hiring manager had to make the choice of what was best for business. During one season, I had to make my case to the rest of the management team about my decisions and they could support me or bring up their own reasons to keep someone or let them go.

One season the hiring manager hired her friend for seasonal work. There was no written policy against this but the person's performance was monitored more closely than other employees. When the season was over, the manager wanted to keep their friend on staff and when bringing up reasons, the final the stats that were brought to the table were higher than were actually achieved that is, the stats were falsified. That manager was brought in for a discussion and disciplinary action. Her behavior was unethical.

EXAMPLES OF LEARNING

Regulate your decision making: In **Chapter 5**, I learned that being able to self-regulate one's decision-making also means they can regulate themselves and set "adaptive targets." Having this skill can in turn help people become more reflective and let them truly think about everything before making a decision. I will try to implement this into my life as well and work on self-regulating myself.

Reflect on judgment made: In **Chapter 5**, I learned that we all will have poor judgment during our lives. No one is perfect 100% of the time. What is important though it that we reflect on the judgments we made. We should see how a different course of action could have resulted in a better result and reflect on why we made the decision in the first place. Being able to reflect on our judgments will help us improve as people and as employees in the workforce. It will also help improve our decision-making in the future.

Broaden my understanding: Developing my innate abilities will be important to my career because in doing so I will broaden my understanding of management roles. In my current job, I must use my innate abilities in delegation, task management, problem-solving, conflict resolution, and time management. I am also responsible for training new and current employees. By continuing to learn and further develop my innate abilities, I will be able to advance my position or seek new job opportunities.

Your innate abilities are traits that are in your genetics. Developing these traits leads to making you a better employee.

I also learned that "the reason for workplace problems is due to poor judgment calls": It doesn't matter how educated a person is, there are going to be times when he or she must make on the spot judgment calls. However, you won't know the impact of that judgment until after the fact. A good example was a sales manager who decided to increase the price of products to meet the company's revenue forecast and getting a big bonus. However, after a few months, customers realized that their products were overpriced and started taking their business elsewhere. As a result, upper management found out and fired him.

Decision-making was described as being the predictor of a person's accomplishment of work tasks: People who are able to self-regulate their decision-making can also set "adaptive targets." Decision-making is something I struggle with because I often find myself feeling indecisive. I think that I have the ability to make moral judgments, but when it comes to making a decision whether it be where to eat, or where to travel to, I struggle.

Moral action and moral judgment are interrelated: This is why managers and supervisors need to be a role model to their subordinates. There can be positive and negative behaviors. The book gives the following examples: helping others, whistle-blowing, resistance to pressure from management personnel or those in authority, and stealing and cheating. By doing things in a moral way and exercising good judgment, we are mirroring positive images to employees. The advantages of doing this goes beyond just showing good moral action and judgment because in the end we will be building a company culture where good moral actions and behaviors are the norm.

"Good judgment is developed from suffering the consequences of bad judgment": I love this quote. It is completely true that bad judgments have consequences and these bad consequences serve to build your experience. The experience you have acquired along the years is a big factor that will determine how you judge specific things. Therefore, it is true that good judgment is developed from suffering the consequences of bad judgment.

Common sense versus judgment: We learned that people with bad judgment do things without thinking and can be described as impetuous. We also learned that there is an absence out in the work world of common sense. Over 500 cases related to workplace deaths were a result of poor judgment where the individuals were skilled workers. There is a lack of common sense nowadays and part of it is due to bad judgment.

Being a great leader: I learned a few things about being a great leader in these chapters. I learned that a leader must always think and make decisions with their head clear. I can relate to this because I am a leader in my job, a captain of an 18,000-lb. aircraft. In order for me to make great decisions my head needs to be "in the game." On the other side of this, I also know that having bad judgment can cost someone their job; in this case, it could cost me my life and other people's lives as well. Another trait you need to have to be a great leader is moral and ethical judgment, for example, if the CEO of a company goes out and commits sexual assault, how do you think the employees feel about that person? If I were in the situation, I would feel like I couldn't trust the CEO and would definitely hesitate to take direction from them. The last trait you need to have as a leader is customer service skills and being able to deal with a rude customer. You have to remember that you are a role model when in a leadership position; if you handle the rude customer in the incorrect manner, employees will follow your lead. This in turn becomes bad for business because you will lose a lot of customers because of this.

Decision makers and ideas: Decision makers must make over 3,000 ideas to obtain one commercial success. This statement found in the reading makes us aware of the insurmountable odds against manager/decision makers. This might be in part due to a lack of common sense and lower ethical values in society as a whole.

The knowledge I acquired will come in handy as I continue to make decisions on how to deal with both subordinates and upper management. I have confirmed that good decision-making skills must be coupled with analytical tools and strategies; furthermore, one must always consider the company's policies when proposing and implementing a decision.

Making moral and ethical decisions: I learned the importance of making decisions that are moral and ethical. An example of this would be whether an employee of a company is involved in a type of crime or assault. This will essentially affect the entire company because this news will spread to the outside world and create a bad reputation for the company. It also will cause other employees to feel uncomfortable around this individual and want to remove themselves from the situation. This series of events would ultimately result from bad judgment and truly reveals the importance of making morally correct decisions. I will use what I learned from this book as a guideline for my decisions in my workplace because I want to refrain from ever being the cause of chaos in my company.

Poor v. good decisions: I learned that sometimes "poor decisions can become good decisions" and I definitely identified with this statement. This means that sometimes we might make an initial decision that is poor, but it can have unexpected results that ultimately changes our perspective such that to believe we made a good decision. I have experienced this firsthand when I made a decision at work based on an encounter with a customer that I immediately regretted because I feared that it was not handled properly. My decision was impulsive, and I was unsure that it would be seen as the right decision. However, I later was thanked for my quick decision and I believe my boss gained a new level of respect for me.

No matter how good or bad the decisions you make in life, that's what helps you grow your abilities to make better decisions and judgments in the future. Any situation that you are presented can go either way and based on the decisions that Dr. Willis used, it is clear that a lot of people have seen the good and the bad with their decisions. What is important is what you take from any experience and what you learned for next time. I will keep this in mind throughout my life and career, so I don't let a bad decision hinder my future.

Decision making model: Maybe what stuck with me the most from either chapter was Miller and Byrnes' decision-making model. It might be the most pragmatic thought and approach to decision-making. If we can be in control while making decisions, chances are we would probably make different ones a certain percentage of the time. I am speaking from personal experience as sometimes I can make decisions that are too much based on emotion. What I need to work on is taking a deep breath and considering all the repercussions of a decision without letting the moment creep in.

CHAPTER 13
A Model to Reflect on and Use

OVERVIEW

Now that you have read the book and completed the exercises, it is time to reflect on what you learned and how you can use the model in Figure 13.1. Each person has a preferred and often distinct style (e.g., visual, discussion, practice, listening to a lecture, other) and for those of you who learn the best with visuals the model will be pleasing. Regardless of your preferred way to learn, I hope you can glean something from the model.

This chapter includes the model in Figure 13.1 and some commentary about each section (e.g., abilities, how measured in book).

Generally, when a person in academia designs a model, they do so to have a visual representation of how they can best empirically validate the concepts represented by the model. This model only includes what I believe are the mediating variables. In my model, I chose to call the variables *mediating*. Because of our individual differences, each person will view and be affected by each variable differently. Regarding *career potential*, I believe that anyone can use what they learned for any of the examples based on the *mediating* variables and what stage they are in their career. The list of *predicted job outcomes* includes the few that I predict will happen to each person because of having read this book.

ABILITIES

Several universal abilities (i.e., those that are relevant to any job) are covered in this book and after you completed the self-evaluation exercise you should have learned something about your own strengths and weaknesses. Additionally, you may have rated yourself higher or lower than you truly are. This is because when a person evaluates him/herself, the evaluation is based on their inner perception and personal life experiences. Other people may have a totally different perception of the person's abilities. Therefore, you should view your scores with some caution. I assume that you were honest when you completed the self-evaluation and now that you have

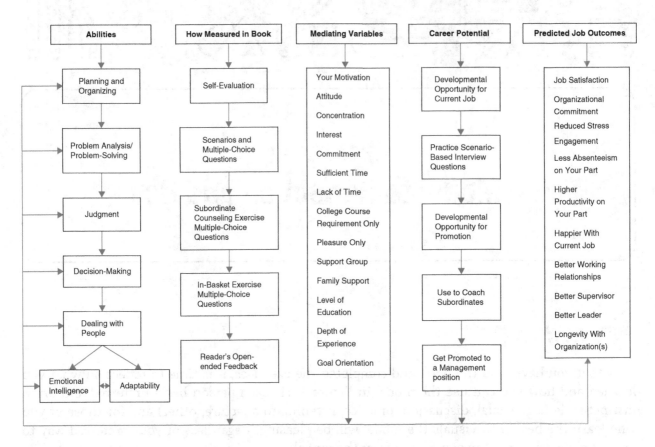

Figure 13.1 Innate Abilities, Measurement, Mediating Variables and the Career Potential and Predicted Job Outcomes

read the entire book and experienced the scenarios, cases, exercises and the quizzes, when you go back and rereview your scores you may rate yourself higher or lower. It all depends on your willingness to stand back and view yourself objectively rather than subjectively.

Regarding your reflection of your abilities, let me suggest that you should think about:

- Whether or not you learned a great deal.
- How you can continue to improve your abilities (e.g., think about critical incidents you have dealt with at work and how you handled them).
- Whether or not you were accurate about your strengths and weaknesses.
- What you can do to be more productive, become a better manager or get promoted.
- Whether or not you will continue to develop yourself because what you learned from this book was a positive experience.

HOW MEASURED IN BOOK

In this book, you have been exposed to several methods for developing your abilities and probably found the quizzes to be the easiest and the exercises a bit more difficult. You also may have liked one method better than the other. I expect that you will put your experience to good use in a number of ways to include:

- Interviewing candidates for a vacant position.
- Participating in an interview process for a new job or a promotion.

- Coaching a subordinate employee.
- Assisting an employee to prioritize and complete their in-basket items.
- Becoming a better planner.
- Recognizing which issues are related and most important and those that are unrelated and not too important.

MEDIATING VARIABLES

Upon reading the list of mediating variables (which are not in rank order), I feel confident that each one has some relevance to your life. **Motivation** is at the top of the list although I did not place the noun at the top intentionally. However, if you are not motivated to develop yourself, then I believe that the remainder of the variables may not be as relevant. First and foremost, you need to be motivated to develop yourself and your innate abilities.

A positive **attitude** is extremely important regarding self-development efforts. For example, if you have a negative attitude about yourself, your abilities, and/or your career, then you may not be successful. Nor would you be willing to put forth the effort it takes to improve your abilities. If you have a positive attitude, you will probably have more determination and energy to put in the time it takes with self-development activities. Furthermore, if you do not have a very positive self-efficacy you may think that you will not be successful at developing yourself.

It took some **concentration** to read the scenarios and complete the quizzes. More concentration was needed for the short cases and exercises. If you are naturally or easily distracted, then concentration is a mediating variable for you.

Those of you who are more **interested** in innate abilities and self-development will probably not become bored or tired of the effort it takes to improve. If you lack interest than this will definitely affect how successful you are at developing your abilities.

We are all busy with work, our family and friends and therefore, we have limited time to spend in time consuming self-development efforts. However, I know from experience that if you are truly committed to improving yourself you will find the time. I am sure most of you have heard of the statement, "If you want to get something done, give it to the busiest person." Overall, if you want accomplish a goal or objective you must be committed and make the time. It is that simple.

Obviously, most readers of this book did so because it was a **college course requirement only**. The latter will serve as a mediating variable because some of you may not remember everything you learned and will move on with your lives. If you did the work and completed the quizzes, you really have learned something.

If you purchased, read, and experienced this book for **pleasure only**, then the pleasure you felt may result in your continued interest and desire to continue to develop your innate abilities. I certainly hope that your experience was pleasurable.

Support group and **family support** are closely related. Many people in college, those preparing for a promotional testing process at work or those who coach other people will undoubtedly gain a great deal from having read this book. Your support group can also be your spouse, significant other, children, entire family, and so on. When people have a support group, they can brainstorm with the members and learn more by engaging in this activity.

Your **level of education** is definitely a mediating variable. This is because for those of you who are working immediately after high school on a college degree, with limited work experience, will probably find the book more difficult than those who already possess a degree and have a great deal of work and life experience. Also, having read and experienced this book may serve as the impetus for some people to pursue additional and/or graduate degrees.

Depth of experience was referenced in the previous paragraph and is also a mediator. The more work experience you have had most likely helped you do better on the quizzes and the opposite is true. Remember that we all learn through life experiences and often make judgment calls based on our past experiences.

Finally, **goal orientation** is a very important mediator. For example, those of you who are goal oriented will probably be more successful in developing your innate abilities, particularly if you make a plan for doing so. The plan will include a timeline for developing your abilities which in reality should be a lifelong effort.

CAREER POTENTIAL

This section of the model includes only some of the ways to enhance or gauge a person's career potential. I included those I believe will help you move up and/or have a successful career. One may ask "Why?" The answers are:

1. Having read and experienced this book was a developmental opportunity for you in your current job.
2. You identified what your strengths and weaknesses were and practiced using your abilities regardless of which ones were strong or weak.
3. You can definitely use what you learned and experienced to prepare for a promotion at your current place of employment.
4. You can definitely use what you learned and experienced to prepare for an interview when applying for a new job.
5. Understanding that being able to coach subordinates is a vital part of being an effective manager.
6. I believe that you can use what you learned and experienced to keep your job and then be promoted!

PREDICTED JOB OUTCOMES

I predict that having experienced the contents of this book you will/may/should (which will be different for each person):

- Be more satisfied at work.
- Be more committed to the organization.
- Be less stressed at work.
- Be more engaged in your work.
- Be absent less.
- Be more productive.
- Become happier with your current job.

- Be able to facilitate/have better working relationships.
- Be a better supervisor.
- Be a better leader.
- Have longevity with the organizations you work for (e.g., not quit or have to leave a job after 1-year).

In summary, I hope that you will be able to make some use of the model and the different mediating variables. Good luck.

List of Universal Abilities

Ability to develop alternative solutions to problems, to evaluate courses of action, and to reach logical decisions. Includes readiness to act or commit oneself to a decision.

Ability to establish efficient and appropriate course of action to accomplish a goal, including recognizing the priorities of major work activities to complete them in a timely fashion, giving attention to detail in the performance of tasks and utilizing appropriate resources.

Ability to establish guidelines for the control of property.

Ability to establish effective worker relationships with coworkers, employees, managers, and other officials and the public.

Ability to foresee the impact and implication of decisions on other components of the organization.

Ability to give constructive criticism.

Ability to guide and direct individuals or a group toward task accomplishment. Takes personal initiative to move events or other persons toward a goal using appropriate methods of influence.

Ability to identify problems in overall management point of view, to recognize clearly underlying issues and possible interrelationships involved, to secure relevant information to identify possible causes.

Ability to identify strengths and weaknesses of subordinates.

Ability to remain fair and objective.

Ability to speak in front of a group (e.g., citizens section or peer group).

Ability to summarize information in written form (e.g., prepare reports).

Ability to summarize information orally.

Ability to work under pressure or stress.

Ability to organize programs, reports, and so on.

Ability to plan programs.

Ability to analyze and evaluate situations/circumstances.

Ability to discipline subordinates effectively.

Ability to counsel subordinates.

Ability to supervise and guide individuals or a group of individuals.

Ability to make analytical judgments where no firm guidelines exist.
Ability to correctly delegate responsibilities and duties.
Ability to make and maintain a decision during stress.
Ability to handle conflicts among subordinates.
Ability to withstand criticism.
Ability to display initiative.
Ability to use diplomacy and tactfulness.
Ability to identify potential problems/deficiencies before they become problems/deficiencies.
Ability to know what to pass on to superiors.
Ability to evaluate the credibility of a customer complaint.
Ability to interpret technical and nontechnical written information.
Ability to follow directions.
Ability to be flexible and to accept new ideas and ways of doing things.
Ability to make sound decisions quickly based on the facts presented.
Ability to gain cooperation and compliance from subordinates.
Ability to favorably influence the activities of others.
Ability to take the lead at risk situations.
Ability to lead by setting an example.
Ability to set priorities and initiate action.
Ability to assist in planning, organizing, and directing management functions.
Ability to display patience.
Ability to display sensitivity to the feelings of others.
Ability to show persistence. Ability to evaluate training needs.
Ability to evaluate budgetary needs.
Ability to obtain needed resources, as appropriate.
Ability to recognize limits of legal action that can be taken.
Ability to work independently.
Ability to interpret department policies and procedures.
Ability to monitor and evaluate program, project, or unit effectiveness and efficiency.
Ability to manage time effectively.
Ability to maintain a balance between employee concerns and management requirements.
Ability to display listening skills.
Ability to understand and explain the provisions of the laws, rules, regulations, procedures, guidelines, policies, and standards governing assigned unit activities and company operations.
Ability to interact with people who are under emotional stress.
Ability to exercise discretion in handling confidential information.
Ability to maintain accurate records.
Ability to give written and oral instructions in a precise and understandable manner.
Ability to follow oral and written instructions.
Ability to adapt to varying work situations. Ability to negotiate with coworkers, peers, subordinates, and customers from different backgrounds.

Innate Ability Definitions and Self-Evaluation Exercise

Instructions: Read the definitions of each innate ability and rate yourself on a scale of 1 to 5. Definitions have been amended to reflect "I" instead of a generic definition.

Based on what you know about yourself, evaluate your strength when answering each question about each dimension using the rating scale. There is no right or wrong score as this is just your assessment as to how strong or weak (aka to what extent) you feel you are in demonstrating each ability. It is highly recommended that you be as honest as possible. No one is strong in every skill dimension and no one is weak in every skill dimension. We all have strengths and weaknesses.

Some of you must complete the exercise as a percentage of your final overall grade in the course.

SELF-ASSESSMENT RATING SCALE

A Great Extent (5)

A great extent rating does not mean that you are perfect or without weaknesses. Rather, a strong rating means that based on your self-assessment, you are likely to be strong in that dimension upon assuming the job. It is expected that you will be able to not only step into the job and perform in a competent manner, but that you are expected to perform in a superior manner almost immediately upon assuming the position, with little training or experience required to achieve that level of performance.

A More than Above Average Extent (4)

A more than average extent rating means that based on your self-assessment, you are likely to perform more than competently upon assuming the position. It is expected, however, that you still can improve your level of performance to a considerable degree, given additional time and training in the position. However, you should only require minimal supervision.

To an Average Extent (3)

To an average extent rating means that based on your self-assessment, you are likely to perform at a competent level when you assume the position. However, additional training and experience will be necessary for you to perform at a more than competent basis, and you will need closer supervision than someone in the first two categories.

To Somewhat of an Extent (2)

To somewhat of an extent rating means that based on your self-assessment, you are likely to perform at a less than a competent level upon assuming the position. Extensive training, experience, and supervision will probably be necessary to bring you up to a competent or higher level of performance.

A Very Little Extent (1)

A weak rating means that you are not prepared to perform in this dimension, based on your self-assessment. If promoted or hired for an entry level position or a supervisory position, your performance is likely to be consistently substandard, even with direct and frequent supervision. You are simply not ready to assume the position now.

PERCEPTION AND ANALYSIS/PROBLEM ANALYSIS

Question 1

To what extent do I demonstrate the ability to quickly identify a problem and to analyze it?

A

1

B

2

C

3

D

4

E

5

Question 2

To what extent do I demonstrate the ability to notice details or phenomena; to sort out pertinent information and to foresee the consequences of various alternatives?

A

1

B

2

C

3

D

4

E

5

Question 3

To what extent do I obtain relevant information from available information and screen out less essential details?

A

1

B

2

C

3

D

4

E

5

Question 4

To what extent do I misinterpret information?

A

1

B

2

C

3

D

4

E

5

Question 5

To what extent do I demonstrate perception of an interaction between various aspects of the problem and between various actions taken or available to be taken?

A

1

B

2

C

3

D

4

E

5

Question 6

To what extent am I able to use data and related information to evaluate a problem?

A

1

B

2

C

3

D

4

E

5

Question 7

To what extent do I logically interpret information to solve problems?

A

1

B

2

C

3

D

4

E

5

JUDGMENT/DECISION-MAKING

Question 8

To what extent do I demonstrate the ability to make sound decisions promptly on difficult problems?

A

1

B

2

C

3

D

4

E

5

Question 9

To what extent am I able to exercise judgment and consideration of all available information?

A

1

B

2

C

3

D

4

E

5

Question 10

To what extent do I demonstrate the ability and willingness to make a decision when required?

A

1

B

2

C

3

D

4

E

5

Question 11

To what extent do I think that I do not or would not overly delegate?

A

1

B

2

C

3

D

4

E

5

Question 12

To what extent do I not delay action on important items?

A

1

B

2

C

3

D

4

E

5

Question 13

To what extent do I take a firm position and make my position clear?

A

1

B

2

C

3

D

4

E

5

Question 14

To what extent do I evaluate a situation to determine the action(s) to be taken?

A

1

B

2

C

3

D

4

E

5

Question 15

To what extent do I or would I assign tasks to subordinates when the nature of the incident requires coordinated efforts of several subordinates?

A

1

B

2

C

3

D

4

E

5

Question 16

To what extent do I make use of all information to take the most appropriate action(s) and exhibit a willingness to make decisions when necessary?

A

1

B

2

C

3

D

4

E

5

DEALING WITH PEOPLE/INTERPERSONAL

Question 17

To what extent do I demonstrate the ability to establish, integrate, and maintain effective and harmonious working relationships with other employees, companies, customers, and peers?

A

1

B

2

C

3

D

4

E

5

Question 18

To what extent am I able to work effectively as a member of an unofficial (i.e., am not assigned to work on a team but feel "we are all in this together") or cross-functional team?

A

1

B

2

C

3

D

4

E

5

Question 19

To what extent do I respect and encourage working cooperatively with subordinates, coworkers, and others without regard to their gender, age, race, beliefs, sexual orientation, or cultural background?

A

1

B

2

C

3

D

4

E

5

Question 20

To what extent do I demonstrate the ability to deal with people beyond giving and receiving instructions?

A

1

B

2

C

3

D

4

E

5

Question 21

To what extent do I demonstrate that I respect the ideas of others, praise subordinates, or would praise subordinates for good and outstanding performance?

A

1

B

2

C

3

D

4

E

5

ADAPTABILITY

Question 22

To what extent do I demonstrate the ability to remain flexible and patient in the face of constantly changing needs, to influence events and to execute the required actions to complete my work?

A

1

B

2

C

3

D

4

E

5

Question 23

To what extent do I demonstrate the ability to modify my behavior to accommodate the needs and feelings of others?

A

1

B

2

C

3

D

4

E

5

Question 24

To what extent do I demonstrate empathy for others?

A

1

B

2

C

3

D

4

E

5

PLANNING AND ORGANIZING

Question 25

To what extent do I demonstrate the ability to plan and organize my daily work routine?

A

1

B

2

C

3

D

4

E

5

Question 26

To what extent do I demonstrate the ability to establish priorities for the completion of work in accordance with sound time-management methodology?

A

1

B

2

C

3

D

4

E

5

Question 27

To what extent do I demonstrate the ability to avoid duplication of effort, estimate expected time of completion of work elements, and establish a personal schedule accordingly?

A

1

B

2

C

3

D

4

E

5

Question 28

To what extent do I demonstrate the ability to know and understand expectations regarding such activities and work to ensure such expectations are met and in a timely manner?

A

1

B

2

C

3

D

4

E

5

Question 29

To what extent do I demonstrate the ability to develop and formulate ways, means, and timing to achieve established goals and objectives?

A

1

B

2

C

3

D

4

E

5

Question 30

To what extent do I demonstrate the ability to effectively and efficiently utilize resources to achieve such goals and objectives?

A

1

B

2

C

3

D

4

E

5

Question 31

To what extent do I demonstrate the ability to break work down into subtasks and prioritize these subtasks, so they can be done effectively?

A

1

B

2

C

3

D

4

E

5

Question 32

To what extent do I demonstrate the ability to anticipate problems before they come up?

A

1

B

2

C

3

D

4

E

5

Question 33

To what extent do I demonstrate the ability to prepare effective plans to control difficulties and problems; to set objectives, priorities, and so on?

A

1

B

2

C

3

D

4

E

5

References

Antonakis, J., Ashkanasy, N. M., & Dasoborough, M. T. (2009). Does leadership need emotional intelligence? *The Leadership Quarterly, 20*, 247–261.

Aristotle. (1953). *The ethics of Aristotle: The Nichmachean ethics* (J. A. K. Thomason, Trans.). New York, NY: Penguin.

Avolio, B. J. (1999). *Full leadership development: Building the vital forces in organizations*. Thousand Oaks, CA: Sage.

Avolio, B. J. (2005). *Leadership development in balance*. Mahwah, NJ: Lawrence Erlbaum Associates.

Bar-Ons, R. (1997). *Bar-on emotional quotient inventory (EQi): Technical manual*. Toronto, ON: Multi-Health Systems.

Barrick, M. R., Mount, M. K., & Judge, T. A. (2001). Personality and performance at the beginning of the new millennium: What do we know and where do we go next? *International Journal of Selection and Assessment, 9*(1–2), 9–30.

Bass, B. M. (1985). *Leadership and performance beyond expectations*. New York, NY: Free Press.

Bass, B. M. (1990). *Bass & Stogdill's handbook of leadership* (3rd ed.). New York, NY: Free Press.

Bass, B. M., & Riggio, R. E. (2006). *Transformational leadership* (2nd ed.). Mahwah, NJ: Lawrence Erlbaum Associates.

Blank, I. (2008). Selecting employees based on emotional intelligence competencies: Reap the rewards and minimize the risk. *Employee Relations Law Journal, 34*(3), 77–85.

Blasi, A. (1980). Bridging moral cognition and moral action: A critical review of the literature. *Psychological Bulletin, 88*, 1–45.

Boss, J. (2015). *14 signs of an adaptable person*. Retrieved from https://www.forbes.com/sites/jeffboss/2015/09/03/14-signs-of-an-adaptable-person/#4e48301616ea

Boyatzis, R. E. (1982). *The competent manager*. New York, NY: Wiley.

Boyatzis, R. E. (2001). How and why individuals are able to develop emotional intelligence. In C. Cherniss & D. Goleman (Eds.), *The emotionally intelligent workplace* (pp. 234–253). San Francisco, CA: Jossey-Bass.

Boyatzis, R. E., Goleman, D., & Rhee, K. S. (2000). Clustering competence in emotional intelligence: Insights from the emotional competency inventory. In R. Bar-On & J. D. A. Parker (Eds.), *The handbook of emotional intelligence* (pp. 343–362). San Francisco, CA: Jossey-Bass.

Bransford, J., Brown, A. L., & Cocking, R. R. (1999). *How people learn: Brain, mind, experience, and school.* Washington, DC: National Academy Press.

Bray, D. W. (1964). The management progress study. *American Psychologist, 19,* 419–420.

Bray, D. W., & Grant, D. L. (1966). The assessment center in the measurement of potential for business management. *Psychological Monographs, 80*(17), 1–27.

Bray, D. W., Grant, D. L., Campbell, R. J., & Grant, D. L. (1974). *Formative years in business: a long-term AT&T study of managerial lives.* Wiley.

Burnaska, R. F. (1976). The effects of behavior modeling training upon managers' behaviors and employees' perceptions. *Personnel Psychology, 29,* 329–335.

Byham, W. C., Adams, D., & Kiggins, A. (1976). Transfer of modeling training to the job. *Personnel Psychology, 29,* 345–349.

Byrnes, J. P. (2013). *The nature and development of decision-making: A self-regulation model.* London, UK: Psychology Press.

Byrnes, J. P., Miller, D. C., & Reynolds, M. (1999). Learning to make good decisions: A self-regulation perspective. *Child Development, 70,* 1121–1140.

Cappelli, P. H. (2015). Skill gaps, skill shortages, and skill mismatches: Evidence and arguments for the United States. *ILR Review, 68*(2), 251–290.

Caruso, D., & Salovey, P. (2004). *The emotionally intelligent manager how to develop and use the four key emotional skills of leadership* (1st ed.). San Francisco, CA: Jossey Bass.

Caudron, S. (1999). The hard case for soft skills. *Workforce, 78*(7), 60–64.

Chaudhry, A. A., & Usman, A. (2011). An investigation of the relationship between employees' emotional intelligence and performance. *African Journal of Business Management, 5*(9), 3556–3562.

Chen, A., Bian, M., & Hou, Y. (2015). Impact of transformational leadership on subordinate's EI and work performance. *Personnel Review, 44*(4), 438–453.

Cherniss, C., & Goleman, D. (2001). *The emotionally intelligent workplace: How to select for, measure, and improve emotional intelligence in individuals, groups, and organizations* (1st ed.). San Francisco, CA: Jossey-Bass.

Choo, A. S., Nag, R., & Xia, Y. (2015). The role of executive problem solving in knowledge accumulation and manufacturing improvements. *Journal of Operations Management, 36,* 63–74.

Clarke, M. (2016). Addressing the soft skills crisis. *Strategic HR Review, 15*(3), 137–130.

Coleman, H., & Argue, M. W. (2015). Mediating with emotional intelligence: When "IQ" just isn't enough. *Dispute Resolution Journal, 70*(3), 15–24.

Conley, C. (2011). *The top 10 emotionally intelligent fortune 500 CEOs.* Retrieved from Huffington-post.com/chip.conley/the-top-10-emotionallyint _b_911567.html, https://www.google.com/search?ei=2XOfXd_jJ4easQWlk574DQ&q=the+top+10+emotionally-intelligent+fortune+500+ceos&oq=top+ten+emotionally+intellgence+fortune+&gs_l=psy-ab.1.0.0i22i30.1980.21061..22905...13.1..0.194.6872.0j49......0....1..gws-wiz.......0i71j0i67j0i131j0j0i10j0i3j0i13j0i8i13i30j33i160j0i13i30j33i299j33i22i10i29i30.8Oop-3RH2Bo#spf=1570730993873

Cullen, K., Edwards, B., Casper, W., & Gue, K. (2014). Employees' adaptability and perceptions of change-related uncertainty: Implications for perceived organizational support, job satisfaction, performance. *Journal of Business and Psychology, 29,* 269–280.

Davidson, J. E., & Sternberg, R. J. (2003). *The psychology of problem solving.* Cambridge, England: Cambridge University Press.

Day, G. (2007). Is it real? Can we win? Is it worth doing? Managing risk and reward in an innovation portfolio. *Harvard Business Review, 85,* 110.

Del Missier, F., Mäntylä, T., & Bruine de Bruin, W. (2010). Executive functions in decision making: An individual differences approach. *Thinking & Reasoning, 16,* 69–97.

Dewey, J. (2002). *Human nature and conduct.* Mineola, NY: Dover Publications.

Di Meglio, F. (2013, May 15). *Want an MBA from Yale? You're going to need emotional intelligence.* Retrieved from https://www.bloomberg.com/news/articles/2013-05-15/want-an-mba-from-yale-youre-going-to-need-emotional-intelligence

Dossey, J. A., O'Sullivan, C. Y., McCrone, S. S., & Gonzales, P. (2006). *Problem solving in the PISA and TIMSS 2003 assessments. [electronic resource]: Technical report.* National Center for Education Statistics, Institute of Education Sciences, U.S. Dept. of Education. http://eds.b.ebscohost.com.ezproxy.fau.edu/eds/detail/detail?vid=5&sid=b5ee8735-810e-40b6-9ac5-06a7ff630516%40pdc-v-sessmgr03&bdata=JkF1dGhUeXBlPWlwLGNvb2tpZSx1cmwsdWlkJnNpdGU9ZWRzLWxpdmUmc2NvcGU9c2l0ZQ%3d%3d#AN=fau.021961403&db=cat06361a

Dulewicz, V., & Higgs, M. (2004). Can emotional intelligence be developed? *International Journal of Human Resources Management, 15,* 95–111.

Einstein, A., & Infeld, L. (1938). *The evolution of physics.* New York, NY: Simon and Schuster.

Feffer, M. (2016). HR's hard challenge: When employees lack soft skills. *HR Magazine.*

Fineman, S. (2004). Getting the measure of emotion-and the cautionary tale of emotional intelligence. *Human Relations; Studies Towards the Integration of Social Sciences, 37,* 719–740.

Fitzgerald, S. P. (2002). *Decision making.* Chichester, England: Capstone Publishing, John Wiley and Sons, Inc. http://eds.b.ebscohost.com.ezproxy.fau.edu/eds/detail/detail?vid=0&sid=ffc59719-a8f3-47d7-9ed5-95a48acac685%40pdc-v-sessmgr04&bdata=JkF1dGhUeXBlPWlwLGNvb2tpZSx1cmwsdWlkJnNpdGU9ZWRzLWxpdmUmc2NvcGU9c2l0ZQ%3d%3d#AN=67246&db=nlebk

Fleishman, E. (1953). Leadership climate, human relations training and supervisory behavior. *Personnel Psychology, 6,* 205–222.

Ford, C. M., Sharfman, M. P., & Dean, J. W. (2008). Factors associated with creative strategic decisions. *Creativity and Innovation Management, 17,* 171–185.

Gardner, L., & Stough, C. (2002). Examining the relationship between leadership and emotional intelligence in senior level managers. *Leadership and Organization Development Journal, 23,* 68–78.

Ginoe, F. (2018, November–December). Case study can you fix a toxic culture without firing people? A CFO wonders how to turn around a struggling division. *Harvard Business Review,* pp. 143–147.

Goleman, D. (1995). *Emotional intelligence: Why it can matter more than IQ.* New York, NY: Bantam Books.

Goleman, D. (1998). *Working with emotional intelligence.* New York, NY: Bantam Books.

Goleman, D. (2006). *Social intelligence: The new science of human relationships.* New York, NY: Bantam Books.

Goleman, D., Boyatzis, R., & McKee, A. (2002). *Primal leadership: Realizing the power of emotional intelligence.* Boston, MA: Harvard Business School Press.

Greenberg, J. (2002). Who stole the money, and when? Individual and situational determinants of employee theft. *Organizational Behavior and Human Decision Processes, 89*(1), 985–1003.

Groysberg, B., & Baden, K. C. (2019). Case study: When two leaders on the senior team hate each other. *Harvard Business Review, 97*(1), 145–149. http://web.a.ebscohost.com.ezproxy.fau.edu/ehost/pdfviewer/pdfviewer?vid=6&sid=b2175009-a607-4b37-993e-85b3c90b328e%40sessionmgr4007

Hart Research Associates. (2015). *Falling short? College learning and career success (Electronic version). Selected findings from online surveys of employers and college students conducted on behalf of the association of American colleges & universities.* Retrieved from https://www.aacu.org/sites/default/files/LEAP/2015employerstudentsurvey.pdf

Himmelsbach, V. (1999). Soft skills are key to success. *Computer Dealer News, 15*(22), 20.

Hopkins, M. M., & Bilimoria, D. (2008). Social and emotional competencies predicting success for male and female executives. *Journal of Management Development, 27*(1), 13–35.

Howard, A., & Bray, D. (1988). *Managerial lives in transition, advancing age and changing times.* New York, NY/London, UK: The Guilford Press.

https://www.onetonline.org/link/summary/53-1031.00, First Line Supervisors of Transportation and Materials Moving and Vehicle Operators">, First Line Supervisors of Transportation and Materials Moving and Vehicle Operators

Huang, X., Chan, S. C. H., Lam, W., & Nan, X. (2010). The joint effect of leader-member exchange and emotional intelligence on burnout and work performance in call centers in China. *International Journal of Human Resource Management, 21*(7), 1124–1144.

John, J. (2009, October/December). Study on the nature of impact of soft skills training programme on the soft skills development of management students. *Pacific Business Review,* 19–27.

Joseph, D. L., Jin, J., Newman, D. A., & O'Boyle, E. H. (2015). Why does self-reported emotional intelligence predict job performance? A meta-analytic investigation of mixed EI. *Journal of Applied Psychology, 100*(2), 298–342.

Katarzyna, P. (2016). Behavioral strategy: Adaptability context. *Management, 20*(1), 256–277.

Kechagias, K. (2011). *Teaching and assessing soft skills*. Thessaloniki, Neapolis: 1st Second Chance School of Thessaloniki, as Part of the Measuring and Assessing Soft Skills (MASS).

Klaus, P. (2010). Communication breakdown. *California Job Journal, 28*(1248), 1–9.

Korn Ferry Institute. (2017). Retrieved from https://www.kornferry.com/insights/latest-news

Kouzes, J. M., & Posner, B. Z. (Eds.). (1993). Credibility: How leaders gain and lose it, why people demand it. *Adult Learning, 3*, 158.

Kyllonen, P. C. (2013). Soft skills for the workplace. *Change: The Magazine of Higher Learning, 45*(6), 16–23.

Laabs, J. (1999). Emotional intelligence at work. *Workforce, 78*(7), 68–71.

Langhorn, S. (2004). How emotional intelligence can improve management performance. *International Journal of Contemporary Hospitality Management, 16*(4/5), 220–230.

Lievens, F., & Thornton, G. C., III. (2005). Assessment centers: Recent developments in practice and research. In A. Evers, N. Anderson & O. Voskuijl (Eds.), *Handbook of personnel selection* (pp. 243–264). Malden, MA: Blackwell.

Likert, R. (1961). *New patterns of management*. New York, NY: McGraw-Hill.

Locke, E. A. (2005). Why emotional intelligence is an invalid concept. *Journal of Organizational Behavior, 26*, 425–431.

London, M. (2002). *Leadership development: Paths to self-insight and professional growth*. Mahwah, NJ: Lawrence Erlbaum Associates.

Lopes, P. N., Cote, S., & Salovey, P. (2006). An ability model of emotional intelligence: Implications for assessment and training. In V. U. Druskat, F. Sala, & G. Mount (Eds.), *Linking emotional intelligence and performance at work: Current research evidence with individuals and groups* (pp. 53–80). Mahwah, NJ: Lawrence Erlbaum Associates.

Loviscky, G. E., Treviño, L. K., & Jacobs, R. R. (2007). Assessing managers' ethical decision-making: An objective measure of managerial moral judgment. *Journal of Business Ethics, 73*(3), 263–285.

MacKinnon, D. W. (1977). From selecting spies to selecting managers. In J. J. Moses & W. C. Byham (Eds.), *Applying the assessment center method* (p. 91). New York, NY: Pergamon Press.

Maes, J., Weldy, T., & Icenogel, M. (1997). A managerial perspective: Oral communication is most important for business students in the workplace. *Journal of Business Communication, 34*, 67–80.

Mandell, B., & Pherwani, S. (2003). Relationship between emotional intelligence and transformational leadership style: A gender comparison. *Journal of Business and Psychology, 17*(3), 387–404.

Martin, W., & LaVan, H. (2010). Workplace bullying: A review of the litigated cases. *Employee Responsibilities and Rights Journal, 22*, 175–194.

Matsouka, K., & Mihail, D. M. (2016). Graduates' employability: What do graduates and employers think? *Industry and Higher Education, 30*(5), 321–326.

Mattingly, V., & Kraiger, K. (2019). Can emotional intelligence be trained? A meta-analytical investigation. *Human Resource Management Review, 29*(2), 140–155.

Mavity, H. (2013). Now let's find out why those employees make those bad decisions. *Workplace safety and health law blog*. Retrieved from https://www.fisherphillips.com/Workplace-Safety-and-Health-Law-Blog/Now-Lets-Find-Out-Why-Employees-Make-Those-Bad-Decisions

Mayer, J., & Salovey, P. (1997). What is emotional intelligence? In P. Salovey & D. Sluyter (Eds.), *Emotional development and emotional intelligence: Implications for educators* (pp. 3–31). New York, NY: Basic Books.

Mayer, J. D., & Cobb, C. D. (2000). Educational policy on emotional intelligence: Does it make sense? *Educational Psychology Review, 12*, 163–183.

Mersino, A. C. (2007). *Emotional intelligence for project managers: The people skills you need to achieve outstanding results*. New York, NY: AMACOM. Retrieved from http://eds.a.ebscohost.com/eds/detail/detail?vid=1&sid=b1f14c78-86ea-4af3-9157-6b0580bfdff1%40sdc-v-sessmgr01&bdata=JkF1dGhUeXBlPWlwLGNvb2tpZSx1cmwsdWlkJnNpdGU9ZWRzLWxpdmUmc2NvcGU9c2l0ZQ%3d%3d#AN=214576&db=nlebk

Miller, D. C., & Byrnes, J. P. (2001). Adolescents' decision making in social situations: A self-regulation perspective. *Journal of Applied Developmental Psychology, 22*, 237–256.

Mitchell, G. W., Skinner, L. B., & White, B. J. (2010). Essential soft skills for success in the twenty-first century workforce as perceived by business educators. *Delta Pi Epsilon Journal, 52*, 43–53.

Mollick, E. (2012). People and process, suits and innovators: The role of individuals in firm performance. *Strategic Management Journal, 33*, 1001–1015.

Morehouse, M. M. (2007). An exploration of emotional intelligence across career arenas. *Leadership and Organizational Journal, 28*(4), 296–307.

Moses, J. L., & Ritchie, R. J. (1976). Supervisory relationships training: A behavioral evaluation of a behavior modeling program. *Personnel Psychology, 29*(3), 337–343.

Mueller, J., Melwani, S., Loewenstein, J., & Deal, J. J. (2018). Reframing the decision-makers' dilemma: Towards a social context model of creative idea recognition. *Academy of Management Journal, 61*(1), 94–110.

Nafukho, F. M., & Mayia, M. A. H. (2014). Emotional intelligence and its critical role in developing human resources. In N. E. Chalofsky, T. S. Rocc, & M. L. Morris (Eds.), *Handbook of human resources development* (pp. 623–640). Hobokent, NJ: Wiley.

Nealy, C. (2005). Integrating soft skills through active learning in the management classroom. *Journal of College Teaching & Learning, 2*(4), 1–6.

O'Boyle, E. H., Jr., Humphrey, R. H., Pollack, J. M., Hawver, T. H., & Story, P. A. (2011). The relation between emotional intelligence and job performance: A meta-analysis. *Journal of Organizational Behavior, 32*(5), 788–818.

Offices of Strategic Services (OSS) Assessment Staff. (1948). *Assessment of men*. New York, NY: Rinehart.

O*Net. (2017). *Summary report for: 11-9111.00—Medical and health services managers* (chap. 3). Retrieved from https://www.onetonline.org/link/summary/11-9111.00

Parker, A. M., & Fischhoff, B. (2005). Decision-making competence: External validation through an individual differences approach. *Journal of Behavioral Decision Making, 18*, 1–27.

Parker, A. M., & Weller, J. A. (2015). Greater decision-making competence is associated with greater expected-value sensitivity, but not overall risk taking: An examination of concurrent validity. *Frontiers in Psychology, 6,* 1664-1078. Retrieved from http://eds.b.ebscohost.com/eds/detail/detail?vid=2&sid=bb8fd6a0-e5db-4041-957c-568c88544d19%40sessionmgr101&bdata=JkF1dGhUeXBlPWlwLGNvb2tpZSx1cmwsdWlkJnNpdGU9ZWRzLWxpdmUmc2NvcGU9c2l0ZQ%3d%3d#AN=edsdoj.822a3108f45f4022b51c8190d7fe7a74&db=edsdoj

Parsons, T. L. (2006). *Definition: Soft skills.* Retrieved from http://searchcio.techtarget.com/definition/soft-skills

Polzer, J. T. (2018, May–June). Case study trust the algorithm or your gut? A VP decides which candidate to promote. *Harvard Business Review, 96*(3), 147–151.

Prati, L., Douglas, C., Ferris, G., Ammeter, A., & Buckley, M. (2003). Emotional intelligence, leadership effectiveness and team outcomes. *The International Journal of Organizational Analysis, 11*(1), 21–40.

Prentice, C., & King, B. (2013). Impacts of personality, emotional intelligence and adaptiveness on service performance of casino hosts: A hierarchical approach. *Journal of Business Research, 66*(9), 1637–1643.

Pulakos, E. D., Arad, S., Donovan, M. A., & Plamondon, K. E. (2000). Adaptability in the workplace: Development of a taxonomy of adaptive performance. *Journal of Applied Psychology, 85*(4), 612–624.

Pulakos, E. D., Schmitt, N., Dorsey, D., Arad, S., Borman, W., & Hedge, J. (2002). Predicting adaptive performance: Further tests of a model of adaptability. *Human Performance, 15*(4), 299–323.

Pure, S. (2019, September–October). Case study your star salesperson lied. Should he get a second chance? *Harvard Business Review, 97*(5), 156–161.

Rest, J. R., & Narvaez, D. (1994). *Moral development in the professions: Psychology and applied ethics.* Hillsdale, NJ: Lawrence Erlbaum.

Riggio, R. E., & Lee, J. (2007). Emotional and interpersonal competencies and leadership development. *Human Resource Management Review, 17,* 418–426.

Robles, M. M. (2012). Executive perceptions of the top 10 soft skills needed in today's workplace. *Business Communication Quarterly, 75*(4), 453–465.

Rubin, R. S., Munz, D. C., & Bommer, W. H. (2005). Leading from within: The effects of emotion recognition and personality on transformational leadership behavior. *Academy of Management Journal, 48,* 845–858.

Salovey, P., & Mayer, J. D. (1990). Emotional intelligence. *Imagination, Cognition and Personality, 9,* 185–211.

Saunderson, R. (2017). Sharpening soft skills with situational learning. *Training Magazine.* Retrieved from https://trainingmag.com/trgmag-article/sharpening-soft-skills-situational-learning/

Schwartz, T. (2000). How do you feel? *Fast Company,* p. 296.

Selingo, J. J. (2015, September 25). Is college worth the cost? Many recent graduates don't think so. *The Washington Post.*

Sharma, V. (2018). Soft skills: An employability enabler. *IUP Journal of Soft Skills, 12*(2), 25–32.

Shoss, M. K., Witt, L. A., & Vera, D. (2012). When does adaptive performance lead to higher task performance? *Journal of Organizational Behavior, 33*, 910–924.

Simpson, S. (2006). *The measurement and recognition of soft factors, developing a common standard.* Guildford, England: University of Surrey.

Smith, L. (2007). Teaching the intangibles. *T+D, 61*(10), 23–25.

Solomon, H. (1999). Soft skills key to success. *Computing Canada, 25*(28), 1–2.

Stevens, G. A., & Burley, J. (1997). 3000 raw ideas = 1 commercial success! *Research Technology Management, 40*, 16–27.

Stogdill, R. M. (1974). *Handbook of leadership.* New York, NY: Free Press.

Stogdill, R. M., & Coons, A. E. (Eds.). (1957). *Leader behavior: Its description and measurement.* Columbus, OH: Ohio State University, Bureau of Business Research.

Thiele, L. P., & Young, M. (2016). Practical Judgment, Narrative Experience and Wicked Problems. *Theoria: A Journal of Social & Political Theory, 63*(148), 35–52. https://doi.org/10.3167/th.2016.6314803

Thornton, G. C., III., & Byham, W. C. (1982). *Assessment centers and managerial performance.* New York, NY: Academic.

Thornton, G. C., III., & Gibbons, A. M. (1982). Validity of assessment centers for personnel selection. *HR Management Review, 19*(3), 169–187.

Thornton, G. C., III., & Krause, D. E. (2009). Selection versus development assessment centers: An international survey of design, execution, and evaluation. *International Journal of Human Resource Management, 20*(2), 478–498.

Thornton, G. C., & Rupp, D. E. (2006). *Assessment centers in human resource management: Strategies for prediction, diagnosis, and development.* Mahwah, NJ: Lawrence Erlbaum Associates.

Trevino, L. K. (1986). Ethical decision making in organizations: A person-situation interactionist model. *Academy of Management Review, 11*, 601–617.

Van den Heuvel, M., Demerouti, E., Bakker, A. B., & Schaufeli, W. B. (2013). Adapting to change: The value of change information and meaning-making. *Journal of Vocational Behavior, 83*, 11–21.

Van den Heuvel, M., Demerouti, E., Schreurs, B. H. J., Bakker, A. B., & Schaufeli, W. B. (2009). Does meaning-making help during organizational change? Development and validation of a new scale. *Career Development International, 14*, 508–533.

Vinchur, A. J., Schippmann, J. S., Switzer, F. S., & Roth, P. L. (1998). A meta-analytic review of predictors of job performance for salespeople. *Journal of Applied Psychology, 83*(4), 586–597.

Watkins, C. (2000). Developing emotional intelligence. *International Journal of Selection and Assessment, 8*(2), 89–92.

Weber, L. (2018, April 20–21). Evolving at work. *The Wall Street Journal*, pp. B1, B6.

Wedell-Wedellsborg, T. (2017). Are you solving the right problems? *Harvard Business Review, 95*(1) pp. 76–83. Retrieved from http://web.a.ebscohost.com.ezproxy.fau.edu/ehost/detail/detail?

vid=4&sid=8d1f7163-eae1-4211-9bd5-8ed3e6c4d5fe%40sdc-v-sessmgr03&bdata=JnNpdGU9Z
Whvc3QtbGl2ZQ%3d%3d#AN=120354891&db=buh

Wilhelm, W. J. (2004). Determinants of moral reasoning: Academic factors, gender, richness of life experiences, and religious preferences. *Delta Pi Epsilon Journal, 46*, 105–121.

Willis, L. C (2017). *Mastering the assessment center process. The fast track to promotion*. Springfield, IL: Charles C. Thomas Publisher, LTD.

Wong, C., & Law, K. S. (2002). The effects of leader and follower emotional intelligence on performance and attitude: An exploratory study. *The Leadership Quarterly, 13*, 243–274.

https://www.forbes.com/search/?q=adaptability-is-key-to-survival-in-the-age-of-digital-darwinism#d423e7f279f4

https://www.forbes.com/sites/forbestechcouncil/2018/05/24/adaptability-is-key-to-survival-in-the-age-of-digital-darwinism/#1d02e2e6408c

https://www.roberthalf.com/research-and-insights/career-development

https://www.roberthalf.com/blog/salaries-and-skills/adaptability-in-the-workplace-the-key-to-a-successful-career-journey

Zeidner, M., Roberts, R. D., & Matthews, G. (2009). *What we know about emotional intelligence: How it affects learning, work, relationships, and our mental health*. Cambridge, MA: A Bradford Book.